Anomalous Experiences

ANOMALOUS EXPERIENCES

Essays from Parapsychological and Psychological Perspectives

Edited by
Matthew D. Smith

McFarland & Company, Inc., Publishers
Jefferson, North Carolina, and London

LIBRARY OF CONGRESS CATALOGUING-IN-PUBLICATION DATA

Anomalous experiences : essays from parapsychological and psychological perspectives / edited by Matthew D. Smith.
    p.   cm.
Includes bibliographical references and index.

ISBN 978-0-7864-4398-7
softcover : 50# alkaline paper ∞

1. Parapsychology.   I. Smith, Matthew D., 1970–
BF1031.A495   2010
130—dc22   2009034199

British Library cataloguing data are available

©2010 Matthew D. Smith. All rights reserved

No part of this book may be reproduced or transmitted in any form or by any means, electronic or mechanical, including photocopying or recording, or by any information storage and retrieval system, without permission in writing from the publisher.

Cover photograph ©2010 Photos.com

Manufactured in the United States of America

McFarland & Company, Inc., Publishers
Box 611, Jefferson, North Carolina 28640
www.mcfarlandpub.com

To the memory of
Professor Robert L. Morris (1942–2004)

Contents

Preface	1

Part One: Parapsychological Perspectives

1. Feeling the Future: Studies of Precognitive Emotional Arousal *Daryl J. Bem*	5
2. Experimenter Effects in Parapsychology: Three Studies with a Remote Helping Task *Caroline Watt*	12
3. The Role of Altered States of Consciousness in Extrasensory Experiences *Chris A. Roe*	25
4. Are Our Assumptions More Anomalous Than the Phenomena? *Paul Stevens*	50
5. Will We Ever Know Whether Extrasensory Perception Exists? *Jezz Fox*	61
6. Towards a Sociological Parapsychology *Robin Wooffitt*	72

Part Two: Psychological Perspectives

7. Anomalous Experiences During Deep Hypnosis *Etzel Cardeña*	93
8. Haunting Experiences: An Integrative Approach *Ciarán O'Keeffe* and *Steve Parsons*	108

9. Apparitions of Black Dogs
   Simon J. Sherwood   120

10. Psychological Aspects of the Alien Contact Experience
    Christopher C. French, Julia Santomauro, Victoria Hamilton, Rachel Fox and *Michael Thalbourne*   136

11. Observing the Impossible: Eyewitness Testimony for Darkroom Séances
    Richard Wiseman   154

12. Developing a Dissociational Account of Out-of-Body Experiences
    Craig D. Murray   161

13. Anomalous Experiences and Boundary Thinness in the Mind and Brain
    Christine Simmonds-Moore   177

About the Contributors   207

Index   211

PREFACE

An experience that might be described as "anomalous" is one that is in some way "out-of-the-ordinary." It can be anomalous in the sense that it may appear as unusual to the person having the experience or in the sense that the processes involved in the experience appear to be "non-ordinary." Non-ordinary processes might either refer to glitches in what are otherwise relatively well understood processes (e.g., memory anomalies) or to processes that appear to fall beyond current scientific understanding (e.g., psychic experiences).

This volume presents a collection of essays that highlight the status of contemporary research on anomalous experiences as we approach the end of the first decade of the 21st century. All the essays formed part of a one-day conference entitled "Developing Perspectives on Anomalous Experience" held at Liverpool Hope University College (now Liverpool Hope University) in June 2005.

Part One focuses on parapsychological perspectives on anomalous experience. The emphasis in these chapters is on research aimed at examining the potentially parapsychological nature of anomalous experiences and the challenges inherent in this approach. Throughout the essays in Part One, the term "psi," from the Greek letter Ψ, is often used to refer to parapsychological experiences or phenomena. Psi is typically used as a neutral term that refers to the apparently unknown factors that underlie these phenomena. One of the main practical (and for that matter theoretical) challenges facing experimental parapsychological research continues to be the replicability of research findings. Positive evidence of anomalous psi processes, such as extrasensory perception (ESP) or psychokinesis (PK), that seem to be as yet unexplained by accepted scientific theory, has so far been difficult to replicate to a level that satisfies many scientists. Evidence for psi phenomena is only likely to be accepted by the scientific community when there is a rigorous experimental procedure that reliably produces an effect.

In Chapter 1, Daryl J. Bem outlines a series of experiments that he believes demonstrate such a procedure (or set of procedures). These experiments examine a set of related effects that seem to demonstrate apparently precognitive effects—that is, information seems to travel back in time in order to influence participants' responses on a range of tasks.

In Chapter 2, the role of the experimenter in parapsychological research comes under scrutiny. It is generally accepted in more conventional psychological research that the person conducting the experiment can affect the outcome of the experiment by influencing the participants' behavior. This influence may be unintentional and often reflects the expectations the experimenter has about the outcome of the study. Parapsychologists have explored how these processes might contribute to the "experimenter effect," which refers to the observation that some researchers seem to be consistently more successful than other researchers in obtaining evidence for parapsychological effects. Caroline Watt examines how research participants' beliefs and expectations about the person acting as the experimenter might influence the results obtained in a parapsychology experiment.

Researchers have long been interested in how anomalous phenomena might be related to altered states of consciousness, such as those experienced while dreaming or under hypnosis. A comprehensive review of this research is presented by Chris A. Roe in Chapter 3.

Chapters 4 and 5 re-examine some of the assumptions that underlie the experimental parapsychological approach to anomalous experiences. In Chapter 4, Paul Stevens calls into question some of the assumptions many researchers may have about the phenomena under investigation, and discusses the implications these assumptions have for research. In Chapter 5, Jezz Fox questions whether experimental research is capable of resolving the question of whether ESP exists. He reminds us of the limitations of what can and cannot be inferred from experiments.

In Chapter 6, the final chapter of Part One, Robin Wooffitt also questions the reliance on the experimental approach that has dominated parapsychological research. He presents an approach to anomalous experiences that draws upon methods from sociology, such as conversational analysis. He shows how adopting methods like these can serve to enable the study of anomalous experiences outside the laboratory as well as cast light on data collected in laboratory based studies.

In Part Two, the focus shifts to more psychologically-oriented approaches to studying anomalous experiences. In recent years the term "anomalistic" psychology has been used to describe this approach. It should be noted without too much surprise, however, that there is some overlap between psychological and parapsychological perspectives. For example, Etzel Cardeña's discussion of anomalous experiences in hypnosis, in Chapter 7, includes reference to research on the relationship between hypnosis and psi phenomena. However, the emphasis of this chapter is very much on the wider range of experiences associated with different "depths" of hypnosis.

Chapters 8, 9 and 10 discuss research on "spontaneous" experiences, which can be contrasted with the kinds of experiences typically studied in an experimental context. In their chapter, Ciarán O'Keeffe and Steve Parsons note the current interest, especially among non-professional researchers, in "ghosts" and associated phenomena. They provide a timely review of research on haunting experiences with an emphasis on likely environmental and psychological influences on such experiences. Simon J. Sherwood, in Chapter 9, focuses specifically on experiences featuring apparitions of black dogs, which are more familiar territory for folklorists than for parapsychologists. In Chapter 10, Christopher C. French and colleagues Julia Santomauro, Victoria Hamilton, Rachel Fox and Michael Thalbourne present a psychological analysis of people who report the experience of being abducted by aliens.

In Chapter 11, Richard Wiseman gives an overview of a series of experiments he and colleagues conducted to examine the reliability of people's accounts of experiences they report in séances. Darkroom séances were especially popular around the end of the nineteenth century and so it interesting to note how a modern group of sitters are affected by these conditions.

In Chapter 12, Craig D. Murray reviews theories that have been put forward to explain out-of-body-experiences, the feeling that one's conscious awareness is somehow separated from one's own physical body. He argues for a dissociaitional account of such experiences, noting that people who are more prone to such experiences have a tendency to be more dissatisfied with their bodies than do people who haven't had an out-of-body experience.

In the final essay, Christine Simmonds-Moore examines the notion that the tendency to have anomalous experiences is associated with the thinness of psychological "boundaries." She argues that thinner boundaries are associated with a less inhibitory style of thinking that is more likely to see connections between things. At a physiological level this is reflected by greater connectivity between neural structures. This approach treats anomalous experiences as inherently linked to the way each of us perceives and interprets the world around us.

Taken together, the essays in this volume represent a range of approaches that may be taken when studying anomalous experiences from a scientific perspective. These have been broadly classified as either parapsychological or psychological approaches, although there is significant overlap between these two approaches. It should be noted that this is still a relatively narrow range of approaches, and that a fuller understanding of anomalous experiences is likely to draw upon a wide range disciplines such as anthropology, philosophy, physics, religious studies, and theology. However, the fact that the focus of this book is on the parapsychological and psychological perspectives reflects that it is these related disciplines that have to date been responsible for the vast majority of research on anomalous experiences. It is hoped that this book will give the reader a flavor of how these approaches have helped to gain a greater scientific understanding of the more unusual and exotic aspects of human experience.

I would like to express my gratitude to all the essay authors for their contributions to the volume.

Matthew D. Smith • Fall 2009

Part One:
Parapsychological Perspectives

1

FEELING THE FUTURE
Studies of Precognitive Emotional Arousal

Daryl J. Bem*

Precognition is the perception of future events. In Lewis Carroll's *Through the Looking Glass* (1899), Alice first learns about precognition from the White Queen:

> "I don't understand you," said Alice. "It's dreadfully confusing!"
>
> "That's the effect of living backwards," the Queen said kindly: "it always makes one a little giddy at first—"
>
> "Living backwards!" Alice repeated in great astonishment. "I never heard of such a thing!"
>
> "—but there's one great advantage in it, that one's memory works both ways."
>
> "I'm sure *mine* only works one way," Alice remarked. "I can't remember things before they happen."
>
> "It's a poor sort of memory that only works backwards," the Queen remarked.
>
> "What sort of things do *you* remember best?" Alice ventured to ask.
>
> "Oh, things that happened the week after next," the Queen replied in a careless tone, [while] sticking a large plaster [band-aid] on her finger as she spoke.
>
> "Oh, oh, oh!" shouted the Queen, shaking her hand about as if she wanted to shake it off. "My finger's bleeding! Oh, oh, oh, oh!"
>
> Her screams were so exactly like the whistle of a steam-engine, that Alice had to hold both her hands over her ears.

---

*The author is grateful to his head research assistants over the past few years; Ben Edelman, Dan Fishman, and Rebecca Epstein, who served both as experimenters and overall coordinators of the Cornell psi laboratory. He is also indebted to his reliable teams of student experimenters: Lea Beresford, Shira Bookin, Maureen Clendenny, Amanda Cohen, Ingrid Edshteyn, Frankie Goldstone, Eric Hoffman, Daniel Huynh, Robert Hutko, Adriana Koeneke, Shehreen Latif, Michelle Michaels, Jordan Terner, Michael Van Wert, David Wilson, and Kimberly Wong.

"What *is* the matter?" she said, as soon as there was a chance of making herself heard. "Have you pricked your finger?"

"I haven't pricked it *yet*," the Queen said, "but I soon shall—oh, oh, oh!"

"When do you expect to do it?" Alice asked, feeling very much inclined to laugh.

"When I fasten my shawl again," the poor Queen groaned out: "the brooch will come undone directly. Oh, oh!" As she said the words the brooch flew open, and the Queen clutched wildly at it, and tried to clasp it again.

"Take care!" cried Alice. "You're holding it all crooked!" And she caught at the brooch; but it was too late: the pin had slipped, and the Queen had pricked her finger.

"That accounts for the bleeding, you see," she said to Alice with a smile. "Now you understand the way things happen here."

"But why don't you scream now?" Alice asked, holding her hands ready to put over her ears again.

"Why, I've done all the screaming already," said the Queen. "What would be the good of having it all over again?"

[Chapter V: "Wool and Water"].

Notice that the White Queen not only perceives a future event (that she will prick her finger) but also feels the future pain it will produce. Suppose the Queen had not foreseen that she would prick her finger. Could she have still felt the pain without knowing why? In other words, is it possible to *feel* a future event in the absence of precognitive knowledge about the event itself?

Evolutionary considerations suggest that it might. If humans and/or other animals really do possess precognitive abilities, then those abilities probably would have appeared first as a simple emotional signal to warn of impending danger, without specifying what the danger might be. It is now well established that we can experience the emotional impact of an event before we become conscious of its actual features (Zajonc, 1984).

This article presents evidence that future events can reach back in time to affect our current feelings, that we can, indeed, "feel the future." Other investigators have already reported some evidence for this. For example, in several "presentiment" experiments, participants were exposed to highly arousing stimuli (e.g. gruesome pictures, erotic pictures, or loud bursts of noise) and to nonarousing control stimuli while their physiological responses were monitored (Bierman and Radin, 1997; May and Spottiswoode, 2003; Radin, 1997, 2003; Spottiswoode and May, 2003). As expected, participants show strong physiological arousal when they are exposed to an arousing stimulus. But the intriguing finding is that participants also show physiological arousal immediately *before* they are exposed to the arousing stimulus—before the computer has even chosen the stimulus to be presented. The researchers termed this effect "presentiment."

The presentiment effect could also be called the "precognitive elicitation of arousal." In my own laboratory, we have been exploring its opposite, the precognitive habituation of arousal.

Precognitive Habituation

The habituation of arousal is a well-known physiological effect. If you see a threatening stimulus or hear a loud noise, your body reacts with the strong physiological arousal known as the "fight-or-flight" response: Your heart rate increases, you start to perspire, your breathing gets shallower, adrenalin is released, and blood flow is redirected to your arms and legs—all responses designed by evolution to prepare you to fight or flee in the face of danger. If the stimulus is repeated over and over, however, you get accustomed to it and your arousal to it diminishes. Technically, you *habituate* to it. Habituation can also occur with positively arousing stimuli. For example, if you are shown an erotic picture, you may experience positive sexual arousal; but, if you are shown the same picture over and over again, it ceases to arouse you and you habituate to it. You get bored with it.

Both of these habituation effects have recently been demonstrated in a laboratory experiment (Dijksterhuis and Smith, 2002). Participants were first subliminally exposed to extremely negative and extremely positive words. When they were subsequently asked to rate those words, they rated them as less extreme than words to which they had not been exposed, that is, negative words were rated less negatively and positive words were rated less positively.

The Precognitive Habituation (PH) procedure tests for precognition by, in effect, running a standard habituation procedure in reverse. Instead of exposing a participant to repeated presentations of a stimulus and then assessing his or her liking for it, the PH procedure reverses the sequence: On each trial of the PH procedure, the participant is first shown a pair of negatively arousing or positively arousing (erotic) photographs on a computer screen and asked to indicate which picture of the pair he or she prefers. The computer then randomly selects one of the two pictures to serve as the "habituation target" and displays it subliminally several times. If the participant prefers the picture subsequently designated as the target, the trial is scored as a "hit." Accordingly, the hit rate expected by chance is 50 percent.

The PH hypothesis is that the repeated exposures to the target can reach back in time to habituate the participant's arousal to it, that is, to diminish the arousal it would otherwise produce, thereby rendering negatively arousing targets less negative and erotic targets less positive. As implied above, this latter effect on erotic targets can be conceptualized as "precognitive boredom." Because the two pictures in each pair are matched, participants are predicted to prefer the target-to-be on trials with negatively arousing pictures and the non-target-to-be on trials with erotic pictures. Preferences on trials with low-arousal control pictures were not expected to differ from chance.

In my laboratory at Cornell University, more than 300 men and women have now participated in variations of the PH experiment. Collectively these studies provided strong support for the two predicted effects. Across the six basic studies, the hit rate was significantly above 50 percent on negative trials (52.6 percent, $p = .0008$) and significantly below 50 percent (48.0 percent, $p = .031$) on the erotic trials.*

THE ROLE OF AROUSAL

In our early experiments, the two PH effects were shown only by women participants; hit rates for the men were at chance levels for both the negative and erotic trials. Because the professional literature does not reveal any systematic sex differences in psi (ESP) ability, it seemed likely that this occurred because the men were less aroused by both the negative and erotic pictures than the women.

Most of the pictures used in the PH studies were selected from the International Affective Picture System (IAPS; Lang *et al.*, 1999), a set of 820 digitized photographs that have been rated on how positive or negative they are and how arousing they are by both men and women raters. The ratings reveal that men rate all of the negative pictures in the set as less negative and less arousing than do women.

Accordingly, we introduced different pictures for men and women in order to better equate the arousal they would experience. In addition, we asked all participants to respond to an "arousability" question before beginning the experiment: "In general, how intense are your emotional reactions to movies, videos, or photographs that are violent, scary, or gruesome?" They indicated their answers by responding on a scale that ranged from 1 (*"Not At All Intense"*) to 5 (*"Extremely Intense"*). Those who rated themselves above 3 on the scale were defined as highly arousable.

With these changes, both men and women identified as highly arousable showed the predicted PH effect on the negative trials: Men who were highly arousable obtained a hit rate of 55.8 percent ($p = .012$); women who were highly arousable obtained a hit rate of 53.6 percent ($p = .0003$). All others scored at chance level.

We also assessed the erotic responsiveness of our participants with two true-false questions: "I enjoy watching erotic scenes in movies," and "I prefer to date people who are physically exciting rather than people who share my values." Those who answered "true" to both questions were defined as "erotically responsive." Both men and women identified as erotically responsive showed the predicted PH effect on the erotic trials. For men, the effect was marginally significant: 45.2 percent ($p = .06$); for women the effect was highly significant: 40.9 percent ($p = .002$). All others scored at chance level.

---

*The p value accompanying each numerical result is the probability that the result could have arisen by chance: the smaller the p value, the less likely it is that the result might be simply a chance finding. By convention, a result may be called "statistically significant" if p is less than .05.

Precognitive Boredom and Aversion

Before my formal research program had begun, I asked a group of psi researchers to try out an early version of the PH procedure. They showed the predicted patterns: 53 percent hit rate on negative trials and 47 percent on erotic trials. The striking finding, however, was that they scored so far below 50 percent on a set of low-arousal neutral pictures that had been included to serve as control trials that they actually achieved statistical significance (37.5 percent, p = .01). They joked about it—"maybe we drank too much beer"—but did not take it seriously. As we shall see, however, the finding was not a fluke.

The earliest studies of the PH effect used only 4 subliminal exposures on each trial. In an attempt to strengthen the PH effect, we kept increasing the number of exposures, moving from 4 to 6, 8, 10, and 12 across the successive experiments. The hit rate on the low-arousal control trials remained essentially at chance until we reached 10 exposures, at which point the hit rate on these trials dropped to (46.8 percent, p = .04). In other words, when the low-arousal targets were exposed very frequently, they behaved like the erotic pictures, showing a precognitive boredom effect. Like a too frequent TV commercial, the many repeated exposures (precognitively) rendered the target picture boring, or even aversive, and hence less attractive than its matched non-target.

This suggested that it might be possible to design an experiment deliberately constructed to produce precognitive boredom as the central phenomenon. This would be desirable for two reasons.

First, there are large sex, cultural, and individual differences in arousal to the gruesome and the erotic pictures used in the PH experiment, making successful replication across different populations more difficult. Moreover, the proportion of highly arousable men in the university populations studied so far is quite low, which means successful replication requires either extensive pre-screening or recruiting many more men into the study to get an adequate sample. In contrast, it seemed likely that precognitive boredom would be most likely to occur among participants who are low in both arousability and in their tolerance for boredom. If true, a potentially larger pool of men would be available in a university population.

Second, several potential investigators have been hesitant to conduct a PH study because of objections to the gruesome and erotic pictures. Because an experiment designed to obtain the precognitive boredom effect would use low-arousal pictures, the objectionable pictures would be eliminated.

Although the precognitive boredom effect was first observed with control pictures that were deliberately selected to be neutral or mildly positive, it seemed likely that low-arousal *negative* pictures would be even more effective. The repeated exposure of a negative picture would render it increasingly unpleasant or aversive not simply boring. Accordingly, I have adopted the term *precognitive aversion* to describe the boredom effect on negative pictures.

THE PRECOGNITIVE BOREDOM/AVERSION PROCEDURE

To identify participants who were low in arousability, we reused the question from the PH experiments that had been used to identify participants who were high in arousability ("In general, how intense are your emotional reactions to movies, videos, or photographs that are violent, scary, or gruesome?"). Those who scored below 3 on the 5-point scale were defined as low in arousability. To identify participants who were low in their tolerance for boredom, we averaged responses to two questions: "I am easily bored" (scored in the reverse direction) and "I often enjoy seeing movies that I've seen before." Those who scored below 3 on the combined scale were defined as low in tolerance for boredom.

The experimental procedure itself was virtually identical to that used for the precognitive habituation studies. On each trial, the participant was shown two matched pictures and asked to click on the picture he or she preferred. The program then randomly selected one of the two pictures to serve as the target and flashed it on the screen 10 times. Unlike the PH studies, however, the target pictures were enlarged to fill the entire screen and were not subliminal; that is, they remained on the screen long enough for the participant to get bored with them. Half of the pictures were low-arousal negative pictures; half were low-arousal positive pictures. Three separate studies were conducted, each with 100 participants. Of the 300 participants, 214 were women and 86 were men.

RESULTS

The precognitive Boredom/Aversion hypothesis is that participants low in arousability and boredom tolerance will select the target picture on significantly fewer than 50 percent of the trials. Over all 300 experimental sessions, the hit rate was 47.5 percent ($p = .001$) on negative trials and at chance level (50.9 percent) on positive trials. Participants defined as low in arousability (103 of the 300 participants) achieved a hit rate of 45.9 percent ($p = .002$) on the negative trials but, again, did not differ from chance on the positive trials (48.9 percent). Finally, we looked at the hit rates achieved by those who were low on boredom tolerance: They showed a significant precognitive boredom effect on the positive trials (45.3 percent, $p = .02$). In general, then, it appears that precognitive aversion on negative picture pairs is a more robust and reliable phenomenon than precognitive boredom on positive picture pairs.

Back to Alice in Wonderland

In my view, the presentiment experiments and the experiments reported in this chapter provide persuasive evidence that we humans are capable of precognition. Whether my colleagues in mainstream psychology will be convinced, however, remains to be seen. Perhaps like Alice, they will exclaim,

> "I can't believe THAT."
> "Can't you?" the Queen said in a pitying tone. "Try again: draw a long breath, and shut your eyes."
> Alice laughed. "There's no use trying," she said: "one *can't* believe impossible things."
> "I daresay you haven't had much practice," said the Queen. "When I was your age, I always did it for half-an-hour a day. Why, sometimes I've believed as many as six impossible things before breakfast."

While I do not urge my colleagues to believe six impossible things before breakfast, I do invite them to consider one improbable thing before dinner, namely, that we can feel the future.

References

Bem, D. J. (2003). Precognitive Habituation: Replicable Evidence for a Process of Anomalous Cognition. In S. Wilson (chair), *Proceedings of Presented Papers From the Forty-Sixth Annual Convention of the Parapsychological Association, 2003 Vancouver, Canada.* 6–20.
Bierman, D. J., and D. I. Radin (1997). Anomalous anticipatory response on randomized future conditions. *Perceptual and Motor Skills*, 84. 689–690.
Carroll, L. (1899). *Through the Looking Glass*. New York: M. F. Mansfield & A. Wessels.
Dijksterhuis, A., and P. K. Smith (2002). Affective habituation: Subliminal exposure to extreme stimuli decreases their extremity. *Emotion*, 2(3). 203–214.
Lang, P. J., M. M. Bradley and B. N. Cuthbert (1999). International Affective Picture System (IAPS): Instruction manual and affective ratings. Technical report A4. Gainesville: Center for Research in Psychophysiology, University of Florida.
May, E. C., and S. J. P. Spottiswoode (2003, August 4). Skin conductance prestimulus response to future audio startle stimuli. Paper presented at the Parapsychological Association 46th Annual Convention, Vancouver, Canada.
Radin, D. I. (1997). Unconscious perception of future emotions: An experiment in presentiment. *Journal of Scientific Exploration*, 11. 163–180.
Radin, D. I. (2003, August 4). Electrodermal presentiments of future emotions. Paper presented at the Parapsychological Association 46th Annual Convention, Vancouver, Canada.
Spottiswoode, S. J. P., and E. C. May (2003). Skin conductance prestimulus response: Analyses, artifacts and a pilot study. *Journal of Scientific Exploration*, 17. 617–641.
Zajonc, R. B. (1984). On the primacy of affect. *American Psychologist*, 39. 117–123.

2

EXPERIMENTER EFFECTS IN PARAPSYCHOLOGY
Three Studies with a Remote Helping Task

Caroline Watt*

Surveys have found that from seventy to ninety percent of people report they can detect when they are being stared at from behind (Coover, 1913; Braud, Shafer and Andrews, 1993a). They may feel slightly uneasy, or feel the hairs standing up on the back of their necks, and on turning round find they are indeed being observed. The earliest research into this question had participants sit with their back to the experimenter and report whether or not they thought they were being stared at by the experimenter (Titchener, 1898; Coover, 1913). However, to rule out the possibility of sensory cues, the methodology has become increasingly sophisticated, for example staring through one-way mirrors (Peterson, 1978) and CCTV (Braud, Shafer and Andrews, 1993a, b). Because people who are being stared at seem to report physiological sensations, parapsychologists have more recently used physiological indicators of autonomic arousal such as electrodermal activity (EDA), which they feel are more sensitive than verbal reports (Braud, Shafer and Andrews, 1993a, b). This research is called direct mental interaction with living systems (DMILS) because it is investigating whether one person can influence another person at a distance through mental intention alone (see Schmidt, Schneider, Utts, and Walach, 2004, for a recent meta-analytic review of EDA-DMILS studies).

---

*The author would like to thank her co-experimenters, Clare Brady, Ian Baker, and Peter Ramakers, as well as Paul Stevens, who programmed the computer for the psi task. She would also like to thank the Perrott-Warrick Fund for providing financial support for these studies.

The basic DMILS procedure involves having two individuals isolated from one another in separate rooms. One acts as the "sender" and one as the "receiver." The receiver's EDA is continuously measured while the sender follows a randomized schedule of influence and control periods. For example, in a remote staring study the sender would stare at a live image of the receiver on a TV monitor during the influence periods and the monitor would go blank during the control periods. Of course, neither the experimenter nor the receiver has any idea of when the influence periods are occurring. Statistical tests are then used to compare the receiver's EDA during the influence periods with EDA during control periods. If there is no remote influence effect, one would find no significant difference between control and influence periods.

This paper summarizes a series of studies looking at experimenter effects in DMILS research. Before going on to describe the methodology used, the issue of experimenter effects will be discussed.

Experimenter Effects in DMILS Research

The experimenter effect, where certain experimenters seem consistently to obtain positive psi results while others do not, is one of parapsychology's most vexing problems. It is perhaps a pivotal question for the issue of replicability of psi effects. One often-cited example in DMILS research comes from the remote staring studies of psi proponent Marilyn Schlitz (MS) and psi skeptic Richard Wiseman (RW). Whereas RW has a history of chance results when he has investigated remote staring detection (Wiseman and Smith, 1994; Wiseman, Smith, Freedman, Wasserman and Hurst, 1995), MS has obtained positive results (Schlitz and LaBerge, 1994). This pattern of results persisted in their two joint studies (Wiseman and Schlitz, 1997; 1999) when using the same participant pool, procedures, and equipment, thus ruling out these factors as contributing to their pattern of results. However, RW and MS differ on many attributes apart from their beliefs about psi, so the reason for their results remains to be discovered.

Many researchers over the years have suggested different factors that may contribute to experimenter effects in parapsychology, and these factors may not be mutually exclusive. The experimenter's own psi may be the source of the results in their experiments (see Stanford, 1981 and 1990, for discussion of this issue). In addition, successful experimenters may create a psi-conducive atmosphere or psi-conducive expectancies in their participants (e.g., Honorton, Ramsey and Cabibbo, 1975; Schneider, Binder and Walach, 2000).

A consistent picture has not yet emerged from the empirical research on the question of experimenter effects. For example, positively-toned experimenter-participant interactions have been associated with significantly higher scores on an ESP task than negatively-toned interactions (Honorton,

Ramsey and Cabibbo, 1975). However, a more recent study that compared neutral (computer-presented) instructions to participants versus personally-presented instructions found an effect size three times larger for the neutral than for the personal condition (Schneider, Binder and Walach, 2000). Disagreement also exists on the question of the characteristics of psi-conducive and psi-inhibitory experimenters. A study by Schmeidler and Maher (1981) asked undergraduate psychology students to judge video-tapes of 5 psi-conducive and 5 psi-inhibitory experimenters (as defined by the authors on the basis of the experimenters' recent research). It was found that the nonverbal behavior of the psi-conducive experimenters was judged to be significantly different from that of the psi-inhibitory experimenters on 14 out of 30 adjectives. However, a recent survey seems to suggest that it is not easy to define "psi-conducive" and "psi-inhibitory." When parapsychologists were asked to rate the psi-conduciveness of 50 named researchers, opinions were inconsistent. There was only low to moderate agreement (i.e., 0 percent to 69 percent agreement on psi-conduciveness ratings) for over half of the researchers being rated (Smith, 2003). Further, perceived psi-conduciveness was found to be unrelated to experimenters' self-ratings of personality, belief that ESP is possible, belief in their own ESP abilities, personal psi experiences, and practice of a mental discipline (Smith, 2003).

Remote Facilitation of Attention Focusing

Psychophysiological research is not easy to conduct. EDA measurements can be affected by factors such as skin dryness, the humidity of the testing room, and the kind of electrode gel that is used. EDA is indeed a sensitive measure, but this can introduce a source of "noise" in the data, for instance if a person moves, sneezes, or yawns, this will affect EDA. For this reason, I decided to investigate experimenter effects with a very simple "cognitive" DMILS task rather than a physiological DMILS task. There are many anecdotal accounts of remote influence over cognitive activities—from remote prayer to help someone do well at their exams, to chess players claiming that their concentration is being affected by the mental intention of a member of the opponent's team hidden in the audience. The three experiments summarized here all used the same cognitive DMILS task: to help someone focus their attention on an object (described below). The studies varied factors that may cause experimenter effects and observed the effect on psi task performance. The first study (Watt and Brady, 2002) had a single experimenter and varied participants' expectancies about her reputation prior to them meeting her by informing participants that she had a history of obtaining positive psi results, or null psi results, in her research. The second study (Watt and Baker, 2002) had a single experimenter who either made psi-supportive or psi-unsupportive suggestions during the session. The third study (Watt and Ramakers, 2003) had multiple experimenters, selected on the basis of their extreme belief, or disbelief, in psi. Before describing each study individually, the psi task will be described in more detail.

For the psi measure in these studies, one individual, the "helper," attempts to help another remote individual, the "helpee," have fewer distractions as they attempt to keep their attention focused on a lit candle in a translucent blue glass holder. This task replicated that used in two previous studies that found significantly fewer distractions during help periods compared to control periods (Braud, Shafer, McNeill, and Guerra, 1995; Brady and Morris, 1997). The helpee is asked to press a button whenever they become distracted from the focus, and the dependent variable is the number of button presses (i.e., self-reported distractions) in the control and help periods. A remote facilitation of attention focusing effect is indicated by the helpee having significantly fewer button presses during help epochs compared to control epochs. All three studies reported here used the same number, duration, and counterbalanced random scheduling of control and help periods as were used in the studies by Braud et al. (1995) and Brady and Morris (1997).

The influence schedule is arranged in 4 pairs of help-control epochs and 4 pairs of control-help epochs, with each epoch lasting 60 seconds, giving a total of 16 minutes. The 8 pairs of epochs were presented in a randomized schedule, with counterbalancing within each pair. The randomization was done by computer once the program was initiated for each session. The program recorded session details including the sum of help presses, the sum of control presses, and the "PIS" (percentage influence score—a ratio calculated from these two sums such that a score of 0.5 represents an equal number of help and control presses, >0.5 represents fewer help than control presses, and <0.5 indicates fewer control than help presses). This PIS measure, as used originally by Braud and Schlitz (1991), can be used as a single outcome measure for each session. The PIS score has limitations (as discussed in Schmidt, Schneider, Binder, Bürkle, and Walach, 2001; and in Watt and Brady, 2002) but for present purposes we use it to enable comparisons between conditions.

Study 1. Experimenter's Track Record of Positive or Null Psi Results

Study 1 (Watt and Brady, 2002) used a single experimenter and influencer (CW) throughout. The aim was to restrict any possible experimenter effect to one factor: the participants' prior perception of the psi research "track record" of their experimenter. This was achieved by asking participants to read a short article that either portrayed CW as having a previous history of positive psi results ("*positive expectancy* condition") or as having a track record of null psi results ("*negative expectancy* condition"). This attempt to influence participants' expectancies about their experimenter's previous psi research track record is similar to several previous parapsychological studies in which participants' expectancies and attitudes have been varied. For instance, Layton and Turnbull (1975) exposed participants to either a positive or a negative evaluation of ESP prior to ESP testing and found, for one of their two experimental series, that the positive group had higher ESP scores than the negative group. Prior to ESP testing, Taddonio (1975) gave participants written instructions that included suggestions about the past performance of participants on the task. As predicted, the group that expected to score above chance scored significantly better than the group that expected chance scoring.

Materials

Priming Article. This simulated one-page article from a fictitious psychology magazine was designed to manipulate participants' expectancy before completing questionnaires and participating in the study. There were two versions of the article. They were identical except that the "positive expectancy" version noted that "*Dr. Watt is one of those who has a history of positive results, saying that 'in my 12 years as a researcher I have generally got positive results in my experiments.'*" The negative expectancy version noted that "*Dr Watt is one of those who has a history of chance results, saying that 'in my 12 years as a researcher I have generally not got positive results in my experiments.'*" For additional emphasis, the quote was repeated in an inset.

Procedure Summary

Participants were sent the priming article to read prior to the experimental session. Participants were otherwise treated the same during the session. CW described the procedure then seated the participant in a sound-attenuated room and lit a candle on which to focus during the session. The participant was instructed to commence the focusing task immediately, but was blind to the exact time of commencement of the influence periods, and to their duration and sequence. After a short delay, CW initiated the computer program that controlled the influence periods, and, seated in a distant room, followed the schedule of help and control periods that was displayed on her computer monitor.

Participants

There were 20 male and 40 female participants, with a mean age of 21.2 years (SD = 5.4) and a range from 17 to 52 years.

Hypotheses

It was hypothesized that there would be a remote helping effect (indicated by significantly fewer distractions in help epochs compared to control epochs) and that those participants in the positive expectancy condition would show greater evidence of remote helping than those in the negative expectancy condition.

Results and Discussion

There were 30 participants in the positive expectancy condition, and 30 in the negative expectancy condition. The mean number of registered distractions in help epochs was 12.58 (SD=8.6) and in control epochs was 12.20 (SD=8.0), which is a non-significant trend in the direction opposite to that predicted. There was therefore no support for the hypothesis that participants would show fewer distractions during help epochs compared with control epochs. This result fails to replicate prior research suggesting remote facilitation of focusing of attention (Brady and Morris, 1997; Braud et al., 1995).

The mean PIS score for participants in the positive expectancy condition was .506 (SD=0.1) and in the negative expectancy condition it was .490 (SD=0.1). This is a trend for greater remote helping in the positive expectancy condition, which is in the predicted direction but is not statistically significant.

The results of Study 1 suggested that in this study at least the prior reputation of the experimenter had little effect on the outcome of the remote helping task. I therefore decided to conduct a second study with what might be considered a stronger portrayal of the experimenter's psi belief or disbelief.

Study 2. Experimenter Making Psi-Supportive or Psi-Unsupportive Suggestions

Study 2 (Watt and Baker, 2002) had the same basic design as study 1: the same psi task was used, and participants were allocated to one of two conditions. A single experimenter (Ian Baker—IB) was used throughout. In a procedural change, participants were asked to bring in a friend to act as remote helper. This procedure had successfully been used by Brady and Morris (1997). Therefore, in the present study participants were working in pairs with a friend rather than a stranger. This procedural change also had the benefit of (as far as it is possible) eliminating the experimenter's role in the psi task. Therefore, it would be more likely that any difference in psi scoring might be attributed to how the experimenter portrayed himself and interacted with participants during the pre-session chat. In another procedural change, participants swapped roles during the session so that each was the helper once and each was the helpee once; there were therefore two psi trials per session. Participant pairs were randomly allocated to session condition (20 positive suggestion pairs, and 20 negative suggestion pairs, giving a total of 40 participants in each condition). This random allocation was prepared in advance of the entire study by CW with random number tables. The condition designation for each session was sealed in separate envelopes so that IB was blind to the condition designation at the time of recruitment and scheduling.

Procedure Summary

Study 2 systematically varied the psi-supportiveness of suggestions made by the experimenter to the participants during the session. In the positive condition, during the pre-session chat, IB actively and explicitly referred to his positive psi belief, and attempted to encourage the participants to consider and discuss possible psi experiences that they might have had. In addition, he referred to previous successful research using the same psi task, and made positive suggestions for success in the session. In the negative condition, the experimenter portrayed himself as a disbeliever in psi, and attempted to encourage the participants to consider and discuss possible "normal" interpretations of their possible psi experiences. He suggested that our own research had not confirmed previous positive results with this psi task. The experimenter attempted to maintain a warm and professional approach to all participants. This contrasts with the approach of Honorton, Ramsey, and Cabibbo (1975), whose experimenter in one condition was "friendly ... casual ... supportive" and in the other condition was "abrupt ... formal ... unfriendly." Thus in the present experiment we attempted to systematically vary the experimenter's professed psi belief and the associated psi-supportive versus psi-unsupportive context of the experimenter-participant interaction, while again holding constant experimenter personality, appearance, and so on.

Participants

There were 53 female and 27 male participants. Ages ranged from 14 to 81 years, with a mean age of 37.9 years (SD = 14.5).

Hypotheses

It was hypothesized that there would be fewer distractions during the help periods compared to control periods overall, and that there would be greater evidence of a remote helping effect for those participants in the psi-supportive condition compared to the psi-unsupportive condition.

Results and Discussion

The mean number of distractions in the Help and Control epochs was 10.35 (SD = 8.3) and 10.76 (SD = 8.8), respectively. This represented a slight tendency for fewer distractions in the Help epochs, as predicted. However, the difference was not statistically significant. The mean PIS score for those in the positive suggestion condition was 0.49 (SD = 0.13), compared with 0.53 (SD = 0.11) for negative suggestion participants. Therefore, there is a non-significant trend in the direction opposite to that predicted: negative suggestion participants showed slightly greater indication of remote helping than positive suggestion participants.

Study 2 therefore failed to demonstrate any effect of the experimenter's making psi-supportive or unsupportive suggestions on psi task performance. Perhaps because the experimenter was merely role-playing, his suggestions were not persuasive. The evidence for this is mixed. All of the participants had been asked to rate their experimenter's degree of belief in psi, in order to check whether the experimenter had successfully communicated this to participants. The mean experimenter psi belief rating for those in the positive suggestion condition was 4.3 (SD = 0.8), which was significantly higher than the mean score of 2.7 (SD = 0.9) for the negative suggestion participants. This suggests the experimental manipulation was fairly successful. However, with a scale midpoint of 3, we can see that those in the negative suggestion condition rated IB as having only moderate disbelief about psi. This may be because of the implicit psi-supportive context overall, given that the study was taking place in a parapsychology unit, or because IB did not convincingly portray a skeptical position.

In the final study, it was decided to select experimenters with strong disbelief or disbelief in psi, in the expectation that this would be an experimental setting closest to real life (where skeptical experimenters seem to obtain null results and believer experimenters obtain positive evidence of psi).

Study 3. Multiple Experimenters Believing or Disbelieving in Psi

A more direct approach to the question of the experimenter's psi belief comes from a preliminary study by Parker (1975) in which the experimenters were 3 ESP-believers and 3 ESP-disbelievers. Each experimenter group was given a talk intended to bolster their prior expectancies (whether positive or negative), and the disbelievers were told to expect scoring around chance level, while the believers were told to expect scores above chance level. Despite the small sample size, the believer experimenters obtained significantly more hits than the disbelievers.

Procedure Summary

The study (Watt and Ramakers, 2003) followed up on Parker's study by using a similar "multi-experimenter" design with the same remote helping task as in studies 1 and 2. The experimenters were selected if their belief or disbelief in psi scores fell in the top or bottom 25 percent of the belief scores from a questionnaire administered to all participants in studies 1 and 2. The study was in two parts: training sessions and psi sessions. For the training sessions, Peter Ramakers (PR) trained the experimenter to conduct a psi session with two participants. All trainee experimenters had previously participated in such a session as participants in the studies with Brady and Baker, so they already had some familiarity with the procedure. Trainee experimenters were encouraged to act naturally during the session and not to deliberately attempt to encourage or discourage psi scoring from their participants. The trainee experimenters then role-played conducting a session with PR. Trainees were given a printed guide to take home and study prior to the psi session. For the psi sessions, the experimenters conducted the psi session with two naïve participants. Participants came in pairs and swapped roles so that each was helper once and helpee once, thus giving two psi trials per session.

Experimenters

There were nine believer experimenters, consisting of three males and six females, mean age = 36.9 (SD = 11.46), range 28–63 years. Seven believer experimenters conducted one session, one conducted two, and one (PR) conducted three sessions, thus giving a total of 12 sessions (24 psi trials. There were five disbeliever experimenters, consisting of three males and two females, mean age = 44.8 (SD = 19.02), range 21–64 years. Four disbeliever experimenters conducted one session and one conducted two, giving a total of six sessions (12 psi trials). As expected, there was a highly significant difference in the believer and disbeliever experimenters' belief scores, thus confirming that our attempt to select trainee experimenters with strongly divergent paranormal belief scores had been successful.

Participants

There were 36 participants, consisting of 21 females and 15 males, mean age = 23.7, SD = 5.9, range 18–43 years.

Hypotheses

It was hypothesized that participants would have fewer distractions in the help epochs compared to the control epochs, and that those tested by believer experimenters would show greater evidence of remote facilitation of attention focusing than those tested by disbeliever experimenters.

RESULTS AND DISCUSSION

Hypothesis 1 predicted an overall remote facilitation of focusing effect. Overall, the mean number of help presses (12.03, $SD = 11.34$) was significantly lower than the mean number of control presses (13.47, $SD = 11.32$). This indicates an effect of remote facilitation on the focusing task, with participants showing significantly fewer distractions during the help epochs compared to the control epochs. Hypothesis 2 predicted an experimenter effect: those participants with believer experimenters would have higher psi scores than those with disbeliever experimenters. Table 1 gives the descriptive statistics for the two conditions, together with the results of related t-tests comparing mean help and control presses within each condition, and mean PIS scores. The table shows that the overall significant psi effect in this study is entirely due to those participants with believer experimenters, who have independently significant psi scoring. Those in the disbeliever experimenter condition scored at chance. A comparison of PIS scores for each condition using an unrelated t-test found a significant difference in the predicted direction. Thus this study found evidence of an experimenter effect on the psi task, with those participants tested by believer experimenters showing greater remote facilitation of attention focusing than those tested by disbeliever experimenters. It is perhaps worth reminding the reader at this point that the experimenters (both PR and the trainee experimenters) were blind to the order of help and control epochs, and that button presses were automatically recorded to computer disk, so it is unlikely that human error or bias could have artifactually produced these results.

Table 1. Mean (and Standard Deviation) Button Presses and PIS Scores, and a Comparison of Help and Control Presses

Condition	H Presses	C Presses	t	p	es(r)	PIS
Believer E (N=24)	12.25 (10.27)	14.54 (10.82)	2.737	.005	.50	.58 (0.12)
Disbeliever E (N=12)	11.58 (13.72)	11.33 (12.46)	-.223	.415	.07	.49 (0.12)

Note: p-values are one-tailed

Conclusions

Study 3 is the latest in a series that examined experimenter effects using as a psi task the remote facilitation of attention focusing. I investigated the effect of the experimenter's psi belief on the outcome of the psi task by preselecting multiple experimenters on the basis of their belief, or disbelief, in the paranormal. An overall remote facilitation of focusing effect was found, with an effect size r = 0.33. This replicates the main findings of two previous studies using the same psi task (Brady and Morris, 1997, r = 0.27; Braud, et al., 1995, r = 0.25), though my own previous studies using this task (Watt and Brady, 2002, r = -.11; Watt and Baker, 2002, r = 0.12) did not find any evidence of remote facilitation of attention focusing. So, the evidence on the question of whether a remote individual can help another to focus attention through mental intention alone is mixed, though there seem to be more significant studies than the one in twenty expected by chance alone.

On closer inspection it could be seen that the effect in study 3 was entirely due to participants who had been tested by believer experimenters. This group obtained independently significant scoring on the psi task, while those tested by disbeliever experimenters scored at chance. This suggests that the "multiple experimenter" method demonstrated an experimenter effect on the psi task, though replication with greater numbers of experimenters in each condition is recommended because it is possible that the different experimenter groups co-vary on other factors apart from their belief in psi. Studies 1 and 2, which attempted respectively to manipulate participants' expectancies of the experimenter's prior track record of positive or null psi results, and to have the experimenter make psi-supportive and psi-unsupportive suggestions during the session, found no evidence of experimenter effects.

An advantage of the multi-experimenter design over other studies (e.g., Schlitz, Wiseman, Radin and Watt, 2005; Watt and Baker, 2002; Watt and Brady, 2002; West and Fisk, 1953; Wiseman and Schlitz, 1997, 1999) is that it allows for a large number of experimenters to interact with their participants in a natural manner (e.g., rather than role playing) in a single study. This enables researchers to measure the experimenters' individual differences on characteristics such as personality and emotional intelligence, measures that would be uninformative when dealing with only one or two experimenters. Taken together with Parker's (1975) findings of significant differences in psi scoring between believer and disbeliever experimenters, these results indicate the potential utility of this kind of multi-experimenter design for the study of experimenter effects in parapsychology.

References

Brady, C., and R. Morris (1997). Attention focusing facilitated through remote mental interaction: A replication and exploration of parameters. *Proceedings of Presented Papers: Parapsychological Association 40th Annual Convention.* 73–91.
Braud, W. G., and M. J. Schlitz (1991). Conscious interactions with remote biological systems: Anomalous intentionality effects. *Subtle Energies,* 2. 1–46.

Braud, W., D. Shafer and S. Andrews (1993a). Reactions to an unseen gaze (remote attention): A review, with new data on autonomic staring detection. *Journal of Parapsychology*, 57. 373–390.
Braud, W., D. Shafer and S. Andrews (1993b). Further studies of autonomic detection of remote staring: replications, new control procedures, and personality correlates. *Journal of Parapsychology*, 57. 391–409.
Braud, W., D. Shafer, K. McNeill and V. Guerra (1995). Attention focusing facilitated through remote mental interaction. *Journal of the American Society for Psychical Research*, 89. 103–115.
Coover, J. E. (1913). The feeling of being stared at. *American Journal of Psychology*, 24. 570–575.
Honorton, C., M. Ramsey and C. Cabibbo (1975). Experimenter effects in extrasensory perception. *Journal of the American Society for Psychical Research*, 69. 135–139.
Layton, B. D., and B. Turnbull (1975). Belief, evaluation, and performance on an ESP task. *Journal of Experimental Social Psychology*, 11. 166–179.
Parker, A. (1975). A pilot study of the influence of experimenter expectancy on ESP scores. In J.D. Morris, W.G. Roll, and R.L. Morris (eds.), *Research in Parapsychology 1974*. 42–44 (research brief).
Peterson, D. M. (1978). Through the looking glass: an investigation of extra-sensory detection of being stared at. M.A. Thesis. University of Edinburgh.
Schlitz, M. J., and S. LaBerge (1994). Autonomic detection of remote observation: Two conceptual replications. In D. J. Bierman (ed.), *Proceedings of the Parapsychological Association 37th Annual Convention*. 352–360.
Schlitz, M., R. Wiseman, D. Radin and C. Watt (2005). Experimenter effects and the remote detection of staring: An attempted replication. *Paper Submitted to the 48th Annual Convention of the Parapsychological Association*.
Schmeidler, G. R., and M. Maher (1981). Judges' responses to the nonverbal behavior of psi-conducive and psi-inhibitory experimenters. *Journal of the American Society for Psychical Research*, 75. 241–257.
Schmidt, S., R. Schneider, M. Binder, D. Bürkle and H. Walach (2001). Investigating methodological issues in EDA-DMILS: Results from a pilot study. *Journal of Parapsychology*, 65. 59–82.
Schmidt, S., R. Schneider, J. Utts and H. Walach (2004). Distant intentionality and the feeling of being stared at: Two meta-analyses. *British Journal of Psychology*, 95. 235–247.
Schneider, R., M. Binder and H. Walach (2000). Examining the role of neutral versus personal experimenter-participant interactions: An EDA-DMILS experiment. *Journal of Parapsychology*, 64. 181–194.
Smith, M.D. (2003). The psychology of the "psi-conducive" experimenter: Personality, attitudes towards psi, and personal psi experience. *Journal of Parapsychology*, 67. 117–128.
Stanford, R. G. (1981). Are we shamans or scientists? *Journal of the American Society for Psychical Research*, 75. 61–70.
Stanford, R. G. (1990). An experimentally testable model for spontaneous psi events: A review of related evidence and concepts from parapsychology and other sciences. In S. Krippner (ed.), *Advances in Parapsychological Research*, 6. Jefferson, NC: McFarland.
Taddonio, J. L. (1975). Attitudes and expectancies in ESP scoring. *Journal of Parapsychology*, 39. 289–296.
Titchener, E. B. (1898). The feeling of being stared at. *Science*, 8. 895–897.
Watt, C., and I. S. Baker (2002). Remote facilitation of attention focusing with psi-supportive versus psi-unsupportive experimenter suggestions. *Journal of Parapsychology*, 66. 151–168.
Watt, C., and C. Brady (2002). Experimenter effects and the remote facilitation of attention focusing: Two studies and the discovery of an artifact. *Journal of Parapsychology*, 66. 49–71.
Watt, C., and P. Ramakers (2003). Experimenter effects with a remote facilitation of attention focusing task: A study with multiple believer and disbeliever experimenters. *Journal of Parapsychology*, 67. 99–116.
West, D. J., and G. W. Fisk (1953). A dual ESP experiment with clock cards. *Journal of the Society for Psychical Research*, 37. 185–197.

Wiseman, R., and M. Schlitz (1997). Experimenter effects and the remote detection of staring. *Journal of Parapsychology*, 61. 197–207.
Wiseman, R., and M. Schlitz (1999). Replication of experimenter effect and the remote detection of staring. *Proceedings of the 43rd Annual Convention of the Parapsychological Association.* 147–153.
Wiseman, R., and M. D. Smith (1994). A further look at the detection of unseen gaze. *Proceedings of the Parapsychological Association 37th Annual Convention of the Parapsychological Association.* 465–478.
Wiseman, R., M. D. Smith, D. Freedman, T. Wasserman and C. Hurst (1995). Two further experiments concerning the remote detection of an unseen gaze. *Proceedings of the Parapsychological Association 38h Annual Convention of the Parapsychological Association.* 480–490.

3

THE ROLE OF ALTERED STATES OF CONSCIOUSNESS IN EXTRASENSORY EXPERIENCES

Chris A. Roe

Charles Tart noted that one of the major problems in attempting to study and understand paranormal phenomena is in having them occur reliably under test conditions; he warned: "If you set up an experiment to test the effects of various variables, but the phenomena don't occur, you have mostly wasted your time" (Tart, 1977, p. 500). Kelly and Locke (1981, p. 2) summarized the state of parapsychology in similar terms: "few would disagree that our most pressing need is for stronger and more reliable psi sources. If we are ever to learn much about these phenomena, we will simply have to make them more consistently available for study." These quotes are over a quarter of a century old and although a number of advances have been made in the intervening years, it can certainly be argued that, in this respect, little has changed. The phenomena of parapsychology seem as inconsistent and ephemeral as ever (cf. Kennedy, 2001, 2003). So how might we engender a more consistent ESP effect in the laboratory, one that can be pinned down and studied more closely? We need to trawl the research literature to identify (or remind ourselves of) optimal conditions for the expression of psi and be sure to insist that those features are a *sine qua non* of future experimental designs. Kelly and Locke's (1981) comments above were part of an introduction to their monograph on altered states of consciousness (ASCs) and psi, and their recommendation was to focus on these states as perhaps not a necessary condition for psychic experience, since ESP can occur in normal waking state (see, e.g., Milton, 1997), but certainly a sufficient one. In this chapter we shall see whether research evidence accumulated since Kelly and Locke's recommendation tends to support or refute their thesis, and will argue that, if anything, ASCs appear even more promising now than they did then.

How we define what counts as an ASC is rather a thorny issue that we will return to at the end of this chapter once we come to interpret the various research findings that have been reviewed. For now we can adopt John Beloff's rather simple definition of them as "any state of mind that differs markedly enough from that which we associate with our normal waking selves" (in Parker, 1975, p. 8), with the caveat that typically researchers will define them operationally (and rather circularly) as the state of mind that results from various practices, rituals or processes that are intended or believed to induce an ASC.

Identifying Conducive Factors from Spontaneous Cases

If we want to explore whether ASCs offer the conditions under which psychic experiences might thrive it seems sensible to begin by looking at the circumstances in which spontaneous instances of psi are reported. There are advantages and disadvantages in looking to spontaneous cases for insights into the nature and mechanism of ESP. Rush (1986, p. 48) notes, for example, that their key advantage is in terms of ecological validity, since "they reflect the involvement of psi in everyday life, in a great variety of situations and subjective modes. To the extent that they are valid accounts, they provide the investigator a sampling of the natural range of psi phenomena without the restrictions on their variety or their physical and psychological contexts that experimental procedures necessarily impose." Starting here therefore ensures that any explanatory models we construct, or any empirical predictions we make about psychic phenomena, will be comprehensive enough to account for the real world occurrences that parapsychology was established to explain, rather than just some subclass of instances that might be found in the laboratory.

Using reports of spontaneous cases as evidence has disadvantages too, however, so that interpretation should always be guarded. For example, where the phenomenon does not recur so that we are not able to investigate it for ourselves, we have only the witnesses' recollections of it. We know that such reports can become distorted or embellished (either consciously or, more usually, unconsciously) due to inaccuracies of perception, attention and memory in ways that tend to increase consistency (cf. Bartlett, 1932), to leave us with an account that becomes more impressive than it originally was. One way of dealing with these problems is to collect direct testimony from as many witnesses as possible along with substantiating circumstantial evidence (including character assessments) much as one might do in presenting a legal case, and this was a feature of early case collections by members of the Society for Psychical Research (e.g., Sidgwick, 1923). When we consider what they discovered we find that, although most of the cases in the classic collection *Phantasms of the Living* (Gurney, Podmore and Myers, 1886) concerned apparitions witnessed while awake, some paranormal events occurred while the percipient was sleeping (149 cases involving dreams in a collection of 702 cases) or in "borderland cases" which represent the transition stage between wakefulness and sleep (see Van de Castle, 1977). The association between ESP and ASCs was sufficiently clear for them to claim:

> It is characteristic of the clairvoyant power that it is generally exercised when the normal powers of sensory percipience are in abeyance, during natural somnambulism, during morbid conditions of trance, or during the sleep-walking state induced by mesmeric passes. It seems as though this supersensory faculty assumed activity in an inverse ratio to the activities of common life [vol. 2, p. 287].

An alternative way of dealing with possible errors or distortions in testimony is to collect sufficient numbers of cases so that we might suppose that the core features of the experience would tend to be reported consistently as an emerging pattern, while errors would be much more erratic and would reduce to background "noise." This was the strategy that was adopted by Louisa Rhine (e.g., 1961) and replicated by others (e.g., Dale, White and Murphy, 1962; Sannwald, 1963). In terms of a role for ASCs in such experiences, about half of Rhine's cases and practically all those that involved imagery had occurred while respondents were dreaming or quietly relaxed or involved with simple, habitual tasks that required little conscious attention. Those that occurred while the experient was actively awake tended to be less explicit, ranging from diffuse uneasiness to intuitions. Very few cases involved occasions where the person was actively involved with others or engaged in mental concentration. Dale (1951) similarly found that of 65 cases collected by the American Society for Psychical Research which she considered to be veridical, 41 percent involved dreams and a further 11 percent borderland states. Schouten (1981) reports that the Sannwald collection of German cases also includes a preponderance of dream experiences (59 percent) and intuitions (24 percent), with only 11 percent of cases involving waking imagery. Rush (1986) has commented on how the relative consistency of these findings is impressive given that they reflect experiences collected during diverse periods from different populations and by different methods. However, when Alvarado (1998) compared the incidence of ESP experiences in dreams and in the waking state across later surveys (1979–1996) the difference in favor of the former was much reduced (51.3 percent versus 48.7 percent) and non-significant, although this was based on questionnaire responses rather than descriptions of specific instances that had been volunteered. This could be interpreted in terms of the tendency we have just noted for ESP-type experiences while awake to be less vivid or detailed, since this could make them sufficiently memorable for respondents to be able to confirm that they occurred when explicitly asked about them as part of a questionnaire, but not sufficiently impressive or evidential for them to take the initiative in sending a description in a letter to one of the parapsychology departments, so that they would not feature in case collections.

In any case, we cannot be sure that the apparent consistency isn't simply a reflection of some systematic bias, for example where reports reflect cultural expectations concerning what "should" happen in a paranormal episode. And without investigating the cases we are unable to evaluate how likely it is that the experience has a mundane explanation, such as coincidence; since the majority of the population dreams each night on a range of topics as diverse as imagination allows, and a significant minority are likely to be able to recall elements of those dreams, there will be plenty of opportunities for capitalizing on chance coincidences.* Rhine was, of course, aware of these limitations, and was very clear that the rationale for pursuing this line of research was "partly in a search for clues, for new insights by which to guide the framing of experiments" (Rhine, 1961, p. 19); once particular aspects were identified from spontaneous cases they would be subject to testing under the more rigorous conditions of laboratory experimentation. Likewise, here we have briefly considered the evidence from case collections not as a proof that ASCs are necessarily implicated in psychic experience, but to see if a *prima facie* justification can be made that the investment of time and resources in experimentation might be worthwhile, and to see what insights it might provide for how those experiments should be conducted.

Experimental Tests of ESP with Meditators

When White (1964) analyzed introspective reports of exceptional psi percipients, she found that a great deal of emphasis was placed on achieving a state of deep physical and mental relaxation. Many cases involved deliberate attempts to still the body and mind as part of some kind of preparatory ritual. If we wished to replicate this type of preparation in an experimental setting then the technique that seems to best fulfill these criteria is some form of meditation practice. Honorton (1974, also 1981) quotes the ancient Yoga Aphorisms of Patanjali as expressing the belief that the states of conscious-

---

*Van de Castle (1977) responds to this concern by noting that paranormal dreams are often described as being unusually vivid and intense, and seem particularly portentous to the dreamer once they waken (and before the event is confirmed) so that explanations simply in terms of after-the-fact capitalizing on coincidence may not apply. See also Hearne (1989).

ness achieved through yoga practices can, as a distracting by-product, lead to the development of *Siddhis* or paranormal powers, and elsewhere he notes that a number of successful ESP subjects such as Lalsingh Harribance and Malcolm Bessent had routinely utilized meditation techniques in preparation for psi testing sessions (Honorton, 1977, p. 441). In summarizing the results from 16 experimental series that tested participants for ESP after they had meditated, Honorton found the combined outcome to be highly significant ($p = 6 \times 10^{-12}$), with 9 being independently significant, and he was moved to conclude, "it appears that meditation is an effective means of producing controlled psi interactions" (p. 442). Schmeidler (1994) subsequently identified a further 6 studies and found that 4 of these gave significant results in the predicted direction, which might be thought of as a confirmation of Honorton's conclusion.

However, if we consider the typical design of such studies we can see that caution is advisable. For example, Dukhan and Rao (1973) reported on three experimental series in which participants were tested for ESP before and after meditation, and found that scores after meditation were significantly higher than those before. This improvement is not straightforward to interpret for a number of reasons. Firstly, participants were not tested for ESP during their meditation and so we can have no guarantee that they were in any form of altered state at the time of the second testing, rather it seems more appropriate to say that improvements in scores were a consequence of *having meditated* rather than a consequence of *being in a meditative state*. Secondly, although some participants showed significant above-chance scores in the post-test, the difference in scores between pre- and post-measures was primarily due to significant below chance scores on the pre-test. Schmeidler (1988, pp. 101–2) accounts for this in terms of the "good participants problem," in which persons recruited to a study that has a simple design and fairly transparent experimenter expectations can be especially susceptible to demand characteristics, where the participant (usually unconsciously) conforms to the behavior that they believe will please the experimenter. Here that can be achieved just as well by underperforming in the pre-condition as it can by (the predicted) overperforming in the post-condition. As such, any significant differences between pre- and post-test scores may have nothing to do with the meditation that takes place in the interim.

These demand characteristics can be addressed by adopting an independent samples design, where participants contribute to only one condition (and indeed may not be informed in advance about the characteristics of other conditions) so that they are much less clear on what outcome might be expected. But what would constitute an appropriate comparison group for meditators? If we use non-meditators as our control group then they may differ in a host of other ways too (such as belief, openness, self-discipline) so that we can not be sure that it is the act or state of meditation *per se* that is responsible for any observed differences in performance. If we have matched groups, with meditators in the comparison group who are simply not given any express instructions to prepare for the session by meditating* there is always a possibility that they will independently decide to meditate as part of their own personal preparation. One way of addressing this is to recruit meditators with different degrees of experience or proficiency to see if this is related to degree of success at the psi task. When Dukhan and Rao (1973) did this, they only found an advantage for senior meditators in one of their three studies, but "seniors" were defined here rather loosely as "one who had already attained some experience in yoga and a fair level of yogic attainment" (p. 149). Roney-Dougal and Solfvin (2006) in contrast worked with a more experienced population who attended an ashram in India. They distinguished between students, Sannyasins and Swamis based on the initiations they had completed so that even students had an average of 3.7 years' practice, Sannyasins had 6 years and Swamis 19.7 years. They found that Swamis had nonsignificant psi hitting at a free response ESP task whereas the other groups scored slightly below chance. In a second study (Roney-Dougal, Solfvin, and Fox, 2008) they reported a significant correlation between years of practice and ESP score ($r = .52$, $p < .05$).

Roney-Dougal and colleagues' research is particularly interesting because they also considered the effects of different forms of meditation to see whether there were any differential effects. This draws attention to the tendency of reviewers to treat all forms of meditation as if they were alike, when it seems naïve to expect that similar beneficial effects will accrue whether one uses yoga meditation or Zen meditation, or whether one is an established swami or a complete beginner. Unless research on the effects of meditation is more systematic in specifying the practices that participants undertake and is clearer in demarcating what level of proficiency is needed with that practice for any effects on ESP to be evident, then it seems unlikely that it will prove especially informative in determining whether ASCs are psi-conducive.

However, many of these practical difficulties can be overcome if we choose to focus on ASCs that are naturally occurring, are regularly experienced by most people, and which they are already very practiced at entering into. The ASC that meets all these requirements is the dream state.

Experimental Tests of Dream ESP

Psychiatrist Montague Ullman established a dream laboratory at the Maimonides Medical Center, Brooklyn, in 1962, prompted by observations in his practice of patients who reported dreams containing material that could be indicative of telepathy (Krippner, 1991). He sought to reproduce this phenom-

---

Instructing them not to meditate draws attention to this as the variable that is manipulated and could easily give rise to the demand characteristics we are trying to avoid with this design.

enon under the more controlled conditions of a dream laboratory. In this he was helped by the then recent discovery that there were certain periods during the sleep cycle when people exhibited bursts of rapid eye movements (REM), and these coincided with EEG readings indicating that the sleeper was in a mentally active state. If woken during such periods, people were more likely to report having been dreaming than if woken at other times.

The general method adopted for Maimonides dream ESP work is described by Van de Castle (1977) and Child (1985). Typically, a subject would come to the lab to spend the night as a percipient or "receiver." He would chat with the person who would later act as "sender," and when he became tired would have EEG electrodes attached so that he could be monitored for REM and would go to bed in a soundproof room. Once the percipient had fallen asleep, the sender would be given an opaque envelope containing an art print as the target picture that had been selected using random number tables. The targets had been prepared by another member of staff so that the experimenters who interacted with the receiver would also not know what the target was. The sender would be housed in a remote room in the building, or even in a separate building, so as to rule out the possibility for normal communication. When notified by the experimenter via a one-way buzzer that the receiver was dreaming, she would open the envelope and concentrate on the target, attempting to communicate its contents to the receiver during each dream phase—the same target picture was used all night. Towards the end of each REM period (i.e. while he was still dreaming) the receiver was wakened and asked to describe the content of his dream. This dream report—termed a *mentation*—was tape-recorded. After this he was allowed to go back to sleep until the next REM phase, and at the end of the night's sleep he had an opportunity to add further impressions or associations that he could recall. He would then be presented with a set of 8 or 12 art prints that included a duplicate of the target and his task was to rank order them in terms of their similarity to the dreams he reported and assign each a correspondence rating out of 100. Once these data had been recorded the actual target would be revealed. If the target picture had been placed in the top half of the ranking table (i.e. 1–4 for 8 alternatives) this was deemed a binary hit, and if in the bottom half it was a binary miss. Apart from screening studies in which a range of people were recruited so as to identify promising participants, most of the experiments involved short series of 7 or 8 trials with the same receiver. At the end of a series, transcripts were also sent to independent judges who repeated the rating process.

Despite this judging method being relatively crude (one would be correct just by chance on 50 percent of trials, which makes it difficult to detect even medium sized effects where the number of trials is quite small), the early series were quite successful. For example, in the first series with a selected participant, the dreamer, Erwin, achieved 7 hits and 1 miss, and in his second series he achieved 8 hits and no misses. The Maimonides research program ran for

16 years and included 13 formal dream ESP studies and 3 separate pilot series. Most followed variants of the basic procedure described above, but they were modified in a variety of ways over time so as to explore different theoretical questions. However, the outcomes seemed quite consistent. The Maimonides research has been reviewed by a number of researchers (Radin, 1997; Sherwood and Roe, 2003; Van de Castle, 1977) and the overall success rate has been estimated at 63 percent (where 50 percent would be expected just by chance), a result that is highly significant ($p < 1 \times 10^{-8}$, Radin, 1997, p. 72). Despite difficulties in replicating these findings at other sleep laboratories (e.g., Belvedere and Foulkes, 1971; Globus, Knapp, Skinner and Healey, 1968), critical evaluations (e.g., Clemmer, 1986; Hyman, 1986) have not been able to offer plausible counter explanations for the original results (see Sherwood and Roe, 2003, pp. 89–90).

But few exact replications have been attempted. This is because most researchers have not had access to the specialist resources that were available to the Maimonides group. Instead investigators have improvised methods that typically sacrifice some degree of control over conditions in favor of greater ecological validity and participant convenience or comfort. Many have followed Braud's (1977) example in allowing participants to sleep in their own homes, to wake naturally and to attempt to recall the content of their dreams then using a dream diary. As the percipient sleeps, the sender attempts to communicate details of the target over an extended period of time in the expectation that this will include at least one REM period, given the normal sleep cycle. Others have adopted a clairvoyant design in which a target (in this case a video clip) was selected by computer and played automatically through the night without a sender (e.g. Dalton, Steinkamp and Sherwood, 1999), or a precognitive design in which the target is only generated after the dream mentations have been discussed and the target set judged (e.g., Sherwood, Roe, Simmonds and Biles, 2002). Both these methods make it more difficult for the participant to gather information about the target by normal means. Sherwood and Roe (2003) reviewed these replication attempts and although they found that they gave an independently significant cumulative outcome, and so could be regarded as a conceptual replication, they had been significantly less successful than the original Maimonides work. To account for this, Sherwood and Roe noted that the replications had been extremely varied in method and heterogeneous in outcome, and this should be able to give pointers to good (and bad) practice.

They made a number of recommendations, including that participants should be monitored and deliberately woken from REM sleep, since this greatly increases the amount and quality of dream material that one can recall, or indeed the likelihood of being able to recall one's dreams at all—it is not uncommon for unselected participants to come to the lab for the judging phase with only the vaguest recollection of any of their dreams. Secondly, they noted that the laboratory climate may be an important factor (Van de Castle, 1977), with some environments or experimenter-participant interactions being much more successful than others in putting the participant at their ease and able to perform naturalistically. Perhaps indicative of this is Sherwood and Roe's finding that some researchers seemed to be consistently successful even where they worked with different research collaborators. And thirdly they pointed out that the Maimonides researchers tended to recruit participants who had done well in screening studies or who had a track record of success in other ESP experiments, whereas many of the later replications involved unselected subjects. Future work might be more consistent if participants were selected for prior experiences, ability to regularly recall their dreams, or for certain psi-conducive personality factors, such as the Feeling and Perceiving dimensions of the Myers-Briggs Type Indicator (Roe, Jones and Maddern, 2007).

Experimental Tests of ESP in the Ganzfeld

Dream research has not been an especially attractive proposition for researchers interested in finding a replicable method for eliciting ESP. This is because the principal approaches in dream research have either required equipment and facilities that allow participants to sleep overnight at the laboratory while their EEG and eye movements are monitored so as to identify REM periods, which can be prohibitively expensive, or else have relied on more ecologically valid arrangements that have varied widely and carry no guarantee that the participant is indeed in any form of non-waking state when they have their impressions of the target.

A method was needed that would reproduce the subjective experience of drifting off to sleep but that could be used in the laboratory during normal working hours. One technique that was adopted independently by three groups of researchers involved ganzfeld stimulation (Braud, Wood and Braud, 1975; Honorton and Harper, 1974; Parker, 1975). The ganzfeld (usually translated from German as "whole field") involves placing halved ping pong balls over the participant's eyes and shining a red (or sometimes pink) light on them. The participant keeps her eyes open and the semi-translucent plastic of the ping pong balls diffuses the light so that she experiences a homogeneous visual field that seems warm and cozy, but because the light stimulus is unpatterned and unchanging her brain habituates to it and she may even experience "blank out" periods in which it feels like she has no visual experience at all. Such an uninteresting visual experience can lead to "sensory hunger," in which the experient is drawn to focus on her own internally-generated mentation, in the form of mild hallucinations that have a dream-like quality. The ganzfeld is thought to facilitate the flow of ideation and imagery (Bertini, Lewis and Witkin, 1964) so that these impressions can seem very spontaneous, creative, and quite independent of any conscious thought processes. A similar auditory effect is achieved by generating a sound signal that evenly represents the whole audible frequency range (called "white noise") or a version that filters out the high frequency aspects that some participants find rather jarring ("pink noise"). This gives an unpatterned hiss that is reminiscent of nothing so much as the rush of cascading water. Again, sensory hunger can lead the participant to incorporate her own internally-generated material into the signal, giving the impression that certain sounds (noises, music, voices) are embedded in the noise just on the edge of hearing.

In a typical ganzfeld study (e.g., Sherwood, Roe, Holt and Wilson, 2005), participants are recruited in pairs, with one to serve as the sender and one as the receiver. The sender's task is to watch a randomly selected target video clip during the time when the receiver is experiencing ganzfeld stimulation, and the prediction to be tested is that the receiver's internally-generated ganzfeld mentation will include elements that had somehow been communicated from the sender, and could be used to identify the target clip. Sessions begin with sender, receiver and experimenter all present in a sound attenuated room as the receiver is prepared for the session. The receiver lies back in a reclining chair and gets as comfortable as she can, removing her shoes and covering herself with a blanket if she wishes. She wears headphones with a microphone attached through which she can communicate with the experimenter and be heard by the sender during the session. Then halved ping-pong balls are placed over her eyes and held secure with micropore tape and a red light shone onto her face. The sender and experimenter then leave her, and the door to the receiver's room typically is locked, partly to ensure that it's not possible for her to be passed information about the target via normal means, and partly to reassure the receiver that no-one will be in the room while she is in this vulnerable sensorily-deprived state (participants sometimes report a sense of presence which can lead them to believe someone is actually in the room with them). The sender is then escorted to his room, where he puts on headphones so that he can hear any comments from the receiver or experimenter as well as the soundtrack to the target clip when it is played. The sender's door is locked and then the experimenter goes to their own room to initiate the computer program that runs the session.

It's quite common for participants to feel a little nervous about this rather unusual protocol, so to encourage them to feel safe and relaxed they firstly follow a series of progressive relaxation instructions played by the computer over headphones. Once these are complete the program selects the target video clip and plays it to the sender repeatedly over the ganzfeld period* as the receiver listens to white noise and reports on any impressions or sensations that she

---

Obviously, the receiver and experimenter would remain unaware of what target had been selected.

experiences. The sender can also hear the receiver's comments as feedback on his sending strategy.

Most ganzfeld sessions last in the region of 25–30 minutes, and after this time the experimenter reviews the receiver's mentation with her to see if anything needs to be added, elaborated or modified while they are both still blind to the target identity. The receiver then removes her eye shields so she can view four video clips consisting of the target and three decoys, all selected and played automatically by the computer. These are rated or rank ordered for their similarity to the receiver's impressions, and once the ratings are saved the actual target is revealed as feedback.

If chance alone were operating and participants were just guessing then they should select the actual target as their first choice 25 percent of the time; so what was the observed hit rate with this method? The first summary reviews of ganzfeld ESP research were prompted by an exchange between parapsychologist Charles Honorton and skeptic Ray Hyman. Honorton initially claimed a 55 percent hit rate in studies from his lab at the Psychophysical Research Laboratories (PRL) in New Jersey, but Hyman suspected that this would reduce to chance levels once they took into account factors that might artificially inflate the apparent level of success. The kind of factors he had in mind included possible multiple analyses—where various outcome measures are taken (such as having the receivers' judgments be supplemented by those from independent judges), but only those that are significant are reported in publications—and file drawer problems, where unsuccessful studies are not published in journals (or perhaps never even written up) so that their data lie hidden in researchers' file drawers.

Hyman (1985) and Honorton (1985) each separately appraised the impact of these possible flaws on a database of 42 ganzfeld experiments contributed by 10 independent research groups, and perhaps not surprisingly came to different conclusions. Hyman felt that the experiments had too many methodological weaknesses to justify the claim that ESP was responsible for any apparently above-chance scoring, whereas Honorton attempted to show that even where there were weaknesses, they were not sufficiently related to the outcomes to be able to account for them, and indeed where they could be addressed in re-analysis (for example, controlling for multiple analysis problems by imposing a consistent measure across all studies) the cumulative outcome remained highly significant. Although there was little hope of Honorton and Hyman agreeing on their interpretation of these data as evidence of ESP, the exchange culminated very positively in a joint communiqué that set the pattern for future work:

> There is an overall significant effect in this data base that cannot reasonably be explained by selective reporting or multiple analysis. We continue to differ over the degree to which the effect constitutes evidence for psi, but we agree that the final verdict awaits the outcome of future experiments conducted by a

broader range of investigators and according to more stringent standards [Hyman and Honorton, 1986, p. 351].

In that paper they outlined what those more stringent standards should be. Honorton himself took up the challenge of producing a gold standard protocol that addressed the various methodological concerns that Hyman had raised; if the significant hit rates were still observed then it would cast doubt on the likelihood that these "flaws" could explain earlier successes. The new protocol placed many aspects of the procedure—such as random selection of targets, presentation of targets along with decoys during judging, and recording of all participant ratings before the target was revealed—under computer control, and so became known as an *automated-* or *auto-ganzfeld*, to contrast it with earlier *manual* ganzfelds, where these were under human control. Bem and Honorton (1994) reported on the results of all the auto-ganzfeld experiments that took place at PRL, consisting of 329 trials involving 240 different receivers and 8 different experimenters. The overall hit rate for these trials was 32–35 percent (depending on how the experiments were divided), and even the lowest of these estimates is statistically significant ($z = 2.89, p = .002$), suggesting that eradicating the flaws that had been identified previously did not reduce performance to chance levels. They also identified a "recipe for success" by looking for internal patterns within this database, finding that dynamic targets such as video clips were more successful than static targets such as postcards, that participants who reported prior personal experiences and those who practiced a mental discipline (such as meditation) fared better than those who did not, and that certain personality types or predispositions—particularly extraversion and creativity—seemed to be associated with more hits. Internal patterns such as these make it more difficult to account for the outcomes in terms of artifacts.

Hyman (1994) was given an opportunity to respond to these new data, and while he accepted that these experiments overcame many of the methodological weaknesses of the earlier series, describing them as "commendable experiments of high quality" (p. 20), and conceded that the result could not be accounted for in terms of the null hypothesis, he particularly questioned the claim that they showed that the effect was replicable. Although a number of experimenters had been involved, it was essentially Honorton's work and used the same basic method and participant pool; what was needed was truly independent replications using the autoganzfeld method.

Setting up autoganzfeld systems was quite difficult technically and so these replication attempts were quite slow to take off. However, by February 1997 Milton and Wiseman (1999) were able to identify publications that described 30 such studies from 7 different laboratories that had been conducted since 1987 (after the communiqué had been published, and hence researchers could be expected to have taken into account its recommendations in their own designs). Taken together, these studies failed to confirm the above chance scoring reported by Bem and Honorton, achieving an overall hit rate of just 27.6 percent, (combined $z = 0.70$, $p = .24$). They also failed to replicate all but one of the internal effects highlighted by Bem and Honorton, the exception being the performance advantage for those who practiced a mental discipline. In accounting for the discrepancy, Milton and Wiseman tended to focus on possible explanations for Bem and Honorton's original claim for an effect, but because they could not substantiate any specific claim for the above chance performance there they were reduced to offering rather vague intimations that those earlier studies were flawed in some way. For example, they claim "this failure to replicate could indicate that the autoganzfeld's results were spurious, with the main effect having been due to very weak sensory leakage" (p. 391) despite earlier conceding that "none of the opportunities for sensory leakage appear sufficiently strong ... to explain away the positive results of the autoganzfeld in any immediately compelling way" (p. 389).

Ganzfeld researchers instead tended to address the discrepancy by raising concerns about the way in which Milton and Wiseman had selected studies for inclusion in their review and also about the way in which the outcomes of these studies had been analyzed so as to lead to their negative conclusion.* In terms of the concern about selection of studies for inclusion, it is worth noting that typically researchers will want to vary a "standard" method in order to explore its limitations, or address theoretical concerns that are not part of the central claim, rather than simply attempt to confirm an earlier finding. The ways in which the method might be adapted will depend on the various interests of researchers so naturally gives rise to a rather heterogeneous group (cf. Bem, Palmer and Broughton, 2001), but this can lead to controversy over which studies are sufficiently similar to the original to be included in reviews such as Milton and Wiseman's and which are not—particularly where reviewers are not blind to the outcomes of those studies. For example, Willin (1996a, 1996b) was interested to see whether the ganzfeld method could be extended to work with purely auditory stimuli, even though ganzfeld stimulation is primarily concerned with enhancing visual imagery—based on his non-significant results, it seems that it can not. During an email discussion among ganzfeld researchers that was prompted by Milton (Schmeidler and Edge, 1999), some researchers complained that this was too radical a departure from the original studies for it to count as a replication and so it (and its negative outcomes) should not have been included. Of course, those calling for the exclusion of these studies were also not blind to their outcomes. But the effects of inclusion or exclusion of individual studies can be dramatic; Milton (1999) updated the meta-analysis to include studies published up to March 1999 and the data-

---

*By this I don't mean their choice of statistical analysis, but rather their interpretation of outcomes from all trials as bearing equally on the claim for an anomalous exchange of information, although Parker (2005, p. 60) has claimed that Milton and Wiseman's database gives a significant above-chance success rate if analysed by z-test rather than the exact binomial test.

base became marginally significant ($p = .011$), although she claimed that this was due to the inclusion of one large, highly significant study (Dalton, 1997). Dalton's study was presented at the conference where Milton and Wiseman first presented their review, so it would have been possible to include it in an updated analysis when revising the paper for journal submission. Nevertheless it is a concern that the effect seems so precarious that the inclusion or exclusion of individual studies can determine whether the null hypothesis is accepted or rejected. Even if the hit rate is accepted as significantly greater than chance expectation, it is also true that the effect size is significantly smaller than that reported by Bem and Honorton (Milton, 1999), and on this basis we may still say that the later database has failed to replicate the findings of the earlier one.

In terms of the concern about how studies included in the review were interpreted by Milton and Wiseman, researchers complained that they were treated as if they were exact replications intended simply to confirm the existence of an effect, and this fails to acknowledge the process-oriented nature of many of them. By process-oriented I mean that they were concerned to investigate the mechanism of any putative effect by manipulating variables to see what effect this might have on performance (to improve it or perhaps impair it), and so can include comparison conditions that were actually hypothesized to be less successful than normal. For example, Williams, Roe, Lawrence and Upchurch (1994) included a baseline condition that had no sender watching the clip and found, as they predicted, that performance here was significantly worse than for conditions with senders. Parker (2000) reported on a series of five studies; in the first of these the sender was not able to hear the participant's mentation and so received no feedback, and the hit rate was just 20 percent; in the subsequent four studies senders could get feedback, and performance improved to an average of 40 percent. In both cases Milton and Wiseman's review combines the effect sizes for these different conditions as if an equivalent ESP effect was expected to occur in all situations.

Of course there is a danger of circularity in pointing retrospectively to particular features of experimental conditions or even whole experiments as being psi-inhibitory or non-standard, since it is likely that those judgments are shaped by our knowledge of the actual outcome as much as by any theoretical concerns, and may simply serve to confirm our *a priori* weightings of whether the effect is real. But this issue can be resolved by having the ratings of "standardness" made by judges who are unfamiliar with the studies and blind to their outcomes. Bem, Palmer and Broughton (2001) conducted just such a study in response to the concerns raised in the email discussion mentioned above. They gave three independent judges Bem and Honorton's (1994) original descriptions of the standard autoganzfeld method along with just the method sections of the 40 post–PRL autoganzfeld studies. The judges' task was to rate the extent to which these studies deviated from the standard ganzfeld method. As they hypothesized, these standardness ratings correlated with study outcome, with more conventional studies being more successful ($r = .31$, $p = .024$). When "non-standard" studies (i.e. those achieving a mean rating of less than 4 out of 7) were excluded, the remaining database gave a combined outcome that is highly significant ($z = 3.49$, $p = .0002$). The rejected studies had a mean hit rate of 24 percent—very close to chance expectation.

There have been no further reviews of ganzfeld research, but in preparing the conference presentation on which this chapter is based, I identified a further 10 ganzfeld studies that had been reported in the period 2000–2004 (Goulding, Westerlund, Parker and Wackermann, 2004; Morris, Summers and Yim, 2003; Parra and Villanueva, 2000; Roe, Holt and Simmonds, 2003; Roe, McKenzie and Ali, 2001; Roe, Sherwood and Holt, 2003; da Silva, Pilato and Hiroka, 2003; Simmonds, 2002; Simmonds and Fox, 2002; Wright and Parker, 2003). These have a combined hit rate of 30.5 percent, which is marginally significant ($p = .04$), and confirms the impression that while we are able to capture an effect that is just large enough to achieve statistical significance, it is some way from the effect sizes originally reported by Honorton.

Lessons to Be Drawn

So does the experimental evidence to date support the claim that ASCs can be psi-conducive? We have considered here the outcomes of studies that incorporate some form of ASC induction procedure, namely meditation, dream ESP and ganzfeld ESP, and together they appear—superficially at least—to give a relatively consistent picture of a small but significant tendency for participants to score above chance. But how reasonable is it to suppose that these different techniques should give rise to an equivalent psi-conducive state? Schmeidler (1988, p. 93) refers to this clumping together of techniques as theoretically embarrassing, since the criterion for inclusion in this category is in terms of what they are *not* (i.e. our normal everyday waking state) rather than what they are, or what properties they share. In terms of method of induction, they do all seem to reflect Ludwig's (1972) first category of ASC, in that they involve the reduction of exteroceptive stimulation and/or motor activity.* But in terms of the consequences of such induction methods, we still need to see if there is enough similarity among them—phenomenologically, cognitively, physiologically—for it to be sensible to class them together, or if they are sufficiently different to warrant separate consideration. Perhaps in this

---

More recently, Vaitl et al. (2005) suggested a classification that distinguishes between spontaneously occurring states (e.g., drowsiness, daydreaming, hypnagogia and dreaming) and psychologically induced states arising from sensory homogenization (such as ganzfeld) and meditation on the other. This distinction seems rather arbitrary, however, given that some "spontaneously occurring" states such as sleep are also typically facilitated by actively reducing or homogenising sensory input (by closing one's eyes, reducing environmental noise, etc.).

respect we might be encouraged by the tendency for meditators to also perform well in ganzfeld studies, suggesting as it does that persons proficient in one domain are also proficient in another, though of course I have already suggested that the kinds of people who are attracted to meditation practice may share other qualities that more directly relate to ESP task success.

Honorton's (1993, p. 245) aim was that "the ganzfeld would provide a way of approximating the kinds of 'altered states' that have traditionally been associated with psi, particularly dreaming." While it is true that the ganzfeld is believed to induce a state of consciousness that phenomenologically is comparable to the dreamlike hypnagogic imagery that occurs during sleep onset (see Pütz, Braeunig and Wackermann, 2006), physiologically the evidence for this equivalence is rather meager. Wackermann, Pütz, Büchi, Strauch, and Lehmann (2002) compared EEG output for participants while in ganzfeld, during sleep onset and with eyes closed while relaxed but awake. They found that the ganzfeld EEG spectrum did not show the expected decrease in signs of vigilance and was very similar to the waking state. Wackermann, Pütz, Miener and Schmitz-Gropengiesser (2001) reported briefly on a follow-up to this study in which they found that the ganzfeld procedure seems to induce a succession of states rather than one stable state, and that there are wide-ranging differences across individuals in their responsiveness to ganzfeld stimulation.

Parker (2005) has suggested that one should not be too hasty in drawing conclusions from Wackermann and colleagues' work, given some key differences between the set-up used here and that which is typical of ganzfeld ESP studies. He criticized the design for not allowing participants any opportunity to become adjusted to the discomfort of wearing EEG electrodes while in ganzfeld given that the removal of physical distractions is such a central aspect of the procedure, for not using a relaxation exercise to begin the session, and for running much shorter sessions than are typical so participants are less able to acclimatize to the ganzfeld situation. As evidence that the ganzfeld does induce a hypnagogic state, Parker points to the numerous participants in his lab who gave characteristically hypnagogic imagery, with some even falling asleep. But interestingly this last observation also highlights the great variation in participants' responses to ganzfeld stimulation noted by Wackermann *et al.* (2001), and alluded to by Stanford (1993, p. 245) when he notes:

> We get people in the ganzfeld in our lab who experience an internal attention state ... who are zonked, plastered to the chair, so to speak, and we have people ... who are very much, by any definition you use, in their ordinary frame of mind when they are talking in there.

This stands in stark contrast to the general presumption that the consequences of ganzfeld stimulation (particularly upon likelihood of being able to access information by ESP) are relatively uniform. Stanford (1993) refers to this as the "delusion of operational omnipotence" and describes it more generally as the belief that if one applies a fixed set of "altered-states-favoring" operations then all one's subjects will develop such a state. This delusion is exacerbated by the tendency of researchers to not include any checks that a shift in state of consciousness has in fact occurred. This is disappointing, since where checks have been made the results have highlighted their importance. For example, Sargent (1982) had participants simply rate whether the ganzfeld had been successful in altering their state of consciousness using a 0–99 scale; the more successful the induction had been the better they performed at the ESP task ($r = .423$, $p < .05$). Similarly, Harley and Sargent (1982) briefly describe how successful participants gave significantly higher scores on a measure of state-shift than did those who were unsuccessful ($U = 16.5$, $p < .05$). And factors that might correlate with state-shift, such as distortions in time perception, also seem to be related to ESP task success (see Stanford, 1984, §6.3 for a discussion).

Perhaps researchers are deterred from using such ratings because they seem quintessentially subjective and open to idiosyncratic responses to a degree that could make them unreliable. However, Pekala and Cardeña (2002) have argued that self reports of inner experience derived from introspection can be valid where participants are primed to provide them and where they are restricted to aspects of experience itself rather than judgments about the bases of that experience. More systematic checks of the subjective state of participants who have undertaken an ASC induction procedure could help explain the variability of outcome in studies that use superficially similar methods. Two measures that could be useful in this respect are Pekala's *Phenomenology of Consciousness Inventory* (PCI) and *Dimensions of Attention Questionnaire* (DAQ) (see Pekala and Cardeña, 2002, for a brief review, but see also Stanford, 1993, for a more critical review).

Participants' verbal accounts of their experience could also indicate the degree to which their state of consciousness has shifted. Sargent (1982), for example, found that greater ESP success was correlated with more bizarre session mentation. And Carpenter (2001) found that success of ganzfeld sessions was related to independent ratings of transcripts as representing relaxation-like experiences, regressed reasoning, reduced intellectualization and conscious control over imagery, primary process imagery, and odd bodily experiences. A single metric that combined these measures was used to split the sample into quartiles and these differed significantly in their hit rates ($p = .006$). These properties are consistent with Sherwood's (2002) description of the hypnagogic state, which he characterizes as involving decreasing awareness of observing the contents of one's own mind, increased absorption, a loss of volitional control over mentation, inaccurate time perception, a reduction of awareness of the environment and a reduction in reality testing. It would be interesting to see if these mentation-based parameters also relate to self-reports of shifts in state of consciousness.

Finally, there may be independent indicators of susceptibility to ASC induction that could be used to screen or select participants. Although Wackermann, Pütz and Allefeld (in press, p. 4) have concluded that "little is known about the psychological conditions or personality correlates of the responsiveness to ganzfeld and virtually nothing is known about the physiological substrate," indirect indicators of susceptibility may already have been identified but have been interpreted as factors more directly affecting ESP performance or experience. For example, Pekala and Cardeña (2000) have argued that assessment of traits such as hypnotizability, absorption and dissociation are of paramount importance to the study of anomalous experience, and individuals with these traits do tend to be more likely to report such experiences (see, e.g., Irwin, 1985). When Targ, Schlitz and Irwin (2000) reviewed individual differences factors that might relate to psi-related experience (PRE), they chose to highlight dissociation, susceptibility to hypnosis and fantasy proneness as particularly promising.

These individual differences factors may be related to each other. Martínez-Taboas (2001) reported that in non-clinical populations dissociation is highly correlated with absorption, and with hypnotizability (albeit to a lesser extent). However, these last two factors may interact; Pekala, Kumar and Marcano (1995) found that respondents with low hypnotic susceptibility but high dissociation reported moderately high levels of anomalous experience, but respondents with high hypnotic susceptibility reported even higher levels of experience for both high and moderate (but not low) levels of dissociation. Relatively few experimental studies of ESP have treated absorption or dissociability as an independent variable, although Stanford and Angelini (1984) did find that prior absorption was related suggestively to participants' reported degree of relaxation in the ganzfeld, and significantly with ESP score, but not with liking for the ganzfeld environment or with overall time estimates (see also Palmer, 1994). The related construct of transliminality has also had some success as a predictor of ESP performance (e.g., Storm and Thalbourne, 1998–9).

These factors may be related to susceptibility to shifts in ASC. Martínez-Taboas (2001, p. 151) explains their relationships with ESP by suggesting that they reflect dissociative tendencies that could invoke psi-conducive states of consciousness. Targ et al. (2000) also interpreted these findings "as suggesting that a capacity to enter altered states of consciousness is a factor in the predisposition to PREs" (p. 228). Indeed, Watson (2001) has shown that dissociative experiences are related to sleep- and dream-related experiences and has speculated that persons who are high dissociators might have more labile sleep-wake cycles such that they more easily pass from normal wakefulness to "more fantasy-based states of consciousness, such as daydreaming, highway hypnosis, episodes of high absorption (e.g., flow states) and hypnagogic/hypnopompic imagery" (p. 533). Two conceptual replications are broadly consistent with this view (Fassler, Knox and Lynn, 2006; Giesbrecht and Merckelbach, 2004). Evans (1999) similarly found that highly hypnotizable individuals reported falling asleep with less difficulty and suggested that hypnotic susceptibility is related to "the ability to switch easily between different psychological states" (p. 144). And where the normal sleep patterns of otherwise healthy persons are disrupted by instructing them to stay awake overnight, this can lead to an increase in waking dissociative symptoms (Giesbrecht, Smeets, Leppink, Jelicic and Merckelbach, 2007). Although this increase was only evident in reports made during the evening and overnight, it was based on just one night's sleep loss rather than some chronic sleep deficiency, and more extensive effects might be expected with more pronounced sleep loss. Thalbourne and Houran (2000) found that high transliminality was associated with incidence of paranormal experiences but also tendency to daydream and to experience altered consciousness.

What can we conclude? Clearly, these results suggest a collection of attributes that are interrelated and that are associated with both paranormal experiences and with unusual sleep experiences. They sound a warning that when exploring possible links between ASCs and ESP it is not simply a matter of providing participants with an environment that encourages a shift into an internal attention state; participants must also have a capacity to freely enter that state under those conditions.* Researchers have access to measures that can be used to identify participants who are most likely to respond to an induction procedure and can gauge the effectiveness of the intervention through self report and qualitative analysis of their mentation. Given that none of these has been used with any consistency in the research discussed above (see also Alvarado, 1998), studies to date have perhaps been more successful in eliciting ESP than they ought to have been. They promise to be even more successful if these steps are followed in future.

But this still leave us with the question of why ASCs might facilitate ESP experiences. There is no shortage of suggestions. When Honorton (1977) described his influential noise reduction model that underpinned his adoption of the ganzfeld technique, he summarized the key requirements for naturally occurring expressions of ESP as a sufficient level of cortical arousal to maintain conscious awareness, muscular relaxation (to reduce somatic noise), reduction of exteroceptive input from peripheral receptors, and deployment of attention toward internal mentation processes. What was particularly innovative about Honorton's approach was his reframing of the question from "how do we get ESP to occur" to "how do we get people to detect already occurring but weak ESP signals." By damping down other sensory and somatic chan-

---

*Irwin (1985) has previously made this point with respect to absorption, but adds participant need as a third necessary component: "psi occurs not only where the experient has the capacity for absorption and prevailing conditions are conducive to this state, but also where the individual has an enduring need for absorbed experience" (p. 7). It remains to be seen if this third element also applies more generally.

nels that constituted "noise" that normally overwhelmed any ESP element, Honorton sought to make pre-existing (and perhaps continuous) ESP signals more salient to the percipient. In contrast, Braud and Braud (1974) have argued that methods for facilitating ESP "are successful to the extent that they produce a shift toward the relaxation state" (p. 242), and showed that physical and mental relaxation alone can facilitate ESP task success. These studies still included very low intensity white noise playing in the background, which could have encouraged attention to be focused internally, but performance was related to self-ratings and physiological measures of degree of relaxation *per se*, suggesting this was a primary factor. Stanford (1993) has similarly questioned whether current evidence from research establishes that it is the presence of an internal attention state that favors ESP task success. Schmeidler (1994, p. 116) adds that these ASCs commonly enhance imagery and also encourage uncritical acceptance of whatever impressions come to mind, and elsewhere she emphasizes their tendency to shift the percipient away from a reality-orientation and towards a suspension of disbelief (Schmeidler, 1988). These speculations fit reasonably well with mainstream characterizations of ASCs generally (e.g., Ludwig, 1972; Vaitl, *et al.*, 2005), and with the phenomenology of specific ASCs (cf. Cardeña, 2005; Sherwood, 2002; Wackermann, *et al.*, in press).

More provocatively, Stanford (1987) has questioned whether *any* of these elements is essential to the action of ESP, suggesting that success might have more to do with lab atmosphere, social interaction and excitement/expectancy rather than ASC induction itself. Typically, induction methods can be quite unusual and involved, and might even be effective only in so far as they constitute an elaborate ritual in which none of the elements plays an active role in facilitating ESP but when combined together they impress upon the participant the belief that ESP can occur in this situation in a self-fulfilling manner akin to a placebo effect. So long as these aspects are constantly incorporated together it is not possible to determine which of the component parts might be effective and which not. Braud (1978, cited in Alvarado, 1998, p. 45–6) alluded to this when he commented:

> While psi does manifest itself ... in the hands of investigators employing these techniques, it is not clear that the techniques themselves are responsible for the high levels of psi obtained. Unfortunately, most research on psi-conducive conditions is not sufficiently analytical to allow us to distinguish fact from artifact. We appear to be at a stage of development in psi research in which we have a general recipe which yields rather efficient paranormal functioning [but] we do not yet know the relative contributions of each of the ingredients of this recipe.

This can be readily achieved in experiments that contrast conditions with and without certain of these elements while holding all other features constant. But although there were some notable early attempts to do just this (e.g., Braud, Wood and Braud, 1975), this kind of analytical approach focusing on the ASC itself has rather fallen out of favor (see Alvarado, 1998, for criticism of this). A return to a more critical analysis of the relationship between ASCs and ESP is certainly needed, but, if lessons are to be drawn from this review, it may be premature. An essential precursor to any such investigation is to be able to show that participants are consistently and reliably entering those ASCs in the first place. Until researchers ensure that participants are actually in the ASCs that the setting is intended to induce, by paying particular attention to selecting suitable persons and monitoring them during the session, then there is a real danger that experiments to identify what it is about ASCs that make them psi-conducive will be, to paraphrase Tart (1977), mostly wasting our time.

References

Alvarado, C. S. (1998). ESP and altered states of consciousness: An overview of conceptual and research trends. *Journal of Parapsychology*, 62. 27–63.
Bartlett, F.C. (1932). *Remembering*. Cambridge: Cambridge University Press.
Belvedere, E., and D. Foulkes (1971). Telepathy and dreams: A failure to replicate. *Perceptual and Motor Skills*, 33. 783–789.
Bem, D. J., and C. Honorton (1994). Does psi exist? Evidence for an anomalous process of information transfer. *Psychological Bulletin*, 115. 4–18.
Bem, D. J., J. Palmer and R.S. Broughton (2001). Updating the ganzfeld database: A victim of its own success? *Journal of Parapsychology*, 65. 207–218.
Bertini, M., H.B. Lewis and H.A. Witkin (1964). Some preliminary observations with an experimental procedure for the study of hypnagogic and related phenomena. *Archivo di Psycologia Neurologia e Psychiatra*, 6. 493–534. Reproduced in C.T. Tart (1969, ed.), *Altered states of consciousness*. New York: Anchor Books. 95–114.
Braud, W.G., R. Wood and L.W. Braud (1975). Free response GESP performance during an experimental hypnagogic state induced by visual and acoustic ganzfeld techniques: A replication and extension. *Journal of the American Society for Psychical Research*, 71. 409–427.
Cardeña, E. (2005). The phenomenology of deep hypnosis: Quiescent and physically active. *Journal of Clinical and Experimental Hypnosis*, 53(1). 37–59.
Carpenter, J.C. (1995). An approach to assessing adjustment to the ganzfeld situation. *Proceedings of the 38th Annual Parapsychological Association Convention*. 65–78.
Child, I.L. (1985). Psychology and anomalous observations: The question of ESP in dreams. *American Psychologist* 40. 1219–30.
Clemmer, E.J. (1986). Not so anomalous observations question ESP in dreams. *American Psychologist*, 41. 1173–1174.
Dale, L.A. (1951). A series of spontaneous cases in the tradition of Phantasms of the Living. *Journal of the American Society for Psychical Research*, 45. 85–102.
Dale, L.A., R. White and G. Murphy (1962). A selection of cases from a recent survey of spontaneous ESP phenomena. *Journal of the American Society for Psychical Research*, 56. 3–47.
Dalton, K. (1997). Exploring the links: Creativity and psi in the ganzfeld. *Proceedings of Presented Papers: The Parapsychological Association 40th Annual Convention*. 119–134.
Dalton, K., F. Steinkamp and S.J. Sherwood (1999). A dream GESP experiment using dynamic targets and consensus vote. *Journal of the American Society for Psychical Research*, 93. 145–66.
da Silva, F.E., S. Pilato and R. Hiroka (2003). Ganzfeld vs no Ganzfeld: An exploratory

study of the effect of Ganzfeld conditions on ESP. *Proceedings of Presented Papers: The Parapsychological Association 46th Annual Convention.* 31–48.
Dukhan, H., and K.R. Rao (1973). Meditation and ESP scoring. In W.G. Roll, R.L. Morris and J.D. Morris (eds.), *Research in Parapsychology 1972.* Metuchen, NJ: Scarecrow Press. 148–151.
Evans, F.J. (1999). Hypnosis and sleep: The control of altered states of awareness. *Sleep and Hypnosis,* 1. 232–237.
Fassler, O., J. Knox and S.J. Lynn (2006). The Iowa Sleep Experiences Survey: Hypnotizability, absorption, and dissociation. *Personality and Individual Differences* 41. 675–684.
Giesbrecht, T., and H. Merckelbach (2004). Subjective sleep experiences are related to dissociation. *Personality and Individual Differences,* 37. 1341–1345.
Giesbrecht, T., T. Smeets, J. Leppink, M. Jelicic, H. Merckelbach (2007). Acute dissociation after 1 night of sleep loss. *Journal of Abnormal Psychology,* 116. 599–606.
Globus, G., P. H. Knapp, J.C. Skinner and G. Healey (1968). An appraisal of telepathic communication in dreams. *Psychophysiology,* 4. 365.
Goulding, A., J. Westerlund, A. Parker and J. Wackermann (2004). The first digital autoganzfeld study using a real-time judging procedure. *European Journal of Parapsychology,* 19. 66–97.
Gurney, E., F. Podmore and F.W.H. Myers (1886). *Phantasms of the Living.* London: Trubner.
Harley, T.A., and C.L. Sargent (1980). Trait and state factors influencing ESP performance in the ganzfeld. In W.G. Roll (ed.), *Research in Parapsychology 1979.* Metuchen, NJ: Scarecrow. 126–127.
Hearne, K. (1989). *Visions of the Future: The definitive Study of Premonitions.* Wellingborough: Aquarian.
Honorton, C. (1974). ESP and altered states of consciousness. In J. Beloff (ed.), *New Directions in Parapsychology.* Woking, UK: Paul Elek (Scientific Books). 38–59.
Honorton, C. (1977). Psi and internal attention states. In B. B. Wolman (ed.), *Handbook of Parapsychology.* New York: Van Nostrand Reinhold. 435–472.
Honorton, C. (1985). Meta-analysis of psi ganzfeld research: A response to Hyman. *Journal of Parapsychology,* 49. 51–91.
Honorton, C. (1993). Commentary on Stanford, R.G. (1993). ESP research and internal attention states: Sharpening the tools of the trade. In L. Coly and J.D.S. McMahon (eds.), *Psi Research Methodology: A Re-Examination.* New York: Parapsychology Foundation.
Honorton, C. (1997). The Ganzfeld novice: four predictors of initial ESP performance. *Journal of Parapsychology,* 61. 143–158.
Honorton, C., and S. Harper (1974). Psi-mediated imagery and ideation in an experimental procedure for regulating perceptual input. *Journal of the American Society for Psychical Research,* 68. 156–168.
Hyman, R. (1985). The ganzfeld psi experiment: A critical appraisal. *Journal of Parapsychology,* 49. 3–49.
Hyman, R. (1986). Maimonides dream-telepathy experiments. *Skeptical Inquirer,* 11. 91–92.
Hyman, R. (1994). Anomaly or artifact? *Psychological Bulletin,* 115. 19–24.
Hyman, R., and C. Honorton (1986). A joint communiqué: The psi ganzfeld controversy. *Journal of Parapsychology,* 50. 351–364.
Irwin, H. J. (1985). Parapsychological phenomena and the absorption domain. *Journal of the American Society for Psychical Research,* 79. 1–11.
Irwin, H. J. (2004). *An Introduction to Parapsychology (4th ed).* Jefferson, NC: McFarland.
Kelly, E.F., and R.G. Locke (1981). *Altered States of Consciousness and Psi: An Historical Survey and Research Prospectus.* New York: Parapsychology Foundation.
Kennedy, J.E. (2001). Why is psi so elusive? A review and proposed model. *Journal of Parapsychology,* 66. 219–246.
Kennedy, J.E. (2003). The capricious, actively evasive, unsustainable nature of psi: A summary and hypotheses. *Journal of Parapsychology,* 67. 53–74.
Krippner, S. (1991). An experimental approach to the anomalous dream. In J. Gackenbach and A.A. Sheikh (eds.), *Dream Images: A Call to Mental Arms.* Amityville, NY: Baywood. 31–54.

Ludwig, A.M. (1972). Altered states of consciousness. In C.T. Tart (ed.), *Altered States of Consciousness*. New York: Anchor.
Martínez-Taboas, A. (2001). Dissociative experiences and disorders. *Journal of Parapsychology*, 61. 279–319.
Milton, J. (1997). Meta-analysis of free-response ESP studies without altered states of consciousness. *International Journal of Parapsychology*, 12(1). 131–162.
Milton, J. (1999). Should ganzfeld research continue to be crucial in the search for a replicable psi effect? *Journal of Parapsychology*, 63. 309–333.
Milton, J., and R. Wiseman (1999). Does psi exist? Lack of replication of an anomalous process of information transfer. *Psychological Bulletin*, 125. 387–391.
Morris, R.L., J. Summers and S. Yim (2003). Evidence of anomalous information transfer with a creative population in ganzfeld stimulation. *Proceedings of Presented Papers: The Parapsychological Association 46th Annual Convention*. 116–131.
Palmer, J. (1986). ESP research findings: The process approach. In H. L. Edge, R. L. Morris, J. H. Rush, and J. Palmer (eds.), *Foundations of Parapsychology*. London: Routledge & Kegan Paul. 184–222.
Palmer, J. (1994). Further studies with the perceptual ESP test: Feast and famine. *Proceedings of Presented Papers: The Parapsychological Association 39th Annual Convention*. 375–388.
Parker, A. (1975). *States of Mind: ESP and Altered States of Consciousness*. New York: Taplinger.
Parker, A. (2000). A review of the ganzfeld work at Gothenburg University. *Journal of the Society for Psychical Research*, 64. 1–15.
Parker, A. (2005). Psi and altered states of consciousness. In M.A. Thalbourne and L. Storm (eds.), *Parapsychology in the Twenty-First Century: Essays on the Future of Psychical Research*. Jefferson, NC: McFarland. 65–89.
Parra, A., and J. Villanueva (2000). Personality factors and ESP during ganzfeld sessions. *Proceedings of Presented Papers: The Parapsychological Association 43rd Annual Convention*. 402–405.
Pekala, R. J., and E. Cardeña (2000). Methodological issues in the study of altered states of consciousness and anomalous experiences. In E. Cardeña, S. J. Lynn, and S. Krippner (eds.), *Varieties of Anomalous Experience: Examining the Scientific Evidence*. Washington, D.C.: American Psychological Association. 47–82.
Pekala, R.J., V.K. Kumar and G. Marcano (1995). Anomalous/paranormal experiences, hypnotic susceptibility and dissociation. *Journal of the American Society for Psychical Research*, 89. 313–332.
Pütz, P., M. Braeunig and J. Wackermann (2006). EEG correlates of multimodal-ganzfeld induced hallucinatory imagery. *International Journal of Psychophysiology*, 61. 167–178.
Radin, D. (1997). *The Conscious Universe: The Scientific Truth of Psychic Phenomena*. New York: Harper Collins.
Rhine, L.E. (1961). *Hidden Channels of the Mind*. New York: William Morrow.
Roe, C. A., A. N. Ali and E. A. McKenzie (2001). Sender and receiver creativity scores as predictors of performance at a ganzfeld ESP task. *Journal of the Society for Psychical Research*, 65. 107–121.
Roe, C. A., N. Holt and C. A. Simmonds (2003). Considering the sender as a PK agent in ganzfeld ESP studies. *Journal of Parapsychology*, 67. 129–145.
Roe, C. A., L. Jones and C. Maddern (2007). A preliminary test of the "four factor model" using a dream ESP protocol. *Journal of the Society for Psychical Research*, 71. 35–42.
Roe, C. A., S. J. Sherwood and N. Holt (2003). Interpersonal psi: Exploring the role of the sender in ganzfeld ESP tasks. *Proceedings of the 46th Annual Parapsychological Association Convention*. 237–256.
Roney-Dougal, S.M., and J. Solfvin (2006). Yogic Attainment in Relation to Awareness of Precognitive Targets, *Journal of Parapsychology*, 70. 91–120.
Roney-Dougal, S.M. and J. Solfvin (2008). Exploring the relationship between two Tibetan meditation techniques, the Stroop Effect and precognition. *Proceedings of Presented Papers: The Parapsychological Association 51st Annual Convention*.
Roney-Dougal, S.M., J. Solfvin and J. Fox (2008). An exploration of degree of meditation attainment in relation to psychic awareness with Tibetan Buddhists, *Journal of the Society for Scientific Exploration*, 22. 161–178.
Rush, J. (1986). Spontaneous psi phenomena: Case studies and field investigations. In H.

L. Edge, R. L. Morris, J. H. Rush, and J. Palmer (eds.), *Foundations of Parapsychology*. London: Routledge & Kegan Paul. 47–69.

Salter, W. H. (1950) *Trance Mediumship: An Introductory Study of Mrs. Piper and Mrs. Leonard*. London: Society for Psychical Research.

Sannwald, G. (1963). On the psychology of spontaneous paranormal phenomena. *International Journal of Parapsychology*, 5. 274–292.

Sargent, C.L. (1982). A ganzfeld ESP experiment with visiting subjects. *Journal of the Society for Psychical Research*, 51. 222–232.

Schmeidler, G. R. (1988) *Parapsychology and Psychology: Matches and Mismatches*. Jefferson, NC: McFarland.

Schmeidler, G. R. (1994). ESP experiments 1978–1992: The glass is half full. In S. Krippner (ed.) *Advances in Parapsychological Research 7*. Jefferson, NC: McFarland. 104–197.

Schmeidler, G. R., and H. Edge (1999). Should ganzfeld research continue to be crucial in the search for a replicable psi effect? Part II. Edited ganzfeld debate. *Journal of Parapsychology*, 63. 335–388.

Schouten, S. (1981). Analysing spontaneous cases: A replication based on the Sannwald collection. *European Journal of Parapsychology*, 4, 9–48.

Sherwood, S. J. (2002). Relationship between the hypnagogic/hypnopompic states and reports of anomalous experiences. *Journal of Parapsychology*, 66. 127–150.

Sherwood, S.J., and C.A. Roe (2003). A review of dream ESP studies conducted since the Maimonides dream ESP programme. *Journal of Consciousness Studies*, 10. 85–109.

Sherwood, S.J., C.A. Roe, N. Holt and S. Wilson (2005). Interpersonal psi: Exploring the role of the experimenter and the experimental climate in a ganzfeld telepathy task. *European Journal of Parapsychology*, 20. 150–172.

Sherwood, S.J., C.A. Roe, C. Simmonds and C. Biles (2002). An exploratory investigation of dream precognition using consensus judging and static targets. *Journal of the Society for Psychical Research*, 66. 22–28.

Sidgwick, E.M. (1923). *Phantasms of the Living: Cases from the Journal of the SPR*. New York: Arno.

Simmonds, C.A. (2002). State, trait and psi: An exploration of the interaction between individual differences, state preference and psi performance. *Proceedings of Presented Papers: The Parapsychological Association 45th Annual Convention*. 223–234.

Simmonds, C.A., and J. Fox (2002). A pilot investigation into sensory noise, schizotypy and extrasensory perception. *Proceedings of Presented Papers: The Parapsychological Association 45th Annual Convention*. 235–246.

Stanford, R.G. (1984). Recent ganzfeld–ESP research: A survey and critical analysis. In S. Krippner (ed.), *Advances in Parapsychological Research 4*. Jefferson, NC: McFarland. 83–111.

Stanford, R.G. (1987). Ganzfeld and hypnotic-induction procedures in ESP research: Toward understanding their success. In S. Krippner (ed.), *Advances in Parapsychological Research 5*. Jefferson, NC: McFarland. 39–76.

Stanford, R.G. (1993). ESP research and internal attention states: Sharpening the tools of the trade. In L. Coly and J.D.S. McMahon (eds.), *Psi Research Methodology: A Re-Examination*. New York: Parapsychology Foundation.

Stanford, R.G., and R.F. Angelini (1984). Effects of noise and the trait of absorption on ganzfeld ESP performance. *Journal of Parapsychology*, 48. 85–99.

Storm, L., and S. Ertel (2001). Does psi exist? Comments on Milton and Wiseman's (1999) Meta-analysis of ganzfeld research. *Psychological Bulletin*, 127. 424–433.

Targ, E., M. Schlitz and H.J. Irwin (2000). Psi-related experiences. In E. Cardeña, S. J. Lynn, and S. Krippner (eds.), *Varieties of Anomalous Experience: Examining the Scientific Evidence*. Washington, D.C.: American Psychological Association. 219–52.

Tart, C. (1972). Introduction. In C.T. Tart (ed.), *Altered States of Consciousness*. New York: Anchor.

Tart, C. (1977). Drug-induced states of consciousness. In B. B. Wolman (ed.), *Handbook of Parapsychology*. New York: Van Nostrand Reinhold. 500–525.

Thalbourne, M.A., and J. Houran (2000). Transliminality, the Mental Experiences Inventory, and tolerance for ambiguity. *Personality and Individual Differences*, 28. 853–863.

Vaitl, D., N. Birbaumer, J. Gruzelier, G. Jamieson, B. Kotchoubey, A. Kübler, D. Lehmann,

W.H.R. Miltner, U. Ott, P. Pütz, G. Sammer, I. Strauch, U. Strehl, J. Wackermann and T. Weiss (2005). Psychobiology of altered states of consciousness. *Psychological Bulletin*, 13. 98–127.

Van de Castle, R. (1977). Sleep and dreams. In B. B. Wolman (ed.), *Handbook of Parapsychology*. New York: Van Nostrand Reinhold. 473–499.

Wackermann, J., P. Pütz and C. Allefeld (in press). Ganzfeld-induced hallucinatory experience, its phenomenology and cerebral electrophysiology. *Cortex*. 1–15.

Wackermann, J., P. Pütz, S. Büchi, I. Strauch and D. Lehmann (2002). Brain electrical activity and subjective experience during altered states of consciousness: Ganzfeld and hypnagogic states. *International Journal of Psychophysiology*, 46. 123–146.

Wackermann, J., P. Pütz, M. Miener and F. Schmitz-Gropengiesser (2001). Electrophysiological correlates (EEG) of ganzfeld stimulation and ganzfeld imagery. *Proceedings of Presented Papers: The Parapsychological Association 44th Annual Convention*. 423–426.

Watson, D. (2001). Dissociations of the night: Individual differences in sleep-related experiences and their relation to dissociation and schizotypy. *Journal of Abnormal Psychology*, 110. 526–535.

White, R.A. (1964). A comparison of old and new methods of response to targets in ESP experiments. *Journal of the American Society for Psychical Research*, 58. 21–56.

Williams, C., C.A. Roe, I. Upchurch and T.R. Lawrence (1994). Senders and Geomagnetism in the Ganzfeld. *Proceedings of the 37th Annual Parapsychological Association Convention*. 429–438.

Willin, M.J. (1966a). A ganzfeld experiment using musical targets. *Journal of the Society for Psychical Research*, 61, 1–17.

Willin, M.J. (1996b). A ganzfeld experiment using musical targets with previous high scorers from the general population. *Journal of the Society for Psychical Research*, 61, 103–106.

Wright, T., and A. Parker (2003). An attempt to improve ESP scores using the real time digital ganzfeld technique. *European Journal of Parapsychology*, 18. 65–72.

4

ARE OUR ASSUMPTIONS MORE ANOMALOUS THAN THE PHENOMENA?

Paul Stevens[*]

One major criticism of parapsychology is that it lacks accepted theoretical models, and that those it does have tend to make use of the more esoteric and speculative areas of physics. Part of the reason for the widespread skepticism and dearth of viable theories is, I think, due to the perceived properties of psi[†] effects rather than properties that are necessarily real. Given our current knowledge, it is difficult if not impossible to model psi effects as the claimed properties rarely appear to be consistent with theory and observation in other areas of science. But are the claims often made for psi phenomena really justified? Here, I look at three of the more common claims made by parapsychologists and critically assess the assumptions that led to them. I will try to show how the different assumptions we make about psi effects can radically alter the physical requirements of any potential mechanisms and suggest alternative perspectives on some parapsychological phenomena.

Claim Number 1: Psi Effects Are Independent of Space

The first assumption is that psi effects are independent of time and space. That is, phenomena such as telepathy work as well when the sender and

---

[*]*The experimental work described was carried out while the author was a Research Fellow with the Koestler Parapsychology Unit, University of Edinburgh.*

[†]*The term "psi" is used in this chapter as a neutral term denoting the unknown factors that underlie parapsychological phenomena. Psi effects refer to observable outcomes attributed to the action of psi. A psi agent refers to a person thought to play an active role in the production of psi effects.*

receiver are separated by thousands of miles as when they are in adjacent rooms. It's a claim that is made in many places, both in popular books and academic papers. For example, Radin (1997, p. 278) states that laboratory data "suggest that psi effects are completely independent of space" and that a good theory must take this into account; Hardy (2000, p. 1) writes that "positive psi results ... show no systematic declines with increases in distance between subject and target" and concludes that this "largely undermines 'transmission' models of psi." Even the FAQ section of the Parapsychological Association (2008) states that "parapsychological phenomena ... do not appear to be limited by the known boundaries of space or time...." So what is the basis for this claim?

Part of the reason comes from theoretical ideas in parapsychology. Schmidt (1975) developed a *Teleological Model of Psi* that suggested that the psi agent need only concentrate on the desired outcome of an event, the psi effect being a skewing of the probability of that event happening. This model meant that any psi effect would not only be independent of space, but also of time and task complexity. A more complex but similar model was developed by Walker (1975), who developed the *Quantum Mechanical Theory of Psi* suggesting that conscious observation somehow affects the system ("collapses the wave-function"). Again, this would mean that psi effects were space-independent: all that is needed is some sort of feedback to the psi agent about the target system. Whether this feedback is about a system in the next room or on the next continent would not matter. Both of these models (usually collectively referred to as "Observational Theories") have had a strong influence on the way parapsychologists conceptualize their research and interpret their results.

There is also empirical support drawn from experimental research. A common reference is to long-range remote viewing (RV) studies. For example, Targ and Puthoff (1977) showed that subjects could successfully identify the location of a remote person over distances of up to 14.5km, noting that "the [RV] phenomenon is not a sensitive function of distance...." Others (Schlitz and Gruber, 1980; Schlitz and Haight, 1984) attempted to replicate this, with their "receiver" and "sender" separated by 854km in the latter study and over 7000km in the former, and found significant results comparable to studies where sender and receiver were separated by only a few meters. Again, they concluded that distance was not a relevant factor.

So do these and similar results mean that psi effects are indeed independent of distance? In making such a claim, there are 3 inherent assumptions:

- The target (person, object, etc.) is the direct source of any information gained.
- The receiver is the active person who is responsible for the psi effect(s).
- Task success is a quantitative measure of the psi effect(s).

So we have to ask whether these assumptions are necessarily valid. As mentioned earlier, the theoretical basis for the claim of spatial independence is accompanied by a prediction of temporal independence, i.e., psi effects can also be seen where the receiver and target are separated by time. In the case of the Observational Theories, then the receiver is not receiving any information about the remote target but is instead selecting the outcome that matches their prediction. In the more general case, if it is possible to receive information from the future, then the receiver may not be getting the information from the distant target but from a future self who is later given sensory feedback about the actual target. In any of these cases, spatial separation would be irrelevant and assumption 1 would not be valid. Although the concept of precognition is one about which it is hard to theorize, and one which exceeds many people's boggle threshold, there is a lot of experimental research that can be interpreted as providing support for precognitive phenomena (e.g., see the meta-analysis of Honorton and Ferrari, 1989). It must therefore be a factor we take into account when designing and evaluating any studies looking at the effect of distance. If we prefer to stick to real-time processes, then we must also consider the possibility of alternative (though still non-sensory) channels of information. If we take the Schlitz and Gruber (1980) study as an example, we find that success was based on the ratings of independent judges, i.e., people otherwise unconnected to the study were given the RV descriptions of the receiver and asked to rate how well these descriptions matched each of the locations used as targets in the study. We would normally assume that the receiver's mentation contained the target information but, in the absence of knowledge of underlying mechanisms, this is just an assumption. We could also posit that the judges were the actual "receivers," in that they were using some ESP faculty that biased their evaluation of the RV descriptions and allowed them to pick out the target-relevant parts of an otherwise random mentation. Perhaps these judges psychically gained this information directly from the sender, or from the site itself (given that they visited each of the target sites and so bypassed the distance aspect)? It is hard to evaluate such possibilities but, with current knowledge, it is as likely that the judges played an active role as it is that the receiver was able to gain the information over large distances. Assumption 2 then may also not be valid. This also highlights an important point about the terms used in parapsychology (and other areas of science): they are used to help the researcher conceptualize a given situation but this does not mean that the system under study is constrained by those terms. Nature does not need to conform our expectations and any experimental model is at best an approximation of what is really going on.

Finally, and perhaps most importantly, success at most psi tasks, remote viewing or otherwise, is rarely a useful measure of how an information channel may have been affected by distance. Saying whether a target has been correctly identified or not does not tell us much about the characteristics of the underlying processes. For example, I could call out my name from in front of you or from a few meters away. In both instances, you could successfully pick my name out from a list but the characteristics of the information you receive would still have been affected by the distance: my voice would be louder when I was closer to you. As I got further away, there would come a point when you could no longer hear me. Up until that point, if you used task success as the key measure, you might conclude that distance had no effect. With psi effects, we similarly have few if any precise measures that might be *expected* to show relationships with distance (or other physical factors). This is a point that has been made before (e.g., Rush, 1986, p. 286), and parapsychologists are starting to show more awareness of it (Irwin, 2003: p. 76; Braud, 2005: pp. 48–9), but it does not yet appear to have had much influence on experimental design or on model-building. Thus, with the possible exception of some physiological measures (although this is as yet far from clear), we can conclude that assumption 3 is definitely not valid.

So it seems that there is still reason to consider a role for distance in our attempts to understand psi effects. Whether there is a parapsychological equivalent to the inverse-square law, or whether psi effects really are "non-local" as the Observational Theorists propose, we cannot afford to treat assumptions as facts. With this in mind, future researchers might consider explicitly stating the distances involved in their experimental set-up, including all parts of the system under study. At the moment, the majority of studies published in parapsychology journals do not provide sufficient detail to even infer such information.

Claim Number 2: Consciousness Is a Requirement for Psi Effects to Occur

The second claim refers to what is seen by many as a fundamental property of psi effects: they are produced by a conscious mind. This is something that is even implicit in the terms we use to describe the phenomena. Psychokinesis literally means "movement by the mind," telepathy comes from "feeling at a distance" and is more commonly described as "transfer of information from mind to mind," DMILS is the direct *mental* interaction between living systems. Suggesting that consciousness may not be necessary for psi effects to occur is at best unfashionable and at worst heretical! I'm not saying that consciousness is not involved at all. I imagine that it would have to be required for any higher level use of psi effects, but only in the sense that having consciousness is the reason humans are so successful at interacting with their environment in general. Consciousness is thought to represent "an integrated response that incorporates [information from] all major bodily systems, including psychological systems" (Thayer, 1989, p. 49). Whatever else it is, consciousness is the current best evolved adaptation for integrating a whole range of information into a unitary structure, enabling humans and other animals to better adapt to, and ultimately alter, their environment. But there seems to be little evidence to suggest that it is any more involved with psi effects than with other processes by which we interact with the world around us. For example, vision involves the detection of light (an electromagnetic "signal") by light-sensitive cells in our eyes. The light enters our eyes and causes retinal cells to momentarily increase their electrochemical activity that is propagated along nerve pathways to the brain (i.e., the signal is detected). If there is enough light, then the electrochemical activity is sufficient to be registered consciously (i.e., the light is perceived). Even then, this perception may be neglected if it is not the current focus of attention (if you are engrossed in a book, you tend not to be aware of all the patterns of light and dark around you). If however, the perception is of something that has immediate relevance to you, you will become very aware of it and your focus will shift (say out of the corner of your eye you see a thrown object rapidly approaching you!). Having consciousness may give us an advantage in the way we use the light to gain information about our surroundings and alter our behavior where necessary, but this does not mean that consciousness is necessary for the light to be detected. Even when there is a change in behavior, this still need not involve consciousness. For example, we may respond to qualities of the light—our pupils will dilate and we will blink if the light is bright—but this is a purely automatic response).

I suggest that we have no reason to think the same does not hold true for psi effects. Whatever the mechanism, it seems likely that there will be a physical process by which psi effects are manifested in the human body and that this will then have subsequent effects on conscious behavior. This does not reduce the psi experience itself to a purely physical phenomenon any more than a knowledge of the way light refracts reduces the experience of seeing a rainbow, but it does differentiate between the physical mediator of information and the experience itself. We are talking about two interrelated but discrete levels of the phenomena. Moreover, it is not clear where consciousness needs to be involved. There are numerous examples of psi effects on target systems to which we would not normally attribute consciousness: Nash (1984) offers results apparently showing a psychokinetic effect on the mutation rate of E. coli bacteria; Barry (1968) conducted experiments on the effects of intention on fungal growth, finding significant results in 85 percent of cases; and Brier (1969) found significant results for the effects of a participant's attention on one of two plants wherein bio-electrical activity was increased only for the focus plant. We could argue that such effects were due to the influence of a consciousness-possessing agent on a wide variety of internal processes within the target systems, but we could equally well (and perhaps more economically) conceptualize the effects as being relevant responses initiated by the target systems themselves when they detected some sort of signal from the agent. If we start thinking of psi effects as being responses to physical signals of some sort, this also widens the range of effects we might expect to find, suggesting the possibility of effects even in the absence of any consciousness-producing agents (e.g., between plants, or even between nonbiological systems).

So perhaps the argument is that there needs only to be an active agent who possesses consciousness? Again, it depends on what we mean by consciousness as there are many studies showing psi effects based on unconscious responses (e.g., Braud, 1975; Ballard, 1980; Schmidt, 1974) including the numerous studies explicitly looking at electrodermal activity as the primary measure of interaction between people (Schmidt, Schneider, Utts, and Walach, 2004). Indeed, the general consensus in the field is that unconscious responses are typically more reliable measures than conscious ones (Sah and Delanoy, 1994).

Claim Number 3: Psi Involves Complex Information Transfer

Even though practically nothing is known about how information might be transferred to give the psi effects we observe, several potential mechanisms are generally considered to have been ruled out purely on the basis of theoretical considerations of the bandwidth needed to transmit complex information. "Mental radio" models are now dismissed by most parapsychologists due to the low emissive capabilities of biological systems (both in terms of the strength of any signal and in the rate at which information could be transmitted) and the problem of noise degrading the intelligibility of any signal's information content over large distances. Most parapsychologists therefore think that psi effects must not be a signal in classical terms, and adjust their theoretical ideas accordingly. However, an alternative suggestion may be that the information transferred is not complex at all, and that much simpler "signalling" may be involved in some apparently complex psi effects.

One good example is the commonly reported experience of telepathy between two people (also the basis for most of the Ganzfeld ESP experiments, one of the most common experimental procedures used in lab-based parapsychological research) wherein the people notice that there is an apparent exchange of thoughts or that some other aspect of their behavior appears to be matched. Ignoring cases where the matching between person A and person B is retrospective—as this is more easily explained by more conventional psychological processes such as selective memory and shared experience—a typical experience would consist of two elements (see Figure 1).

1. Person A talks about, or otherwise indicates by their behavior, their current thoughts (either spontaneously or as part of an ongoing conversation). Meanwhile, Person B is "broadcasting" their thoughts in some manner.

56   Part One: Parapsychological Perspectives

2. Person B hears Person A and, if their thoughts correspond in some way to what they were thinking, they get excited, thinking telepathy had occurred.

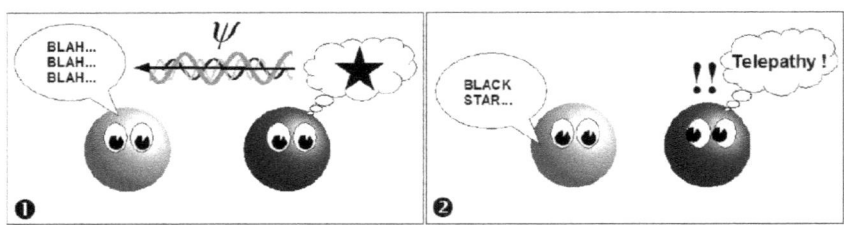

Figure 1: Traditional view of telepathic experience.

If chance occurrences, external cues and conventional sensory cues such as body language have been ruled out, it is unsurprising that such experiences might lead people to think that the thoughts of one person had somehow been transferred to the other. But think what this would really mean. Even with the simplest information (e.g., thinking about a black star), there is a lot of information which needs to be transferred. Whether it is a visual image (the most commonly reported experience), the semantic concept or just the words, we would have to come up with a theory that would (a) allow this information to be packaged ("encoded") in a form that could be transmitted, (b) specify a physical signal that a person can emit that would be able to carry this information, and (c) allow the information to be unpacked ("decoded") by the receiving person in such as way that it would be understandable. No wonder that parapsychology lacks viable theories!

So let's think about the same situation in a slightly different way (see Figure 2).

1. Person A talks about, or otherwise indicates by their behavior, their current thoughts (either spontaneously or as part of an ongoing conversation).
2. Person B hears this and, if those thoughts happen to correspond in some way to what they were also thinking, they get excited. This act of getting excited generates a very simple signal (i.e., some increase in the energy emitted from person B, perhaps in terms of the magnetic field generated by their increased physiological arousal).
3. Person A detects this signal on an unconscious level (perhaps they also experience a change in physiological arousal).
4. Person A then looks for a reason for this change within themselves and attributes it to what they were just saying (i.e. the signal reinforces their current behavior), perhaps thinking of it as a telepathic "hunch."

Figure 2: Simple information transfer view of telepathic experience.

So how is this different? There is still information transfer and it would still count as a telepathic experience. However, here the hypothetical signal need not contain any complex information about the thoughts of either person—it simply exists. No matter what the situation, the signal in step 2 could have the same characteristics and would cause the same initial reaction when detected by person A. All the complexity of the experience is transferred by the conventional senses: person A verbally describes the complex information (step 1) and it is reinforced by a simple "telepathic" signal (steps 2–4) if it is relevant to person B.

If this is a valid idea, then it changes the way we think about a lot of parapsychological experiences. Any experience that involves some kind of sensory feedback between the people involved could be conceptualized in this way, whether it is a spontaneous event or a lab-based study. The conventional senses provide the complexity and richness of the experience while the psychic part may actually be one of the simplest components, involving some sort of signal with relatively low information content. So could this be a valid perspective? Well, there is some support from general findings within parapsychology. Analyses have shown that a "free-response" protocol, where people are free to describe the target as they see fit, is more successful than a "forced-choice" protocol, where people are asked to choose from a small set of possibilities (Utts, 1995). The kind of model proposed would suggest that you need a wide-range of thoughts to be expressed, giving the greatest chance for any of those thoughts to happen by chance to be relevant and so get reinforced by the "psi signal." Forced choice protocols would therefore restrict the possibility of this reinforcement being able to occur. It has also been noted that emotional targets do best (Bem and Honorton, 1994), a suggestion which ties in with anecdotal reports of spontaneous ESP. This is usually interpreted as showing that emotionally-charged events are the best psi targets, but perhaps the success is because emotional states are associated with high levels of arousal and physiological activity. Such states might therefore generate stronger or more consistent "psi signals." Finally, the basic process involved with the model—that person A will show a measurable response when person B simply gets excited—is an effect that has received empirical support in the experimental parapsychology literature (Schmidt et al., 2004).

Additionally, I carried out an experimental series specifically looking for this kind of effect during Ganzfeld ESP sessions (Stevens, 2004). This is a common technique in parapsychology, usually involving a "receiver," who describes their thoughts and feelings ("mentation") at the time a "sender" is watching a randomly selected video clip in a remote room. The receiver then uses their mentation to try to pick the correct target video clip from among 3 other decoy video clips. The sender can hear what the receiver is saying but has no way of communicating with the outside world via the conventional senses. It was hypothesized that the receiver in the Ganzfeld (a mild state of sensory deprivation involving audio white noise, low level red light and a relaxed physical state) would show a change in skin conductance (a measure of physiological arousal) every time the sender decided that they were producing verbal mentation relevant to the target. The sender indicated this by pressing a button that recorded the exact time and was later matched to the record of the receiver's skin conductance. The change in skin conductance at these times would reflect a change in the baseline arousal of the receiver (due to the hypothetical "psi signal") and would hopefully act to reinforce the theme of whatever the receiver was describing at the time.

What was found did indeed suggest that the proposed model of simple information transfer was valid. Receivers did show an increase in their arousal at times of sender button presses and this was significantly different from times of no button presses (see Figure 3). The appearance is very much what would be expected if the receiver were responding to a sensory stimulus, even though no such stimulus was present. Unfortunately, the conscious responses of the receivers (their choice of which video clip was the target), was less successful. Even though they appeared to be responding to the sender on some level, they were not able to make use of this enough to significantly demonstrate successful ESP. Again this goes back to the point I made earlier: there is a difference between the detection of a signal and being aware or able to make use of it. Even then, the information it conveyed may be ignored if it is not judged to be relevant.

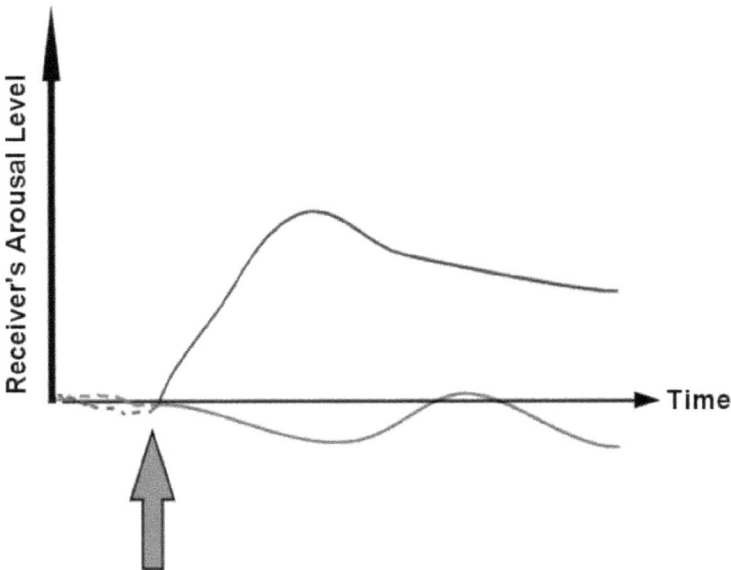

Figure 3: Comparison of averaged receiver arousal levels at times of sender button presses. The arrow indicates the time when the sender thinks the receiver has said something relating to the target (i.e., presses the button) and the topmost line shows the subsequent average change in receiver's skin conductance. The lower line shows the receiver's resting level of arousal (i.e., at time when there were no button presses).

Conclusions

Most parapsychology researchers would agree that the experimental literature demonstrates that the anomaly we term psi needs to be taken seriously and does not simply represent methodological flaws or statistical errors. It is equally true that few of us agree on what psi effects do represent. The years of careful research have not enabled us to explain the erratic nature of the phenomena or to develop useful theoretical models. I think this strongly indicates the need for a return to first principles, a questioning of the assumptions that have become part of accepted doctrine in the field. Here, I have tried to highlight three areas that I feel are important to our understanding of psi phenomena. My hope is that the questions raised might offer incentive to other researchers, current and future, to think again about the nature of parapsychological phenomena.

References

Ballard, J. (1980). Unconscious perception of hidden stimuli enclosed with ESP cards. *Journal of Parapsychology*, 44. 319–339.
Barry, J. (1968). General and comparative study of the psychokinetic effect on a fungus culture. *Journal of Parapsychology*, 32, 237–243.
Bem, D.J., and C. Honorton (1994). Does psi exist? Replicable evidence for an anomalous process of information transfer. *Psychological Bulletin*, 115. 4–18.
Braud, W.G. (1975). Conscious versus unconscious clairvoyance in the context of an academic examination. *Journal of Parapsychology*, 39. 277–288.
Braud, W. (2005). The farther reaches of psi research: future choices and possibilities. In Michael A. Thalbourne and Lance Storm (eds.), *Parapsychology in the Twenty-First Century: Essays on the Future of Psychical Research*. Jefferson, NC: McFarland. 38–62.
Brier, R. (1969). PK on a bio-electrical system. *Journal of Parapsychology*, 33, 187–205.
Hardy, C. (2000). Psi as a multilevel process: semantic fields theory. *Journal of Parapsychology*, 64. 73–94.
Honorton, C., and D. C. Ferrari (1989). "Future telling": a meta-analysis of forced-choice precognition experiments, 1935–1987. *Journal of Parapsychology*, 35. 281–308.
Irwin, H.J. (2003). *An Introduction to Parapsychology*. Jefferson, NC: McFarland.
Morris, R.L. (1977). Parapsychology, biology, and anpsi. In B. Wolman (ed.), *Handbook of Parapsychology*. Jefferson, NC: McFarland. 687–715.
Nash, C.B. (1984). Test of psychokinetic control of bacterial mutation. *Journal of the American Society for Psychical Research*, 78, 145–152.
Parapsychological Association (2008). *FAQ: What Do Parapsychologists Study?* http://www.parapsych.org/faq_file1.html#4. Accessed: 11 March 2008.
Radin, D.I. (1997). *The Conscious Universe: The Scientific Truth of Psychic Phenomena*. New York: HarperCollins.
Rush, J. H. (1986). Physical and quasi-physical theories of psi. In H. L. Edge., R.L. Morris, J.H. Rush and J. Palmer (1986). *Foundations of Parapsychology*. London and Boston: Routledge & Kegan Paul.
Sah, S., and D. Delanoy (1994). Cognitive and physiological psi responses to remote positive and neutral emotional states. *Proceedings of the Parapsychological Association 37th Annual Conference*. 128–352.
Schlitz, M., and E. Gruber (1980). Transcontinental remote viewing. *Journal of Parapsychology*, 44. 305–317.
Schlitz, M.J., and J.M. Haight (1984). Remote viewing revisited: an intrasubject replication. *Journal of Parapsychology*, 48. 39–49.
Schmidt, H. (1974). Observation of subconscious PK effects with and without time displacement. *Research in Parapsychology*. New York: Scarecrow. 116–121.
Schmidt, S., R. Schneider, J. Utts and H. Walach (2004). Distant intentionality and the feeling of being stared at: two meta-analyses. *British Journal of Psychology*, 95. 235–247.
Stevens, P. (2004). Experimental evaluation of a feedback-reinforcement model for dyadic ESP. *Journal of Parapsychology*, 68. 65–92.
Targ, R., and H. Puthoff (1977). *Mind-Reach: Scientists Look at Psychic Ability*. New York: Delacorte.
Thayer, R.E. (1989). *The Biopsychology of Mood and Arousal*. Oxford: Oxford University.
Walker, E.H. (1975). Foundations of paraphysical and parapsychological phenomena. In L. Oteri (ed.) *Quantum Physics and Parapsychology*. New York: Parapsychology Foundation. 1–44.

5

WILL WE EVER KNOW WHETHER EXTRASENSORY PERCEPTION EXISTS?

Jezz Fox

Western culture is increasingly based upon the storage, transmission, and manipulation of information. This has been aided by the development and proliferation of digital systems that reduce complex objects and concepts to simple streams of binary data (ones or zeros). It increasingly seems as though people expect to apply such a "yes" or "no" understanding to all issues in life. In this chapter I examine whether we will ever have a definitive "yes" or "no" answer as to the question of whether Extrasensory Perception (ESP) exists.

Research into ESP is considered from the initial work in the late nineteenth century, through the development of experimental protocols to test such abilities "scientifically," to a contemplation of the current situation in which some researchers believe in ESP as a genuine human ability and others do not. At each stage we see that there are shortfalls in applying the "scientific method" to this issue.

Complications begin at the earliest stage in which we assume that the scientific method can be used to determine whether a particular phenomenon exists or not through the use of experiments. This is not the case; experiments can only be used to determine whether there is sufficient evidence to suggest that something is happening, not that nothing is happening. Even if we conclude that something is happening, the results of an experiment do not allow us to conclude that the something that is happening is the same thing that we set out to investigate. Conclusions relating to the causes of the observations are embellishments applied by researchers as part of the scientific process. These embellishments occur at a point at which subjective opinion is allowed to enter an ostensibly objective process, and therefore may result in erroneous conclusions being drawn.

The validity of the conclusions drawn by a researcher during this stage of embellishment is based upon a number of assumptions concerning the experiment that has been performed. These assumptions include the notion that the experimental protocol being used is appropriate for testing ESP, that the task set for the participants is reasonable based upon our knowledge of the phenomenon that we are testing, and that the participants are actually participating during the experimental procedure.

This chapter examines six assumptions that I think are held by the general public when considering the existence of ESP and the research that is being performed in order to test for it. These assumptions are questioned through a contemplation of features of real-life ESP, and evidence that has been gained through my own research. Firstly we see that experimental tests of ESP differ markedly from the real-life experiences upon which notions of ESP were derived; in the case of telepathy, in real-life scenarios telepathy happened *to* people whereas experimental protocols participants are asked to *be* telepathic. Secondly, we see that from our current knowledge relating to people's experiences during ESP experiments we may be expecting participants to achieve a greater level of success than could reasonably be expected. Finally, evidence is presented that suggests that researchers may be being naïve in assuming that participants are in fact "participating" during experiments.

It is concluded that whilst it is not possible to use experimental findings to conclude that ESP does not exist, it is also unlikely that we will ever be able to use these findings to conclude that ESP does exist. This is not to say that the studies have no value; they do provide researchers with additional information to further their own understanding of ESP. However, it seems as though the experimental research being performed will not help to unify researchers in their opinions relating to ESP as a genuine human ability.

Assumption 1: Experiments Can Provide Yes/No Answers

When it comes to considering scientific evidence, many people seem to follow the train of thought that science is a source of facts, these facts are based upon experimentation, and experiments are capable of producing yes/no answers. The reality is somewhat different; the results of experiments are reported in terms of the probability of the observed results having occurred by chance alone. It is then through the application of conventions that an interpretation is made and an inference drawn. By convention it is stated that a probability of occurrence through chance of less than one in twenty provides sufficient evidence to (tentatively at least) claim a genuine effect. More stringent criteria of 1 in 100 or 1 in 1,000 are also often used either in situations in which researchers want to be more cautions in their conclusions (e.g. when making claims that may have medical implications) or to highlight that the evidence is more compelling than simply the 1 in 20 that is used as a baseline. When these criteria are met the findings are said to be statistically significant. This translates to meaning that they are so unlikely to have occurred by chance that they provide evidence for the proposed phenomenon. These claims are tentative as the conclusions may be challenged at a later date by other evidence. The rationale behind using these criteria is that they provide an objective decision-making process that all researchers may agree upon. Even if they have personal grievances about these conventions there can be agreement that these are the conventions by which the discipline operates. As can be seen in other chapters in this volume, and in any journal reporting findings from experimental research, present-day research relies heavily upon this method of drawing conclusions from the data gathered. This, however, has not always been the case.

One of the earliest researchers to apply probabilities to ESP research was Charles Richet. One area of research that interested him was the study of sensitives (now more commonly referred to as mediums) and their alleged ability to communicate with the deceased. In one report Richet describes how a medium correctly ascertains that the person for whom the reading was being performed has a dead son named Louis, and that her son has left behind two sons and a daughter. The medium also provides various other pieces of apparently accurate information including her grandmother's love of writing.

In his analysis of this session he states that the probability of ascertaining a dead son named Louis was 1 in 200, that the information concerning the knowledge of a sudden death leaving two sons and a daughter took the total probability to about 1 in 40,000, and that taking into account the other information such as the grandmother's love of writing resulted in a total probability of "in round figures, 1 in eight million." Bearing in mind that current day research uses 1 in 20, 1 in 100, or 1 in 1,000 as criteria for evidence, these claims of 1 in 8 million from a single reading might, by today's standards, be considered virtual proof of the existence of ESP.

Naturally there are many factors that would need to be taken into consideration in assessing the accuracy of the claim of 1 in 8 million. For instance, elsewhere in the book Richet mentions that the "probability of a common Christian name is one in thirty" (p. 203) whereas in order to get an accurate overall probability one would have to include the actual probability of the name Louis in the original calculation rather than an estimate. Interested readers should also note that there are many issues relating to the assessment of readings such as this and could consult relevant literature for more information (e.g. Hyman, 1989). What is perhaps more interesting is the cultural change in the use of probabilities between then and now. As has already been mentioned, probabilities are now used as the decision-making tool in research. However, when looking at Richet's approach to the use of statistics he introduces his statistical analysis of the reading with "If we attempt, in a very arbitrary fashion, to calculate the probability of these various replies" (p. 127), indicating that he does not intend accuracy in his assessment, and ends the assessment with "In reality, as has already been frequently said, there is not the slightest authority in this kind of calculation of probabilities. It is just one way of looking at things" (p. 127). Therefore it would seem apparent that the use of probabilities would not be seen as a method of assessing a phenomenon in the manner in which it is in current research.

Assumption 2: Experiments Are Testing ESP

The second assumption made by many people is that the experiments being used by researchers are testing ESP. Here we consider simply the case of studies into telepathy.

In a basic telepathy set-up we have the following components:

- a "sender" who acts as the source of the telepathic information.
- a "target" that is an object or other item whose identity the sender is intended to "send" to the receiver.
- a "receiver" whose job it is to pick-up on the telepathic information being sent by the sender.
- an experimenter whose role it is to oversee the whole situation.

A study would consist of a number of trials. Each trial is an attempt to send information telepathically and consists of a number of stages:

- the preparation period in which participants get ready to "be telepathic." This may include special preparations such as a relaxation procedure.
- the trial period in which it is intended that the telepathy "takes place."
- the judging period in which an assessment is made as to whether there is any evidence for telepathy having occurred.

By running a number of trials it is then possible to see whether the receiver can identify the target from a limited set of options. For example, in recent experiments using the ganzfeld procedure, the target is typically a video clip. The receiver is presented with 4 video clips, the target and 3 decoys, and asked to give each a rating of how likely it is to be the target). So by chance alone one would expect correct identification of the target (a direct hit) 1 in every 4 trials. Once a study is complete an analysis can be made that result in the probability of the observed level of successes having been due to chance factors alone.

Looking back to the work of Richet we see an important distinction between the perceived nature of ESP abilities in sensitives and in the general population. In the case of sensitives it would appear that they have the ability to use their abilities at will, i.e. their abilities were under their conscious control. This, however, is not the case when we consider the research that resulted in Myers' coining of the term telepathy in the early 20th century (see Myers, 1927). Most of the reports of telepathic occurrences involve spontaneous cases. Such cases include cases of "crisis telepathy" in which, for example, a mother might gain, without the use of conventional channels of communication, information that her son or daughter has been killed or seriously injured. Case collections of reports of ESP communications (most notably Louisa Rhine, 1961) reveal that an equal number of cases are far more mundane and often involve quite trivial information in which the information has no import. The important feature of these spontaneous cases is that they do not involve people trying to be telepathic. In spontaneous cases telepathy happens *to* people whereas in the experimental protocols participants are being asked to *be* telepathic.

This is a far from trivial distinction; it means that there is little reason for believing that participants should be successful in experiments designed to explore telepathic experiences. If such experiments lead to above-chance scoring then one might conclude that something "anomalous," perhaps telepathy, has been demonstrated. However, if they do not then this in no way provides any evidence to back the notion that the spontaneous, cases are not genuine.

The introduction of experimental methods of testing ESP not only introduces the assumption that ESP is being tested, it also necessitates a number of further assumptions. The first to be considered is that the participants in studies are actually participating.

Assumption 3: Participants Are Participating

A fundamental assumption that is made when conducting experiments with human participants is that the participants are, indeed, participating (i.e., that they are behaving in a manner consistent with the instructions given to them). In the telepathy protocol outlined above this would mean that the sender is trying to "send" information telepathically and that the receiver is trying to "receive" the telepathic information. Whilst the behavior of the receivers is often monitored as part of the protocol (e.g., in the ganzfeld protocol they are asked to report anything that they are experiencing) this is not so often the case for the sender in modern day protocols. It is for this reason that one study in which I have been involved (Fox, 2004) included as part of the protocol a request for the senders to vocalize what they were trying to do and what they were experiencing throughout the session. Whilst in many cases the senders were behaving in a manner that could be considered consistent with attempting to "send" information this was not always the case. Here one example will be provided. In this case the sender was repeatedly presented with a video clip describing a quasar with a visual representation comprising of a blue sphere with blue "flames" dancing around its surface. These visuals were accompanied by an audio track providing information such as the fact that quasars were discovered in the 1960s and the vast distances involved when considering such stellar entities.

During the 20-minute trial period the sender had the following train of thought. They began by talking about the manner in which the quasar reminded him of a football, before concentrating on how it looked liked a stormy planet. Moving on from this he mentioned that the quasar reminded him of a conker, and in turn about the day when he had been cycling along a country lane with the conker in his back pocket before falling off his bicycle and hurting his backside. He then remarked upon how the voice of the person doing the narration on the track irritated him as he did not like the American accent. From here he focused on the spherical nature of the quasar again, how it reminded him of playing golf, and how he should find time to play again.

Then he reflected upon the situation in which he found himself in terms of wearing a headset with a boom microphone and how he, therefore, felt like an airline pilot. Following from this he returned to the notion of a stormy planet before turning his attention to information contained in the soundtrack of the clip giving information concerning the discovery of quasars in the 1960s. This led him along the train of thought of associating the 1960s with the hippie culture and drugs, and from this to his thinking that the existence of quasars was pretty unlikely, that the "discovery" was nothing more than the bi-product of drug-induced hallucinations and that they did not really exist. Following from this he relates to the large distances involved when considering quasars by thinking that he really should go to Australia for a holiday. From here he ends the session by thinking about *Star Trek* and space travel before concluding with some thoughts on the spherical nature of the quasar and how it reminded him of marbles.

There are two main conclusions that are of relevance to us here. The first relates to the assumption currently being considered that participants are actually participating in the trials. Here it is quite apparent that there are at least some periods in which the participant is not participating in the intended manner and is involved in other activities. The second conclusion relates to our next assumption that protocols allow a fair chance of success.

Assumption 4: Protocols Allow a Fair Chance of Success

There seems to be an assumption that the protocols used to test for ESP allow the participants a fair chance of success. To take a specific example we may consider the task that is given to the receivers in ESP tests. The receiver's ESP "success" is assessed through their ability to provide information that matches the target for the session. In the case of a telepathy protocol the task is somewhat complicated by the fact that the receiver is being asked to discern the thoughts of the sender whilst their success at doing so is not measured through a correspondence with the thoughts of the sender but with the target that has been give to the sender to concentrate upon. Therefore, in order for the receiver to be given a fair chance of demonstrating a telepathic ability it would be important for the thoughts of the sender to be as closely related to the features of the target as possible. In the example provided above this is clearly not the case throughout sections of the trial period. Therefore whilst it may be theoretically possible for the receiver to pick up on "telepathic" information such as the notion of being an airline pilot, this information would in no contribute towards a positive assessment of telepathic ability using the experimental protocols that are currently being used and may in fact (depending upon the decoy items) be detrimental to such an assessment (e.g. if one of the decoys had an aviation theme). Thus we may conclude that a "purity" of source information may be needed in order for the receiver to have a fair chance of success.

Next we consider the same assumption from the slightly different perspective of the receiver's experiences during ESP trials. For this we shall give a single example from a study in which I acted a receiver in a clairvoyance task (the same as the telepathy protocol described earlier but without a sender). In this series of 12 trials I had 5 direct hits (i.e. gave the target the highest rating 5 times), 6 second places, 1 third place and no fourth places. The point of interest, however, relates to the thoughts that a receiver may experience during the trial. It is often assumed that when people are trying to use ESP any thoughts that they have would be related to their potential ESP ability. However, this is unlikely to be the case. People naturally have many diverse thoughts, and asking people to think of nothing is arguably one of the most difficult things to ask of a person.

In one of the trials in this series I awarded one of the items in the judging set a high rating and the other three lower ratings. It was only when I came to look at the clips again that I noticed a particular stance adopted by a person in one of the clips. The clip was an advert for a casino in which an elderly lady spins a friend around in a chair. At one point there are a few frames in which the lady has her arms in the air. This provoked an emotional reaction as it bore similarities to some imagery that I had experienced that had lasted for only a few seconds of the 20 minute trial. This similarity was not enough to warrant me awarding the clip the highest rating as the one that I had given the highest rating to seemed to match my thoughts more for the session as a whole. Therefore I decided to give this clip the second highest rating. As it turned out, this clip was the target for the session. Whilst acknowledging that this is purely anecdotal, it was a scenario that was repeated in several trials of the series. Therefore it serves as a basis for postulating that it may be unreasonable to expect untrained participants to be able to interpret their thoughts and feelings in a manner in which they are capable of distinguishing ESP–based information from "normal" thoughts and feelings that they may be expected to experience if asked to relax and relate their thoughts during a 20 minute period.

Taking these two examples together, we may question the assumption that the protocols currently used by researchers allow the participants a fair chance of success in a trial.

Assumption 5: Experiments Can Detect ESP If It Exists

Our fifth assumption follows on from those that have preceded it. In essence it acts as an "umbrella" assumption that covers many of the issues already mentioned. This assumption is that experiments can detect ESP if it exists. Here we return to the notion of using probabilities as our objective tool for making decisions concerning the existence of postulated phenomena through the analysis of gathered data. In order for it to be concluded that a study provides evidence supporting the notion of ESP existing we would have to have probabilities of less that one in twenty ($p<0.05$), one in a hundred ($p<0.01$), or less than one in a thousand ($p<0.001$). These probabilities are determined by two factors, the effect size and the sample size. The effect size relates to the strength of an observed effect. The sample size refers to the number of data points available for inclusion in the analysis. For a given effect size an increase in sample size will lead to an increase in confidence that the observed effects result from something other than natural, chance, variation as indicated by a reduction the probability that the observed effects are due to chance. Similarly for a given sample size, an increase in effect size results in a reduction in probability.

Some reviews of ganzfeld research (e.g., Bem and Honorton, 1994) have concluded that there is an overall increase in identification of the target compared to what would be expected by chance alone. This is a relatively small effect (though large by ESP standards) of increasing the hit-rate from the chance level of 1 success in 4 to around 1 success in 3. (Note that the debate surrounding the interpretation of ganzfeld research has continued, e.g. Milton and Wiseman, 1999; Storm and Ertel, 2001.) With an effect of this size even running 100 trials does not guarantee observing a statistically significant effect. In fact it leaves the probability of obtaining a significant effect the same as that of tossing a coin (Utts, 1991). Due to the resources needed to run ganzfeld trials, studies typically have far fewer than 100 trials and often have around 30 trials. This further decreases the probability of obtaining significant results in any given study. This leads us to the next assumption to be considered, namely that absence of evidence is evidence of absence.

Assumption 6: Absence of Evidence Is Evidence of Absence

Due to the considerations described above it is rare for individual studies to result in the conclusion that ESP exists, or even that evidence in favor of ESP has been obtained. However, one has to be careful in how to interpret this. For many people, the train of thought seems to take the following path. First, let us assume that the study has not resulted in statistically significant findings, therefore if we were to ask "Does this study back the notion that ESP exists?" we would have to answer "no." As we have answered "no" to this we might answer "yes" to the question "Does this study suggest that ESP does not exist?" and as a consequence many people seem to be left with the impression that studies seem to be showing that ESP does not exist. Put in other words, this translates to the notion of absence of evidence being evidence of absence.

The reality, however, is that the study does not back the notion that ESP does exist, but neither does it back the notion that ESP does not exist. In view of the postulated effect size the chosen sample size would be doomed to produce inconclusive results. Indeed one may go so far as to say that in many cases even researchers who believe that ESP exists would be surprised if the study produced statistically significant results as the observed effect would have to be markedly higher than that which is typically observed in experimental settings. Thus we may call into question our assumption that absence of evidence provides evidence of absence.

Conclusions

In this chapter we have examined a number of assumptions that many people seem to make when considering the issue of whether we will ever know whether ESP exists. Whilst it may seem as though these assumptions paint a negative view of the prospects for ESP research this is not the case. For example, meta-analysis has the potential to address some of the concerns raised in this chapter. A meta-analytic approach allows data from different studies to be grouped together and analyzed as though, to some extent at least, they were performed as one large study. Such meta-analyses have been performed on ESP data and do overcome this issue of the impracticality of running a sufficient number of trials for the postulated effect size (e.g., meta-analyses of ganzfeld research have been conducted by Bem and Honorton, 1994, and Milton and

Wiseman, 1999). That said, there are other issues and debates that surround the use and interpretation of meta-analysis (see e.g., Utts, 1991).

In addition, it must be remembered that the examples used in this chapter to illustrate the issues raised have themselves been selected to highlight the intended issues. This is not to say that these examples are typical of all the studies performed. If we take as an example the session used to illustrate the thoughts that the sender has during the trial, the example provided was one example from a study. Whilst there were others trials that displayed similar examples of drifting away from the intended behavior for the trial, there were also others in which the senders appeared to be behaving in a manner that would be consistent with the notion of sending.

The aim of this chapter has been to provide some context for people who are not familiar with research into ESP when considering the outcomes of such research. This raises the question of how much weight is given to such research in the formulation of people's beliefs about the existence of ESP. A small, unpublished, study conducted by myself explored this question and suggested that the findings from experimental ESP research did not rate highly on people's lists. Instead, it seemed that beliefs about the existence of ESP were likely to be influenced by (a) people's personal experiences and (b) information from what I would term "trusted others." Trusted others are primarily friends and family, though this may be extended to media sources that people trust and sometimes research findings.

In this context we might conclude that the research will not lead to swaying people's beliefs concerning the existence of ESP. The role that the research seems to play is to provide information to create a framework of understanding around that fundamental belief. When it comes to considering the impact that the research has on researchers we may conclude that the present practical limitations involved in the study of ESP, as outlined in this chapter, will not generate sufficient data to allow conclusions to be drawn that would allow researchers to agree upon whether or not ESP exists.

Added to this, we should not forget that researchers themselves are as susceptible to the influences on human decision-making processes as the rest of us. Researchers may ultimately place as much of the emphasis of their decision-making process upon personal experience or information received from "trusted others" as from the data gathered from their empirical studies. Therefore research findings may never ultimately unite researchers in their opinions on ESP.

My Assumption

In this chapter, there is an underlying assumption that the aim of conducting research on ESP is to determine whether or not ESP exists. This, however, need not necessarily be the case.

I have had a number of experiences that have resulted in me "knowing" that ESP exists. In the research that I have performed since then I have never seen the studies as testing this fundamental belief. Instead my assumption is that ESP does exist and that the purpose of performing experimental studies is to develop a protocol that can detect this ESP in the laboratory despite the intrinsic limitations of using experimental protocols. More specifically, I see the purpose of such experiments as tackling each of these limitations and trying to maximize the possibility of detecting ESP. In the case of whether the participants are participating I have argued that some form of monitoring of the sender's behavior and actions would be beneficial (Fox, 2004). If this is performed, two of the courses of action available to researchers would be to remove trials in which senders are deemed not to be participating from the analysis, or to develop measures of performance and include these in the analysis with the expectancy of "good" performance being associated with demonstrations of ESP and "poor" performance being associated with trials in which there is little or no evidence of ESP being demonstrated. By taking such approaches it may be possible to develop protocols that do allow participants a fair chance of success and in turn that the size of the effect observed in trials will be greater than at present. In turn, fewer trials would be needed to achieve statistical significance, which, may lead to the possibility of being able to run studies that would have a genuine chance of detecting ESP if it does exist.

References

Bem, D. J., and C. Honorton (1994). Does psi exist? Evidence for an anomalous process of information transfer. *Psychological Bulletin*, 115. 4–18.
Fox, J. (2004) An initial categorization of the behavior of senders during ganzfeld trials. *Journal of the American Society for Psychical Research*, 98. 68–92.
Honorton, C. (1985). Meta-analysis of psi ganzfeld research: A response to Hyman. *Journal of Parapsychology*, 49. 51–91.
Hyman, R. (1989). *The Elusive Quarry: A Scientific Appraisal of Psychical Research*. New York: Prometheus.
Hyman, R. (1985). The psi ganzfeld experiment: A critical appraisal. *Journal of Parapsychology*, 49. 3–49.
Hyman, R. and Honorton, C. (1986). A joint communiqué: The psi ganzfeld controversy. *Journal of Parapsychology*, 50. 351–364.
Milton, J., and R. Wiseman (1999). Does psi exist? Lack of replication of an anomalous process of information transfer. *Psychological Bulletin*, 125. 387–391.
Myers, F. W. H. (1927). *Human Personality and Its Survival of Bodily Death*. London: Longmans, Green.
Rhine, L. E. (1961). *Hidden Channels of the Mind*. New York: William Morrow.
Richet, C. (c.1928). *Our Sixth Sense*. London: Rider.
Storm, L., and S. Ertel (2001). Does psi exist? Comments on Milton and Wiseman's (1999) Meta-analysis of ganzfeld research. *Psychological Bulletin*, 127. 424–433.
Ullman, M., S. Krippner and A. Vaughan (1973). *Dream Telepathy*. London: Turnstone.
Utts, J. (1991). Replication and meta-analysis in parapsychology. *Statistical Science*, 6. 363–378.

6

TOWARDS A SOCIOLOGICAL PARAPSYCHOLOGY

Robin Wooffitt*

Parapsychology is a sub discipline of psychology, and the relationship between the two is close (if not always untroubled). Institutionally, parapsychology research centers have been based in psychology departments: the Rhines' laboratory at Duke University, for example, was part of the Department of Psychology. And, although in the U.S. some key research centers now have less formal relationships with universities, elsewhere the institutional link between psychology and parapsychology is very strong. So, in the UK, most centers for the study of anomalous or paranormal experiences are based in psychology departments. And substantively, parapsychology reflects the characteristics of its parent discipline. Conceptually, the focus of analysis is the (aggregate) individual and her (anomalous) cognitive processes; moreover, empirical research is largely based around laboratory-based, experimental studies.

This is a curious state of affairs, for two reasons. First, as there is so little consensus about psi—what it is and how it might work—it seems premature to try to devise laboratory-based experiments to study how it works. For example, while ganzfeld experiments may present evidence of anomalous communication, it is unclear as to the mechanisms which may underpin that process. So, does the participant successfully identify the target clip by virtue of some telepathic connection with the sender? Or is it due to precognitive awareness of which target was to be selected? Or is it evidence of some precognitive psychokinetic principle that allows the participant to interact with

---

*The author thanks Nicola Holt, who provided very helpful comments on an earlier version of this chapter.

the experimental technology so as to influence the target selection prior to the experiment? Sociological studies of new or controversial claims in the natural sciences show that, in the absence of a consensually agreed framework of knowledge—for example, about what exactly is being tested, or what precise aspect of its functioning is being explored—it is difficult to interpret the significance of any statistical evidence from experimental studies (Collins, 1992). It has been argued that parapsychology has not developed the kind of cumulative empirical evidence nor theoretical framework that characterizes established scientific disciplines (for example Kurtz, 1985). And this is perhaps why parapsychology has difficulty in gaining recognition from mainstream scientists, and, indeed, from psychologists with whom they tend to share university accommodation (McClenon, 1982).

The second reason is that the home environment for spontaneous anomalous experiences is not the laboratory, but everyday life. They occur to people as they are enmeshed in a range of cultural, social and interpersonal activities. The parapsychological response has been to regard reports of spontaneous experiences as suggestive of particular kinds of anomalous cognitive capabilities and then to test for those capabilities through laboratory-based experimental procedures. But anomalous experiences, whatever their nature, are inextricably implicated in precisely the social processes and contexts which cannot be reproduced in laboratory conditions.

It is perhaps appropriate, then, that parapsychology broaden its methodological horizons, and develop methodologies and lines of empirical research associated more with the social sciences. This is not a call to abandon experiments, but to explore the value of empirical perspectives and theoretical positions more associated with research in the social sciences.

Of course, this is not an original position. Rhea White (1990) suggested that parapsychology develop a more interpretative approach to what she calls exceptional experiences, and identified particular approaches common to sociology, and the social sciences more generally. (Her argument, however, seems to have fallen on deaf ears, perhaps in part because it was coupled with a strong call for parapsychologists to abandon experiments altogether.) Similarly, much of the work of Robert Morris and his colleagues at the Koestler Parapsychology Unit was directed to investigating the broader contexts of psi experiences, which invites consideration of distinctly social processes (for example, Delanoy, Watt and Morris, 1993; Morris, 2005). And parapsychologists have regularly made use of data gathering techniques commonly used in social science research, such as surveys (for example, Irwin, 1993).

However, I think the social sciences can offer much more. In this chapter I outline three research projects which draw on methodologies from the social sciences, in which sociological and parapsychological concerns merge, and from which findings may be generated that are relevant to both disciplines. These projects concern the geodemographic or spatial features of spontaneous experiences, and, in experimental conditions, the discourse of participants' introspective reports, and the interpersonal dynamics of experimenter-participant interaction.

Spontaneous Experiences and Spatial Parapsychology

I have suggested that the home environment for psi-related experiences, or PREs (Targ, Schlitz and Irwin 2000, p.220) is not the laboratory experiment; but neither is it the laboratory itself: the physical space in which the experiment takes place. PREs happen to people in other places. They may be at home, or at work. They may be in transit, or they may have just ended a journey and be at a destination, or they may be about to embark on a journey, and be at the point of departure. But experients are always somewhere. Whenever they occur, therefore PREs always have a geographical dimension; this fundamental component of the PRE, however, has not been systematically explored in the analysis of spontaneous psi experiences.

The degree to which the spatial and geographic dimensions of spontaneous PREs have been largely overlooked in parapsychology can be gauged by considering two strands of parapsychological research and writing: the analysis of collections of accounts of spontaneous cases; and theoretical or conceptual writings on the value of spontaneous case research.

Analysis of collections of accounts of spontaneous cases has been a significant feature of the emergence of the formal scientific study of PREs. However, these analyses have focused primarily on substantive thematic continuities inherent in the nature of the reported experience. For example, the classic study by Gurney, Myers and Podmore (1886) focused on types of cases where it appeared that the mind of one human being had influenced another without the apparent use of the ordinary five senses. Saltmash's (1934) analysis of 349 reports of precognitions focused on two primary criteria: form (whether the experience occurred as a dream, a waking experience or an hallucination) and content (whether it concerned illness, death or more trivial incidents). More recently, L.E. Rhine's analysis of 14000 unsolicited accounts sent to the Parapsychology Laboratory at Duke University focused on the identification of recurrent themes (summarized in Rhine, 1981). What is consistent across these qualitative analyses of case collections is the relative lack of concern with the spatial organization and geographic correlates of psi related experiences.

Quantitative analyses have similarly neglected the relevance of the spatial dimension to spontaneous PREs. For example, Schouten quantitatively examined case collections from studies by Gurney et al. (1886), Sannwald (1961, cited in Schouten, 1981) and L.E. Rhine (1981). To permit statistical analysis, each collection was coded into a variety of categories according to characteristics such as the type of experience reported, the seriousness of the event, the relationships between the individuals concerned, the gender and age of the experient, the time interval between the event and the subsequent reporting, and so on (Schouten, 1979, 1981, 1982). The relevance of the geographic location of the experient at the time of the experience (as opposed to, say whether they were in bed, sitting in an armchair, and so on), nor their domestic, residential location at the time of reporting the experience, are not given any systematic analytic consideration.

Conceptual and theoretical assessments of the value of spontaneous case analysis also overlook the potential significance of the location of the experient. For example, the section devoted to the role of spontaneous case analysis in Irwin's (1991) introduction to parapsychology does not raise the possibility that geographical variables may be important factors in psi experiences or their distribution among a designated population. Similarly, Watt's (1990) assessment of the value of spontaneous case research explicitly draws on Morris's argument (Morris, 2005) that to understand psi phenomena it is necessary to take account of all the possible relevant factors "within which the spontaneous psychic experience is embedded [and which] might suggest new process related hypotheses" (Watt, 1990, p.275). Indeed, Morris argued that it "seems appropriate to regard parapsychology settings, be they the natural settings of spontaneous cases, or the controlled environment of experiments, as complex open systems.... We may need to focus more on the strategies for evaluating ... psi conducive systems" (Morris, 2005, p.31). Morris was not referring specifically to the geographic dimensions of psi experiences. But his call for analysis of the complexity of psi conducive circumstances draws our attention to the fact that we know so little about a fundamental feature of the context of psi related experiences: that they happen somewhere. This alone invites at least preliminary analysis of the relationship between geographical variables and psi experiences.

This line of research may be developed by exploring the use of sophisticated computer hardware and software such as Geographical Information Systems, or Geodemographic Information Systems (GIS/GDIS). A geographic or geodemographic information system is "a computer system for capturing, managing, integrating manipulating, analyzing and displaying data which is spatially referenced to the Earth" (McDonnell and Kemp, 1995, p.42). It allows a spatial mapping of the distribution and location of classes of experiences or behaviors, such as the kind of information that may be collected in large scale social surveys. A GIS/GDIS is a tool by which the analyst can develop a spatial representation of various dimensions of experiential and behavioral phenomena. GIS/GDIS systems were designed to allow analysis of the spatial organization and distribution of a range of experiences and behaviors; but they can also be applied to the investigation of PREs, and can contribute to experient profiling: identifying the characteristics of people who experience spontaneous psi phenomena.

It is at this point that we need to consider why it may be useful to explore the relationship between geographic and geodemographic variables and PREs. There are three arguments.

First, anecdotally, it is common to hear that some geographical locations are associated with a range of anomalous or psi phenomena. Anthropological studies have identified that shamanic ceremonies and experiences often cluster around traditionally sacred sites; but in contemporary western societies also, particular kinds of PREs are associated with locations: hauntings and houses, mystical experiences and ley lines and so on. While these observations are anecdotal, or have their origins in folklore, it is reasonable to explore the root of stories that so consistently link PREs with particular spaces or locations. Rigorous exploration of geographical variables may explicate the scientific relationships which underpin folklore and anecdote, thereby suggesting new lines of inquiry for parapsychological research.

Second, there is empirical scientific evidence that some kinds of anomalous phenomena may be related to the effects of recognized forces, the occurrence of which are crucially connected to particular locations. For example, Persinger's work on the relationship between electrical distortions to the temporal lobe and anomalous or mystical experiences suggests that energies locally displaced by tectonic movement may influence the consciousness of people in that location (Cook and Persinger, 2001; Persinger and Healey, 2002; Persinger, Koren and O'Connor, 2001; see also Braithwaite, 2004a, 2004b; Braithwaite, Perez-Aquino and Townsend, 2004; Wiseman, Watt, Greening, Stevens and O'Keeffe, 2002; Wiseman, Watt, Stevens, Greening and O'Keeffe, 2003).

Third, GIS/GDIS have proved extraordinarily useful in gaining new insight to behaviors that have traditionally been understood in terms of individual psychological factors, or explained by reference to the relationship between personality and social context. Take for example, crime. A criminal act is to an important degree the outcome of an individual's decision, motive or predisposition to commit an illegal act. However, most western police and law enforcement agencies now routinely use GIS/GDIS analysis to better understand the broader geographical context of criminal behavior, be they minor burglaries (for example, Young, 1999; Neighbourhood Renewal Unit, 2002) or more serious crimes (for example, Canter, 2003), and to assist in the prosecution of criminals (for example, Moland 1998; see also, Chainey and Ratcliffe, 2005; Harris, 1999). The use of GIS/GDIS by law enforcement agencies shows that there is a significant geographical and spatial dimension to events which intuitively seem primarily psychological, cognitive or individual in nature.

It is important to note that GIS/GDIS do not merely allow the analysis of geographical data. Other forms of electronic data may be entered into a GIS/GDIS to facilitate complex statistical analysis of the relationship between geographic and geodemographic variables and other kinds of variables. For example, census data about national or local populations allow correlational analysis between geographic variables and social class, occupation, education, religiosity, gender, age and so on. GIS/GDIS therefore allow us to explore and develop sophisticated profiles of experients.

The analysis of the characteristics of experients has been a key dimension to parapsychological research. Studies have focused on psychological variables such as belief in the paranormal (for example, Clarke, 1995; Irwin, 1985), dissociative tendencies (for example, Zingrone and Alvarado, 1994), personality (for example, Alvarado, Zingrone and Dalton, 1996), and the impact of cognitive style (for example, Irwin, 1979). There have also been studies of the relationship between PREs and sociological variables such as social class and class mobility (Nelson, 1975), education (Hay and Morisy, 1978) religion (Bourque, 1969; Hay, 1982; Rice, 2003), cultural expectations (McClenon, 1990, 1994), and social values (Bourque and Back, 1968). Again, though, there has been little systematic investigation of the geographical correlates of experiences. GIS/GDIS allow us to explore precisely this relationship between the geographic dimensions of PREs and the characteristics of experients, thereby contributing to our understanding of the kind of people who have spontaneous psi experiences and the sociological and geodemographic conditions under which these experiences occur.

Discourse and Parapsychological Experiments

Sociological methods are important resources in understanding ostensible psi experiences in everyday life. But they may also provide insight to what happens in parapsychology laboratories. To illustrate, we will consider some data from a series of autoganzfeld experiments conducted at the Koestler Parapsychology Unit at the University of Edinburgh.

There are variations in the autoganzfeld procedure, but, typically, a sender tries mentally to send or project images of a target, usually a short video clip from a large database chosen randomly by specifically modified software. This clip is shown several times during the sending part of the experiment. During the sending period the experimental subject (hereafter, the receiver) is asked to report verbally whatever images or sensations they are experiencing. This is called their *mentation*. These are noted by an overhearing (but at this point non-participating) experimenter in another room. After the sending period, the experimenter makes contact with the receiver (they can communicate via an intercom system and headphones, but are in different rooms) and the *mentation review* commences. In the review the experimenter goes over his or her notes of the images and sensations reported by the receiver during the sending period. During the judging phase that follows, the receiver is shown four video clips: the target and three others. On the basis of the images and sensations experienced during the sending phase, the receiver has to nominate which clip they think the sender was trying to project. Both the mentation and the mentation review are important steps in the procedure. If there are psi processes operating during the sending period, the participants' reports of their phenomenal consciousness may provide insight as to how anomalous cognition interacts with ordinary cognitive processes. And the review is significant because it allows the experimenter, where appropriate, to correct his or her record of the mentation; it is also an opportunity for the receiver to expand upon their imagery.

Both the mentation and the mentation review are discursive events. In the first, the participant provides a description of their contemporaneous conscious imagery and sensations. In the review, the experimenter and participant interact verbally to ensure a final record of the mentation experiences.

One of the pre-eminent methods in the social science for the analysis discourse and interaction is Conversation Analysis, or CA. Despite its name, CA it may be applied to any form of unscripted or naturally occurring interaction, even of the kind which may occur in such formal settings as a (para)psychological experiment. The goal of CA is to describe the tacit communicative skills that inform the turn-by-turn unfolding of interaction. It is a qualitative method based on detailed, formal description of recurrent properties of (audio and/or video) recordings of interactional episodes. Analysis is aided by detailed transcripts which capture the way talk is produced, the natural "messiness" of verbal interaction (such as false starts to words, or the speed of delivery), non lexical sounds (such as breathing), the gaps in talk or periods of silence (measured in tenths of seconds), and structural aspects of talk (for example, the way that a turn may be initiated while on-going turn is still continuing, leading to periods of overlapping talk). (For introductory overviews of conversation analysis, see Heritage, 1984; Hutchby and Wooffitt, 2008; Sacks, 1992; Schegloff, 2007).

In this section, I illustrate briefly how a conversation analytic approach can illuminate the conduct of experimenter and participant in ganzfeld experiments.

The Poetics of Introspection on (Potentially) Parapsychological Experiences

During the sending period of the ganzfeld experiment, the receiver is required to describe out loud their experiences. This is called their mentation narrative. Although the experimenter can hear the mentation and make notes of it, they do not at this stage interact with the participants. The mentation, then, is a monologue.

Monologic discourse raises some interesting questions. In everyday interaction, we monitor others' turns as a resource to make sense of the collaborative nature of our conduct. So, as the analysis in the previous section illustrates, hearing someone produce a turn which performs a particular kind of action, such as an "acceptance," provides grounds to infer that they heard our prior turn as performing the action of "inviting," as opposed to "questioning," "complaining" and so on). In this sense, the turn-by-turn production of talk may be said to be the building blocks of intersubjective understanding (Heritage, 1984). That is, the to and fro of ordinary interaction is a resource for the production of intelligible discourse. But what resources are available in the absence of the turn-by-turn infolding of interaction, such as in monologic discourse?

Nicola Holt and I have been studying mentation narratives to investigate the communicative skills that underpin how people describe their inner phenomenological experiences (Wooffitt and Holt, 2008). One feature that has emerged from this analysis may be termed the *poetic relationships* in mentation narratives.

One striking kind of poetic relationship is alliterative: stretches of talk in which discrete images or imagery clusters are reported, in which particular sounds seem to occur as the first sound of a word with conspicuous frequency. To illustrate, consider the following extract, which comes from a transcript of a mentation narrative from an experimental participant who produces minimal, one or two word reports of imagery. Note how frequently the sounds "f" and "s" occur in this sequence of descriptions.

(1) ("R" is the receiver in the experiment.)
R: foo:tprints
(35.2)
((clicking sound)) (.8) 's=like a (.) a wrought ir:on ga:te
(13.1)
fer:ns:
(42.1)
for:k:
(15.5)
sunse:t
(32.8)
sta:rs
(32)
°s:nowfla:kes°
(9.6)
(fie:lds)

It is noticeable that reports of conscious imagery tend to be temporally distributed, or clustered (Wooffitt and Holt, 2008), with periods of silence in between report of discrete images. In this stretch of eight discrete reports, there are four words that begin with "f" and three with "s." One word, "snowflakes," seems conspicuously fitted to this sequence in that it contains both sounds.

In some of his early lectures on social interaction, Harvey Sacks, the founder of conversation analysis, made some observations on the poetic features of mundane conversation. For example, he noted that some kinds of alliteration seemed to be conspicuously prominent. He speculated whether a particular sound of a start of a word may sometimes predispose on-going word selection procedures so that subsequent words also begin with that sound (Sacks, 1992, vol II: 306). That is, poetical structures in talk, such as the kind of alliterative relationship identified in extract 1, are not happenstance, but orderly outcomes of the operations of particular (tacit) communicative competencies.

The mentation narratives provide considerable evidence of the designed quality of poetical features in descriptions of imagery. For example, an alliterative relationship can be seen to obtain in the construction of longer reports.

(2)
    (27.1)
R: well °there's° a load've windo:ws, (0.9) in a wa::ll
    (35.1)

(To demonstrate that this is a discrete report, the periods of silence before and after have been included in this extract.) This cluster exhibits two recurrent sounds: the "w" in "well," "window" and "wall." There is also recurrence of "l" sounds in "well," "load" and "all."

There are two features of this cluster that suggest poetical ordering has a strong influence on the composition of this report. The "well" that prefaces the report is interesting. In everyday interaction, "well" has a clear interactional orientation, in that it signals that the turn which follows displays a particular stance towards a prior turn. So, for example, it routinely occurs in turns in which some (albeit minor) disagreement is expressed (Pomerantz, 1984). Its occurrence here at the start of this cluster is therefore puzzling as, in this kind of extended monologue, there are no prior turns to which any cluster is a response. Moreover, it is not an idiosyncratic feature of this participant's discourse; this is the only time "well" occurs at the start of a descriptive cluster. We may say then, that, this "well" is a conspicuous feature of the cluster.

Consider also the adjectival and vernacular "loads" to describe the number of windows. There are numerous synonyms, vernacular and formal, that could have been selected to capture the noticeable or large number of windows in the imagery: "tons," "many," "heaps," "masses" and so on (Schegloff, 1972). However, the word that was selected bears a poetical relationship to one of the dominant sounds within this cluster.

Here, then, is evidence of a design procedure for the receiver's report of their conscious imagery. Word selection establishes or maintains a poetical resonance across the cluster.

The poetic construction of mentation narratives is not only to be found in conspicuous recurrence of particular sounds. It may also inform more lexical and semantic considerations.

(3)
R: u:m: (2.4) something: about (0.3) .h butterflies (3.8) .h and there's somebody swimming
(27.0)
u:m: (2.6) an: engine

This extract comes from the start of the mentation, and "something: about (0.3) .h butterflies (3.8) .h and there's somebody *swi*mming" is the participant's report of their first imagery. Evidence of a poetical ordering is found in the symmetry of the two components, in that they are of similar length and composition. This is clear if non-lexical sounds are removed, leaving only the spoken words: "something: about butterflies" has common sounds with "there's somebody *swi*mming," namely, recurrent "b", "m" and "s" sounds. There is also repetition of "some" in "something" and "somebody." At a semantic level, in both components there is a matched imprecision: it is an unspecified "something" about butterflies, and it is an unspecified "someone" doing the swimming.

Poetic relationships within mentation descriptions may be surprisingly complex. In the following extract, the participant produces a description of discrete imagery.

(4) 01-18
R: anima:ls: °it's° a- (.) a dogs a horse
(5.4)
white noise is making me think've (.) trains and planes:, °but uh(h)° .hh (0.6)
°(hh)=>I c'n see-< u:::=I c'n see° a book
(6.6)
OLD lady passing (2.8) >>'s a<< walking stick (2.3) 'er's an indian dancer
(6.7)
>>there's a<< old lady walking towards me now
(6.9)
song::, called tw(r)igs and see:ds,
(14.0)
a song called (pink=pig slats)
(6.6)
→ °>I c'n<° see things (.) pa:ssing >sort've< (2.4) patterns in the dogs 'n co:nes,
(33.0)
.hh there's a river

This is the start of this participant's mentation. The cluster we are focusing on here is arrowed. As in the previous extract, this report has two components. There is a preliminary report and then, after a 2.4 second silence, an extension of that description (it is an extension rather than a report of new imagery because the truncated "sort of" before the silence projects that what follows is a continuation of the current topic).

A first point to make is that the extended part of this report does not seem to address the topic introduced in the first part. And although there are earlier references to animals, and specifically to dogs, there is no *topical* relationship between the first part of this cluster and the second. But there is a strong *poetical* relationship. There is alliteration of the "p" sound in the words "passing" and "patterns," and assonance occurs with the repetition of the "o" sound in the words "dogs" and "cones." It is as if the extended part of this report is designed solely to develop a poetic extension of dominant sounds in the words used to compose the first part.

There is another poetic feature to this cluster. In his lectures, Sacks noticed that in everyday interaction, there would be occasions in which words or word sounds would be reversed. So, he examined a taped recording of interaction in which one speaker produced a turn which contained the phrase "that's just," which was then followed in the next turn by a different speaker that contained the phrase "just that"; other cases included the occurrence of "how, now" in one turn, and in the next, "now how" was a component.

There is some degree of sound reversal in the passing/patterns cluster. The first component contains the sound of a hard "c," and then a "p"; the second component reverses this: there is the "p" sound in "patterns" and then the hard "c" repeated in "cones."

Why might these poetical relationships be significant to parapsychologists? There are two issues. In the ganzfeld procedure, what the receiver says during the sending period is very important: it is recorded by the experimenters, used as the basis for the mentation review, and will inform the receiver's assessment of the video clip and three target decoys in the judging phase. But the analyses presented here, informed by Sacks' observations on the poetics of ordinary talk, suggest that what is described during the mentation narrative may not be a simple expression of an inner experience, but may be the outcome of socially-organized tacit communicative practices, such as a poetically oriented word selection procedure. In this sense, then, the communicative resources by which the receiver can articulate their conscious experiences may function in much the same way as demand characteristics, and, as a consequence, potentially complicate the experimental procedure. More optimistically though, the poetical ordering may itself reflect a dimension of anomalous communicative processes, thereby providing an insight into the mechanisms by which psi processes interact with conventional psycholinguistic procedures.

Experimenter-Participant Interaction in the Mentation Review

The mentation review allows the experimenter to ensure that his or her record of the prior mentation is accurate, and it follows a step-wise procedure. The experimenter reads out from his or her notes one discrete image or sensation. After each item is introduced the experimenter momentarily withholds further talk, thus establishing a "slot" in the interaction in which the participant may either correct the experimenter's record, if relevant, or expand upon that imagery. When participants do provide more information, there are two ways in which experimenters acknowledge that expansion. In most cases, they use "okay" or some variant, and withhold further talk in case the participant intends to add more information. If no further talk is forthcoming, they move to the next item in their record.

For example, in extract 5 we see the experimenter introduce three images reported during the mentation. The subject uses a minimal turn, "mm" to pass on the opportunity to expand on the first (the boat in the water), but expands on the second (the pile of something). The experimenter receipts the expansion with an "okay" and, after a half second delay, introduces the next item (the frog).

(5) (01-05: E3/F. "E" is the experimenter, "R" is the receiver/experimental participant. In the data identification codes, the number following "E" indicates which of the three experimenters taking part is featured in the extract, and the gender of the subject is designated by /F or /M. Transcription conventions are explained in the appendix.)

E: ˙hh boat=in=the=water=leaving=a=wake,
R: m:m::
   (0.6)
E: (tk) ˙hh a pile of something?
   (1.1)
R: >˙h yeah< it was like a pile of pla:tes or:: ˙ (0.7) um:: (1.1) °something like that°
E: °okay:?° (0.5) ˙h a fro:g(h) >a big one?<

The experimenter may also use "mm hm" to acknowledge the participant's expansion on the imagery. However, as acknowledgment tokens, "okay" and "mm hm" are not equivalent, in that if there is a "mm hm" token, the subsequent interaction has a very different trajectory and outcome. In extract 6, the experimenter introduces the final item of the mentation review. This is confirmed by the receiver, who then goes on to offer further information about that item.

(6) (01-21: E3/M)
E: °°·(n)hh°° °o:kay,° (tk).·hh and then I think the final thing you said was uh:: (.) ·h something like a chair (.) >in< in a pyramid?
R: °(n)hh° yeah, >saw the< (.) the triangle thing again and then (.) °.·h° >something< which reminded me of like, (.) um, (0.5) ·h an upright chair like um:, (1.5) °(n)hhh° (.) um:? >°so-°< like a black chair, (1.4)
E: → m:hm
(0.5)
R: not like the one I'm sitting on or °anything° jus:::t °uh:° (3.5) >I don't know,< it was >sort of< °uhm:(h)° (2.1) >like a s-< like a sort of padded chai(hh)r or something °·h° >it was just< from the side that I saw it, so >it was like< an ell shape (.) °.·h° [that =
E: [°mhm°
R: = suggested a chair:

There are two immediately noticeable differences. First, after the (arrowed) "mm hm" token, the review does not proceed to the next item on the experimenter's record, but instead the receiver provides further description of the current imagery. Second, that further talk exhibits a degree of circumspection or cautiousness: there are, for example, hesitations in the speech; and the "I don't know" formulation is an explicit marker of doubt with regards to certainty or confidence in his reflections on the imagery. The receiver interprets the experimenter's "mm hm," as inviting a modulated or downgraded claim about his imagery.

This is not a unique case: receivers routinely interpret a "mm hm" acknowledgment as exhibiting the experimenter's expectation that there should be some expression of cautiousness or doubt about their imagery (Wooffitt, 2007). As an illustration, consider the next extract, in which the experimenter produces two "mm hm" acknowledgment tokens.

(7) (01–28: E2/F)
E: and you said you felt you could see for mi:les (.) across countryside,=
R: =yea°f-s°, ( ) ·hh like I was flying across it
(0.5)
E: → (h) m↑hm
R: ·hh looking down over ( ) ·hhh hhh fields a- >I don't know:< it was very odd hh yeah,
E: → °m°↑h
R: °°·hhhh hhhh°°
(0.3)
R: (°mus:-°) >I'd-< ↑hh (.) ·h ↑I'M NOT VERY GOOD AT DESCRIBING IT it's a very weird >sort of< va:gue (.) ·hh (1.2) >°it°< just felt like (>sort of you<) so::: (0.3)) ·hh body's just: (1.2) taking off

The imagery being reviewed here is the receiver's sense of "seeing miles across countryside." After the first "mm hm" receipt (arrowed), the participant returns to the imagery, reporting that she was "looking down over (0.5) ˙hhh hhh fields." In her subsequent talk she produces an explicit doubt marker, "I don't know"; and then, by way of closing summary formulation, she explicitly mentions to the strangeness of the image, "it was very odd hh yeah." Both these turn components establish a degree of uncertainty in the receiver's current recollection and understanding of the imagery. There is another experimenter continuer (also arrowed), and when the participant speaks again she reports, with a marked upwards intonation and at louder volume that the surrounding talk, "↑I'M NOT VERY GOOD AT DESCRIBING IT"; she then says "it's a very weird >sort of< va:gue." These reports unequivocally establish a basis for circumspection about her confidence in her recollection of the imagery.

Space limitations prevents a fuller analysis, and these analytic observations are therefore offered only to sketch some broad properties of recurrent interactional patterns in the ways in which experimenter and participants conduct the mentation review. How may these kinds of sociological observations on the nature of experimenter-participant interaction contribute to parapsychological concerns?

There is a general contribution. Parapsychologists have had a long standing interest in the way that the experimenter's interpersonal style may have a bearing on the outcome of experiments. This is because there is anecdotal and experimental evidence that broadly suggests that experimenters who are able to develop a rapport with their participants, obtain better results than negative experimenters who do not (for example, Honorton, Ramsey, and Cabibbo, 1975; Parker, 2000; Schlitz and Honorton, 1992; Schlitz, Wiseman, Radin and Watt, 2005; Schmeidler and Edge, 1999; Sherwood, Roe and Holt, 2005; Watt, 2002; Wiseman and Schlitz, 1998). However, rapport, defined as a "sympathetic relationship or understanding" (Collins Shorter English Dictionary, 1993) is a vague definition, as it broadly characterizes a kind of relationship, but tells us little about the practices through which that relationship is generated and sustained. Rapport is thus an interpretative term, not a descriptive one. Conversation analytic research can offer a formal and detailed description of the interactional practices through which positive mutual regard, or alignment, may be established and maintained. This could provide the basis by which to specify formally how it is that one experimenter's conduct in the laboratory context differs from another's.

With regards to the ganzfeld experiment more specifically: after the review, participants go to the judging phase of the experiment. They will see four video clips and will be asked to identify which of these they think the sender was concentrating on. During this process it is assumed that participants rely (at least in part) on their imagery to guide them in deciding which of the four clips was the focus of the sender's attention. The preliminary analyses presented here suggest, however, that interactional details (the choice of "mm hm" instead of "okay" to acknowledge further talk about imagery) may encourage participants to express their doubt or uncertainty about their imagery. The implication: it is at least possible that, when they come to view the video clips, they will have less confidence in relying on their imagery to identify significant events or themes. A participant's decision about the target clip, then, may be tacitly informed by a position or stance toward their imagery which was *interactionally* generated, in that it was an outcome of the participant's inferences about the significance of the way in which the experimenter acknowledged the prior turn.

Conclusions

In this chapter I have briefly reviewed three lines of research which suggest a rapprochement between traditional parapsychological concerns and the broad goals and methods of the social sciences. These are not the only projects that stand at the juncture of social and parapsychological science. For example, Holt's studies of ostensible psi experiences in everyday contexts draws on experience sampling methodologies, techniques which have their roots as much in social science as in psychology (Holt, 2006; 2007). Lamont's studies of accounts of belief and skepticism draw from social science discourse analytic perspectives that emphasize the constitutive and functional nature of communication (Lamont, 2007).

Parapsychology, though, remains a predominantly experimental discipline. But parapsychology laboratories are not just places where (a particular kind of) science gets done. They are themselves social environments, in which people use everyday communicative skills to interact, develop (albeit brief) interpersonal relationships, and collaboratively work through particular kinds of institutional or work related tasks. Parapsychologists have recognized that the social dimensions of laboratory experience may have a bearing on parapsychological experiments. There are numerous methods available in the social sciences by which parapsychologists could better understand the relational dynamics that underpin experimental work as social practice. In the second and third sections of this chapter I have briefly tried to illustrate the kind of findings that may be yielded by a conversation analytic approach to data from parapsychology laboratories. Of more general relevance, this kind of analysis exposes the subtle but organized intricacies naturally occurring in interaction which parapsychologist must address if they are to develop a sophisticated and empirically rigorous appreciation of the interpersonal dynamics between experimenter and experimental participant.

Ostensible psi related experiences happen to social beings in social contexts, not brain mechanisms isolated in artificial and environments for research purposes. This has been long recognized by some parapsychologists. Louisa Rhine's analysis of the 14000 unsolicited written accounts submitted to the laboratory at Duke was extremely sensitive to the emotional and relational aspects of experiences (Rhine, 1981). Yet this work was done primarily to help develop hypotheses about the operation of psi that could subsequently be explored in the laboratory. Even here, then, the experimental approach was primary; the analysis of non experimental data was accorded a secondary importance, even when those data were reports of people's own first hand experiences.

But in the absence of a consensually agreed and well tested theoretical framework, and in the absence of a robust and cumulative set of empirical findings, it seems premature to assume that the experimental laboratory is naturally the most important place in which to try to understand ostensible psi phenomena. It is for this reason that research outside the laboratory should be accorded equal significance with laboratory research. The key to understanding these phenomena may lie in hitherto overlooked spatial and geodemographic conditions, or in the influence of particular social or cultural contexts, and or the mechanisms of interaction through which we live our lives as social beings. But while parapsychology faces inwards, towards the laboratory, we may never know.

Appendix: Transcription Symbols

The transcription symbols used here are common to conversation analytic research, and were developed by Gail Jefferson. The following symbols are used in the data.

(.5)	The number in brackets indicates a time gap in tenths of a second.
(.)	A dot enclosed in a bracket indicates pause in the talk less then two tenths of a second.
.hh	A dot before an "h" indicates speaker in-breath. The more h's, the longer the inbreath.
hh	An "h" indicates an out-breath. The more h's the longer the breath.
(( ))	A description enclosed in a double bracket indicates a non-verbal activity. For example ((banging sound))
-	A dash indicates the sharp cut-off of the prior word or sound.
:::	Colons indicate that the speaker has stretched the preceding sound or letter. The more colons the greater the extent of the stretching.
( )	Empty parentheses indicate the presence of an unclear fragment on the tape.
(guess)	The words within a single bracket indicate the transcriber's best guess at an unclear fragment.
.	A full stop indicates a stopping fall in tone. It does not necessarily indicate the end of a sentence.

Under	Underlined fragments indicate speaker emphasis.
↑↓	Pointed arrows indicate a marked falling or rising intonational shift. They are placed immediately before the onset of the shift.
,	A comma indicates a continuing intonation.
?	A question mark indicates a rising inflection. It does not necessarily indicate a question.
CAPITALS	With the exception of proper nouns, capital letters indicate a section of speech noticeably louder than that surrounding it.
° °	Degree signs are used to indicate that the talk they encompass is spoken noticeably quieter than the surrounding talk.
°° °°	Double degree signs have been used to indicate whispered or extremely quiet talk.
Thaght	A "gh" indicates that word in which it is placed had a guttural pronunciation.
> <	"More than" and "less than" signs indicate that the talk they encompass was produced noticeably quicker than the surrounding talk.
>> <<	Additional "more than" and "less than" symbols mean that the talk they encompass is extremely quick relative to the surrounding talk.
=	The "equals" sign indicates contiguous utterances.
[]	Square brackets between adjacent lines of concurrent speech indicate the onset and end of a spate of overlapping talk.

A more detailed description of these transcription symbols can be found in Atkinson and Heritage (1984, p. ix–xvi).

References

Atkinson, J.M., and J. Heritage (eds.) (1984). *Structures of Social Action: Studies in Conversation Analysis*. Cambridge: Cambridge University.

Alvarado, C.S., N.L. Zingrone and K. Dalton (1996) Out of body experiences, psi experiences, and the "Big Five": relating the NEO-PI-R to the experience claims of experimental subjects. *Proceedings of the 39th Annual Convention of the Parapsychological Association*.

Bourque, L. B. (1969). Social correlates of transcendental experiences. *Sociological Analysis*, 30. 151–163.

Bourque, L. B., and K.W. Back (1968). Values and transcendental experiences. *Social Forces*, 47. 34–38.

Braithwaite, J. J. (2004a). Magnetic variances associated with "haunt-type" experiences: a comparison using time-synchronized baseline measurements. *European Journal of Parapsychology*, 19. 3–28.

Braithwaite, J. J. (2004b). Putting magnetism in its place: a critical examination of the weak-intensity magnetic field account for anomalous haunt-type experiences. *Journal of the Society for Psychical Research*, 890. 34–50.

Braithwaite, J. J., K. Perez-Aquino and M. Townsend (2004). In search of magnetic anomalies associated with haunt-type experiences: pulses and patterns in dual time-synchronized measurements. *Journal of Parapsychology*, 2. 255–288.

Canter, D. (2003). *Mapping Murder: The Secrets of Geographical Profiling*. London: Virgin.

Chainey, S., and J. Ratcliffe (2005). *GIS and Crime Mapping*. Chichester: Wiley.
Clarke, D. (1995). Experience and other reasons given for belief and disbelief in paranormal and religious phenomena. *Journal of the Society for Psychical Research*, 60. 371–384.
Collins, H.M. (1992). *Changing Order: Replication and Induction in Scientific Practice*. Chicago: University of Chicago.
Collins Shorter English Dictionary. (1993). Glasgow: HarperCollins.
Cook, C.M., and M.A. Persinger (2001). Geophysical variables and behavior: XCII. Experimental elicitation of the experience of a sentient being by right hemispheric, weak magnetic fields: interaction with temporal lobe sensitivity. *Perceptual and Motor Skills*, 92(2). 447–8.
Delanoy, D., C. Watt and R. Morris (1993). A new methodology for free-response ESP testing out with the laboratory: Findings from experienced participants. *Proceedings of the 36th Annual Parapsychological Association Convention*. 204–223.
Gurney, E., F.W.H. Myers and F. Podmore (1886) *Phantasms of the Living*. London: Trubner. Two volumes.
Harris, K. (1999). *Mapping Crime: Principles and Practice*. Washington, D.C.: United States Department of Justice. http://www.ojp.usdoj.gov/nij/maps/.
Hay, D. (1982). *Exploring Inner Space: Science and Religious Experience*. New York: Penguin.
Hay, D., and A. Morisy (1978). Reports of ecstatic paranormal, or religious experience in Great Britain and the United States—a comparison of trends. *Journal for the Scientific Study of Religion* 17 (3). 255–268.
Heritage, J. (1984). *Garfinkel and Ethnomethodology*. Cambridge: Polity Press.
Holt, N. (2006). Developing experience-sampling methodology to explore psi in "everyday life." *Proceedings of Presented Papers: The Parapsychological Association 49th Annual Convention*. 235–238.
Holt, N. (2007). Are artistic populations "psi-conducive"? Testing the relationship between creativity and psi with an experience-sampling protocol. *Proceedings of Presented Papers: The Parapsychological Association 50th Annual Convention*. 31–47.
Honorton, C., M. Ramsey and C. Cabibbo (1975). Experimenter effects in extrasensory perception. *Journal of the American Society for Psychical Research*, 69. 135–139.
Hutchby, I. and R. Wooffitt (2008). *Conversation Analysis*. Second edition. Oxford: Polity Press.
Irwin, H.J. (1979). Coding preferences and the form of extrasensory experiences. *Journal of Parapsychology*, 43. 205–220.
Irwin, H.J. (1985). *Flight of Mind: A Psychological Study of the Out-of-Body Experience*. Metuchen, NJ: Scarecrow Press.
Irwin, H. J. (1993). Belief in the paranormal: a review of the empirical literature. *Journal of the American Society for Psychical Research*, 87. 1–39.
Irwin, H. J. (1999). *An Introduction to Parapsychology*. Jefferson, NC: McFarland.
Kurtz, P. (1985). Is parapsychology a science? In P. Kurtz (ed.), *A Skeptic's Handbook of Parapsychology*. Buffalo: Prometheus. 503–518.
Lamont, P. (2007). Paranormal belief and the avowal of prior scepticism. *Theory and Psychology*, 17(5). 681–696.
McClenon, J. (1982). A survey of elite scientists: their attitudes towards ESP and parapsychology. *Journal of Parapsychology*, 46. 127–152.
McClenon, J. (1990). Chinese and American anomalous experiences: the role of religiosity. *Sociological Analysis*, 51. 53–67.
McClenon, J. (1994). "Surveys of anomalous experiences: a cross cultural analysis" *Journal of the American Society for Psychical Research*, 88. 117–135.
McDonnell, R. and K. Kemp (1995). *International GIS Dictionary*. Cambridge: GeoInformation International.
Moland. R.S. (1998). Geographical display of murder trial evidence. In N. LaVigne and J. Wartell (eds.), *Crime Mapping Case Studies: Successes in the Field*, volume 1. Washington, D.C.: Police Executive Research Forum.
Morris, R.L. (2005). Parapsychology in the Twenty-First Century. In M.A. Thalbourne and L. Storm (eds.), *Parapsychology in the Twenty-First Century: Essays on the Future of Psychical Research*. Jefferson, NC: McFarland. 21–27. (Originally published as "Parapsy-

chology in the 1990s: Addressing the Challenge" in the *European Journal of Parapsychology*, 1990-91, 8. 1-26.)
Neighbourhood Renewal Unit. (2002). *Alley-Gating*. London: Office of the Deputy Prime Minister. http://www.renewal.net.
Nelson, G.K. (1975). Toward a sociology of the psychic. *Review of Religious Research*, 1(3). 166-173.
Parker, A. (2000). A review of the ganzfeld work at Gothenburg University *Journal of the Society for Psychical Research*, 64:1. 1-15.
Persinger M.A., and F. Healey. (2002). Experimental facilitation of the sensed presence: possible intercalation between the hemispheres induced by complex magnetic fields. *Journal of Nervous and Mental Disorders*, 190(8). 533-41.
Persinger, M.A., S.A. Koren and R.P. O'Connor (2001). Geophysical variables and behavior: CIV. Power-frequency magnetic field transients (5 microtesla) and reports of haunt experiences within an electronically dense house. *Perceptual and Motor Skills*, 92(3) Pt 1. 673-4.
Pomerantz, A. (1984). Agreeing and disagreeing with assessments: some features of preferred/dispreferred turn-shapes" in J.M Atkinson and J. Heritage, J. (eds.) *Structures of Social Action: Studies in Conversation Analysis*. Cambridge: Cambridge University Press. 79-112.
Rhine, L. E. (1981). *The Invisible Picture: A Study of Psychic Experiences*. Jefferson, NC: McFarland.
Rice, T.W. (2003). Believe it or not: religious and other paranormal beliefs in the United States. *Journal for the Scientific Study of Religion*, 42. 95-106.
Sacks, H. (1992). *Lectures on Conversation*. Volumes I and II, edited by G. Jefferson and E. A. Schegloff. Oxford and Cambridge, MA: Basil Blackwell.
Saltmarsh, H.F. (1934). Report on cases of apparent precognition. *Proceedings of the Society for Psychical Research*, 42. 49-103.
Sannwald, G. (1961). Parapsychishen erlebnissen und Personlichkeitsunerkmalen. [Relations between paranormal experiences and personality traits]. Unpublished Dissertation, University of Freiburg.
Schegloff, E.A. (1972). Notes on a conversational practice: formulating place. In D. Sudnow (ed.), *Studies in Social Interaction*. New York: Free Press. 75-119.
Schegloff, E.A. (2007). *Sequence Organisation in Interaction*. Cambridge: Cambridge University Press.
Schlitz, M. J., and C. Honorton (1992). Ganzfeld psi performance within an artistically gifted population. *Journal of the American Society for Psychical Research*, 86. 83-98.
Schlitz, M., R. Wiseman, D. Radin and C. Watt (2005). Of two minds: Skeptic-proponent collaboration within parapsychology. *Proceedings of the 48th Annual Convention of the Parapsychological Association*. 171-177.
Schmeidler, G.R. and H. Edge (1999). Should ganzfeld research continue to be crucial in the search for a relicable psi effect? Part II: edited ganzfeld debate. *Journal of Parapsychology*, 63. 335-388.
Schouten, S.A. (1979). Analysis of spontaneous cases as reported in *Phantasms of the Living*. *European Journal of Parapsychology*, 2. 408-454.
Schouten, S.A. (1981). Analysing spontaneous cases: a replication based on the Sannwald collection. *European Journal of Parapsychology*, 4. 9-48.
Schouten, S.A. (1982). Analysing spontaneous cases: a replication based on the Rhine collection. *European Journal of Parapsychology*, 4. 113-159.
Sherwood, S., C. Roe and N. Holt (2005). Interpersonal psi: Exploring the role of the experimenter and the experimental climate in a ganzfeld telepathy task. *European Journal of Parapsychology*, 20. 150-172.
Targ, E., M. Schlitz and H.J. Irwin (2000). Psi-related experiences. In E. Cardena, S. J. Lynn and S. Krippner (eds.), *Varieties of Anomalous Experience: Examining the Scientific Evidence*. Washington, D.C.: The American Psychological Association. 219-252.
Watt, C.A. (1990). The value of spontaneous cases. *Journal of the Society for Psychical Research*, 56. 273-286.
Watt, C. (2002). Experimenter effects with a remote facilitation of attention focusing task:

a study with multiple believer and disbeliever experimenters. *Proceedings of Presented Papers, 45th Annual Parapsychological Association Convention.* 306–318.

White, R.A. (1990). An experience-centred approach to parapsychology. *Exceptional Human Experience,* 8. 7–36.

Wiseman, R. and M. Schlitz (1998). Experimenter effects and the remote detection of staring. *Journal of Parapsychology,* 61. 197–208.

Wiseman, R., C. Watt, E. Greening, P. Stevens and C. O'Keeffe (2002). An investigation into the alleged haunting of Hampton Court Palace: Psychological variables and magnetic fields. *Journal of Parapsychology,* 66. 387–408.

Wiseman, R., C. Watt, P. Stevens, E. Greening and C. O'Keeffe (2003). An investigation into alleged "hauntings." *British Journal of Psychology,* 94. 195–211.

Wooffitt, R. (2007). Communication and laboratory experience in parapsychology experiments: demand characteristics and the social organization of interaction. *British Journal of Social Psychology,* 46(3). 477–498.

Wooffitt, R. and N. Holt (2008). Reporting on Consciousness: communication in mentation narratives. *Proceedings of the 51st Annual Convention of the Parapsychological Association.*

Young, C. A. (1999). The Smithdown Road "Alleygating" project. Evaluated on behalf of the Safer Merseyside Partnership (unpublished).

Zingrone, N.L., and C.S. Alvarado (1994). Psychic and disassociative experiences: a preliminary report. *Proceedings of the 37th Annual Convention of the Parapsychological Association.*

Part Two:
Psychological Perspectives

7

ANOMALOUS EXPERIENCES DURING DEEP HYPNOSIS

Etzel Cardeña

Harking back to the exuberant collective healings of *Docteur* Mesmer in Paris in the late eighteenth century, much has been speculated and researched about the constellation of phenomena and techniques that we refer to as hypnosis. Despite current interest in the therapeutic uses of hypnosis, other areas have received scant attention, among them the appearance of spontaneous anomalous experiences within the hypnotic context. An anomalous experience can be defined as a very uncommon experience (e.g., synesthesia), or one that, although statistically not uncommon, seems to deviate from the culture's conception of reality (e.g., psi phenomena; Cardeña, Lynn, and Krippner, 2000). The gist of this paper will revolve around spontaneous experiences within the hypnotic context, including some recent data by the author, after a very brief discussion of mesmerism, hypnosis and reputed psi (parapsychological) phenomena. I will not review the literature on physiological correlates of hypnotic depth, which suggests that it is related to cortical desynchronization and higher EEG frequencies (Cardeña, Lehmann, Jönsson, Terhune, and Faber, 2007), and to parasympathetic vagal components of heart rate variability, probably mediated by lower respiration rate (Diamond, Davis, and Howe, 2008).

Mesmerism, Hypnosis, and Psi

Although debatable, it is often assumed that what we now know as hypnotic phenomena and procedures originated with the techniques of the 18th Century Viennese physician Franz Anton Mesmer, although not in his theory of animal magnetism that posited a magnetic invisible substance that could be used to heal. However, Mesmer's procedures and ensuing phenomena differed greatly from current hypnosis. They could involve music and a grand entrance by Mesmer himself, "magnetic passes" of the hands over the patient's body, or being in indirect contact through rods with "magnetized" water. Healings occurred in an emotionally charged setting in which there could be crying, fainting, and other dramatic crises, not unlike the exorcisms that the secular Mesmer wanted to replace (Laurence and Perry, 1988). These exuberant manifestations became far more subdued after one of Mesmer's disciples, the Marquis de Puységur, found that one of his magnetized peasants, Victor Race, went into what looked like a sleep-like "trance." Both Mesmer and Puységur wrote that in a hypnotic state individuals exhibited what would now be called various forms of psi phenomena including precognition and clairvoyance. Later authors described more systematically that mesmerism enhanced the creativity and paranormal abilities of hypnotically gifted individuals, allowing them to sense what the hypnotist was experiencing at a distance or know his or her thoughts, be hypnotized at a distance, and various other phenomena (Gauld, 1992; Moreau and Rogez, 1977). With few exceptions most early reports of enhanced paranormal abilities under hypnosis would fail contemporary criteria for good scientific reporting and experimental controls. The exceptions include the demonstrations of reputed psi by Alexis Didier, who was endorsed by Robert Houdin, the foremost magician of his time (Méheust, 2003), or the descriptions by Pierre Janet's of experiments with his patient Mme. B (Gauld, 1992). These and other cases justify Dingwall's (1967–68) conclusion regarding a possible connection between psi phenomena and hypnosis that "[A]n attitude of suspended judgment both as regards the past and the present is perhaps the most judicial" (V. 1, p. 297).

Although most hypnosis researchers in the 20th century made a concerted effort to distance themselves from any whiff of paranormality or mysticism, there have been controlled studies, although not programmatic research, on the reputed link between psi phenomena and hypnosis (Honorton, 1977; Moreau and Rogez, 1977). The initial lack of attention by parapsychological researchers to hypnosis is partly based on J. B. Rhine's disinterest in the subject, despite the significant effects produced in his own laboratory (Van de Castle, 1969). Two meta-analyses of all published studies to that date (Schechter, 1984; Stanford, 1992) have provided support for Gauld's assertion (1992) that the early mesmerism/hypnosis authors were "on to something." The most salient results of the meta-analyses are:

- psi performance was higher in hypnosis than control conditions in 16 of 20 studies ($p < .006$, one-tailed);
- results in the hypnosis condition were significantly higher than mean chance expectation in 9 studies, and non-significantly higher in 6 others, out of 19 studies;

- methodological flaws were not significantly related to results although, as in some other areas of psi research, there might have been a significant experimenter effect (Stanford and Stein, 1994).

Questions that clearly deserve further exploration include whether reputed enhanced psi performance during hypnosis depends on the hypnotic procedure (context), high hypnotizability (a trait denoting high responsiveness to suggestions after a hypnotic induction), or an interaction between those two variables as facilitated by an enthusiastic and positive researcher (cf. Schlitz, 1992).

Anomalous Experiences and Hypnotic Phenomena

In this section, I concentrate on spontaneous phenomena within a hypnotic context, rather than on how high hypnotizable individuals experience specific suggestions (e.g., McConkey and Barnier, 2004). Whether or not interpreted as referring to paranormal phenomena, reports of alterations of consciousness were yoked to mesmeric and hypnotic procedures from the very beginning, and there were initial attempts to categorize them. One of the most important synthesizers of the 19th Century, Kluge, described six degrees (or levels) of the magnetic state, including phenomena such as "darkness," "self-contemplation," and "universal clarity" (Ellenberger, 1970). When reviewing the more recent literature on phenomena described within the hypnotic context, a distinction must be made between consciousness alterations in response to specific suggestions and spontaneously occurring phenomena. The former are also of great interest, such as in inductions of quasi-mystical experiences (e.g., euphoria, expansion of time and space, unspeakable beauty; Aaronson, 1967; Sacerdote, 1977). However, they do not allow us to distinguish between the "artifact" (e.g., specific inductions and suggestions) of hypnosis and its "essence" (i.e., phenomena intrinsically associated with the hypnotic context; Orne, 1959). Multifactorial experiential models of hypnosis or hypnotic depth involving increased suggestibility, lack of reflective awareness/dissociation, and alterations in consciousness/absorption have been proposed (Ås and Ostvold, 1968; Cardeña and Spiegel, 1991; Evans, 1963; Field, 1965; Pekala, Kumar, Maurer, Elliot-Carter, and Moon, 2006), but there has been little research, especially among "ultraresponsive" individuals (Weitzenhoffer, 2000, p. 227). It has been established, though, that hypnotizability, even outside of the hypnotic context, is positively correlated with mystical, psi-related, near-death, and other anomalous experiences (Cardeña, Lynn, and Krippner, 2000).

Research on spontaneous hypnotic phenomena has been carried out by various authors. Gill and Brenman (1959) reported that while entering hypnosis many participants reported changes in body image (e.g., swelling of the head, mouth and arms) and body sensations (e.g., dizziness and sensations of floating) and a fading of the sense of external reality. As hypnosis continued, the specific configuration of the changes became more idiosyncratic. Ludwig (1965) administered a questionnaire to participants before and after a long hypnotic challenge procedure (i.e., suggestions in which participants are told to do something they have been given suggestions that they cannot do). In contrast with a no-hypnosis condition, the hypnotic experience fostered reports of phenomena such as a sense of unreality, merging with the surroundings, and unusual sensations, which the author interpreted as alterations in thinking and time sense, sense of loss of control, increased meaning, decreased affect, and changes in body image and somatic sensations. Ernest Hilgard (1968) interviewed 159 participants after their first standard hypnotic induction. Reports of non-suggested experiences included disinclination to speak, move or think, feelings of compulsion in response to suggestions, changes in body image (in appearance and size) and body sensations (e.g., dizziness, floating, spinning) and a similarity to sleep. Pekala (1991), using a standardized questionnaire, found that during hypnosis participants experienced alterations in the following areas: body image and sensations, time sense, perception, meaning, affect, and imagery, accompanied by a general sense of being in an altered state of consciousness. As compared to hetero-hypnosis, self-hypnosis is characterized by greater imagery, free-floating attention, and receptivity to "internal stimuli" (Fromm, Brown, Hurt, Oberlander, Boxer, and Pfeifer, 1981). Research has also shown that physical activity and/or suggestions for alertness instead of relaxation within a hypnotic context can produce similar responses to hypnotic suggestions (Bányai and Hilgard, 1976; Mallot, 1984), although there has been scant attention as to how the experience in physically active versus relaxation hypnotic contexts may differ.

Some authors have taken seriously the notion of levels of hypnosis and have investigated alterations of highly hypnotizable people during "deep" levels of hypnosis. Probably the first well-known modern author to dedicate a work specifically to deep hypnosis was Milton Erickson (1952) who defined it as an "unconscious level of awareness without interference by the conscious mind." He described loss of contact with the body during *plenary* (very deep) hypnosis and explained it as a pattern of retarded psychological and physiological functioning with lack of spontaneity. In a later article (1965), Erickson described author Aldous Huxley's experience of hypnosis and other states. Huxley described the beginning of hypnotic experience as a withdrawal from outer reality concerns which at later stages was characterized by changes in body sensation culminating in synesthesia, a sense of loss of personal identity, and lack of mental content.

In a more systematic fashion, Tart (1970) devised a deep hypnosis procedure (i.e., asking a hypnotically responsive participant to go as deeply as possible without other overt suggestions or instructions) and published a report about the phenomenology of a hypnotic "virtuoso." He described the participant's experience thus: (1) his body became very relaxed until awareness of the body was lost, (2) awareness of breathing gradually disappeared, (3) absolute blackness was perceived, (4) sense of identity and ego-awareness waned and gave rise to a sense of potential, (5) time slowed down until it became meaningless, (6) spontaneous mental activity was lost, and (7) a sense of oneness with the universe ensued. Tart's case study was subsequently replicated in within-subject designs. Using a sample of highly hypnotizable volunteers, Sherman (1971) found statistically significant clusters of phenomena associated with deep hypnosis. Characteristic features of the deepest level of hypnosis include difficulties in talking, a feeling of oneness with everything, loss of individual identity, blankness, episodes of absolute mental quietitude and voidness, feeling in a different level of reality, and great brightness. The very deep hypnotic state was also correlated with occurrences of reductions in EEG amplitude. Reports from medium hypnosis included emotional experiences, simple images and body sensations (e.g., relaxation, wavelike experiences, and motion). Light hypnosis was characterized by ideas, worries and "normal verbal thinking."

Feldman (1976) replicated the basic design of Sherman and addressed some particular questions of his own. He obtained a similar pattern of results as Sherman (i.e. mainly changes in body image and bodily sensations at the beginning of hypnosis; and phenomena such as feeling one with the surroundings, being immersed in blackness, a sense of awe and wonder, in deeper hypnosis). He also reported that participants' expectations were negligible predictors of deep hypnosis phenomena and that mood did not seem to change significantly during the hypnosis session. Ernest Hilgard (1986) carried out some informal research and also found that deeply hypnotized individuals spontaneously reported losing contact with their body and experienced an altered sense of time and mystical phenomena such as a sense of oneness and ineffability.

Despite the consistency of the findings on "very deep," minimal suggestion hypnosis, the studies reviewed have had various methodological shortcomings, including no control for relaxation effects, no quantitative analyses and reliance on case studies, no comparison conditions, and lack of a previously validated instrument to evaluate alterations in consciousness. To correct these shortcomings, I carried out a study (Cardeña, 2005) using a "neutral" deep hypnosis procedure (i.e., no specific suggestions other than asking the person to go into a very deep, and undefined state of hypnosis) with 12 highly hypnotizable participants. Ten of the 12 participants had a global, intuitive type of information processing, consistent with the proposals that hypnotic virtuosos tend to be imaginative and creative (J.R. Hilgard, 1979), and that hypnosis involves a holistic type of thought (Crawford, 1981).

The study employed a repeated measures factorial design with a two-level factor (state: hypnosis versus no hypnosis sessions) and a three-level factor (types of physical stimulation: motionless on a bed, pedaling a stationary bicycle at a comfortable rate, and having a motor do the pedaling at a comfortable rate). In the hypnosis sessions participants were administered the physical conditions in counterbalanced order, while a 1–30 induction count was used, the only suggestion being that as the count progressed participants would go into an increasingly deeper state of hypnosis. At the end of the induction and at 5 minute intervals the experimenter repeated the word "state," to elicit a numerical depth report, and asked "what are you experiencing?" Participants were also free to report their experience at any point. After the hypnosis session, control sessions were conducted with a 1–30 count, but without a suggestion to go into deep hypnosis and asking participants not to use self-hypnosis or similar procedures. After every session participants were interviewed about their experience and completed the Phenomenology of Consciousness Inventory (PCI; Pekala, 1991) and a checklist with various possible alterations in psychological processes (including "no change" from normal) in reference to their "deepest state."

As compared with the control condition, during very deep hypnosis participants reported significant alterations in body image, time sense, perception and meaning, and the sense of being in an altered state of awareness. They also described increases in affect, attentional focus, and amount and vividness of imagery, but less self-awareness, rationality, voluntary control, and memory. Variables that seem irrelevant to hypnosis such as "sexual excitement" did not show differences across conditions.

Frequency analyses of session reports elucidated the content of these alterations. For the level of *no hypnosis and feeling slightly different than normal*, participants did not report any change from normal experience other than a minor increase in relaxation. The next level, *light/medium hypnosis,* was mentioned at the beginning of the hypnosis sessions and involved primarily body sensations and, less frequently, changes in body image. Relaxation increased, especially in the quiescent condition (e.g., participant #11: "Slowly relaxed. I can't really feel my body"), along with somesthesias and vestibular alterations such as tingling (e.g., P #12: "Darkness, tingling sensations"), "feeling light," and "spinning." There were also changes in body image (e.g., P #2: "My hands have been growing, they are like big rocks") and an increasing sense of well-being (e.g., P #1: "Feeling mellow, both physical and emotional"). Respondents also mentioned increased concentration on their inner experience and losing touch with the environment.

Most of the significant differences were found during *deep and very deep hypnosis*. The sensation of "lightness" became more pronounced with reports of the body floating, flying, and leaving the physical body (e.g., P #9: "It's just sort of me floating," P #2: "I don't have a physical body anymore"). There were also, paradoxically, frequent reports of the body falling down (e.g., P #3: "Sinking deep, deep"), sometimes into a dark liquid. After a while, if there was an experience of a body it was of a phenomenal, but not physical, body. Somatic sensations were often incorporated into ongoing, imaginal events (e.g., P #8: "Walking down in a spiral staircase"), with a shift from conceptual thinking to spontaneous imagery. Overall there was a change of modality from concepts to images, often including geometric designs such as prisms, grids and tunnels (e.g., P #10: "[Pictures] like nothing else in this world: geometric"), which became more elaborate and vivid, sometimes in a cross-modal or synesthetic way (e.g., P #4: "Lines of different colors that stretch infinitely ... making music that I have never heard before"). There were also common reports of "having no thoughts" (e.g., P #9: "For a while I was just total nothing"). Various categories referring to imagery were endorsed at this level, including "increased quality," "sustained sequences," spontaneous imagery," "greater realness," and "imagery not referable to a sensory modality," sometimes interpreted as similar to "dreaming." Especially important seemed to be very common reports of "flashes of light" or "brightness" (e.g., P #5: "Colors with lots of light and energy"), and also, paradoxically, "great obscurity" (e.g., P #3: "Complete black, no sense of clearness").

Emotions were overall positive (e.g., P #4: "All the feelings that are good just surround me"), although a few reports indicated fear about the unusualness of the experiences encountered. With respect to cognition, participants mentioned "difficulties remembering" everyday activities but "suddenly remembering" forgotten events, along with "greater control" over their mental states while maintaining a "free floating" attention. Many categories related to transpersonal/spiritual experiences were reported including "being one with everything," "greater relatedness," "loss of identity," or being "in touch with one's inner self" (e.g., P #5: [after merging with light] "The best place to be"). There was as well a sense of "being in a different reality" that entailed "profound personal insight," "increased sense of potentiality," and "increased meaningfulness."

A general sequence of events from the session transcripts is that at the beginning stage participants just felt more relaxed. Light/medium hypnosis was mostly characterized by alterations in body sensations and body image. They typically included experiences of floating or flying (and sometimes sinking), and an increasing disconnection from the body and the environment. Somatic sensations gave rise to a disembodied phenomenal self, with a shift from conceptual thinking to spontaneous imagery. This imagery became either dreamlike (and experienced as very real) or gave rise to atemporal experiences of pure light and love, no thought and cognitive emptiness, and an overall sense of euphoria, potentiality, meaningfulness, insight, and connectedness. Respondents felt as thought they were "in another plane of reality" during deep hypnosis.

Analyses by physical activity showed that quiescence was the state most conducive to "deep" experiences, probably because of a faster experiential detachment from the body; a reduction in self-awareness characterized the motor condition, and sadness and arousal were associated with self-pedaling.

In follow-up interviews at the end of the experiments and 8 months later there was only mention of positive sequelae (e.g., greater perceptual vividness and dream recall, increased personal insight and inner peace, decrease in anxiety and nightmares) suggesting that, in addition to its research potential, deep hypnosis can be of great benefit in therapeutic and self-growth contexts, at least with individuals with reasonable psychological stability. Although the effect of expectations on hypnosis was not statistically evaluated, participants answered an open question as to what they expected would happen at the deepest level of hypnosis. As Table 1 shows, descriptions tended to be general and somewhat vague; some of them were accurate ("being in another plane of reality," "no body sensations"), others were not (e.g., "relive repressed situations," "the hypnotist will be in control"). Although Feldman (1976) did not find that expectations were good predictors of deep hypnotic experiences, the findings in this study are mixed and recommend a systematic evaluation of expectancies in future research. There was remarkable consistency in the phenomena reported, but their manifestation showed individual variations. For instance, although episodes of darkness were common, they might have been experienced as an imaginal adventure in a dark cave, or as being submerged in a black substance. Participants' reports of free-floating attention to "inner" experiences and, at times, increased imagery, are consistent with research by Fromm et al. (1981) on self-hypnosis (and indeed participants in this study were mostly responsible for the hypnotic process).

This study included methodological improvements over previous ones, but has some limitations. First, the findings are generalizable only to highly hypnotizables in the context described earlier. Although some phenomena (e.g., changes in body sensations and image) have been reported in more typical contexts of hypnosis, others (e.g., experiencing the void or merging with the light) have only been described in deep hypnosis procedures or non-hypnotic contexts. Second, although some readers may object to the choice of a within-subjects design, Barabasz and Barabasz (1992) have argued that this design may be optimal in detecting differences resulting from a hypnotic intervention. Nonetheless, it has also been argued that highs may "hold back" their reports during the control sessions, especially considering that the hypnosis sessions preceded the control ones (cf. Braffman and Kirsch, 1999). Another criticism is that demand characteristics might have influenced the results. I sought to reduce them by requesting honest reports and employing a simple count induction and a neutral query. Furthermore, meta-analyses of various research areas show that a similar context to this (i.e., laboratory interviews of sensory restriction) had a very small interpersonal expectancy effect ($r=.07$; Rosenthal and Rubin, 1978). The request that participants not use self-hypnosis in the control sessions took into consideration the finding that "highs" may engage in self-hypnosis during control sessions, thus invalidating them (Tart and Hilgard, 1966).

To investigate the effect of hypnotizability on hypnotic experience and evaluate EEG activity concurrent to the hypnotic procedure, a second study was recently conducted with low, medium, and high hypnotizables (Cardeña et al., 2007). Comparing groups with the PCI as a function of hypnotizability at baseline showed few significant differences across the groups. A different pattern was found for the self-rated deepest hypnotic state. Lows differed from both mediums and highs in reporting significantly less alterations in altered experience, body image, perception, and being in an altered state. They differed only from highs in reporting smaller changes in time sense, enhanced meaning, positive affect, love, self-awareness, and voluntary control. Medium hypnotizables differed only from highs in reporting less time alterations, positive affect, and love. These results point to an interaction between a trait (hypnotizability) and a state (hypnosis). A content analysis evidenced that reports of high hypnotizables more often reflected primarily self-transcendent or intense emotional experiences than those of the other two groups; they were also more likely to experience imagery as a primary dimension than low hypnotizables, but not than medium hypnotizables. The reports of low hypnotizables were more likely than the other two groups to have "normal/no change" as the primary phenomenological dimension, and there was a suggestive result that the reports of mediums were more often of body alterations than those of highs.

Discussion

Earlier observations of a possible connection between mesmerism/hypnosis and psi phenomena would not, in general, stand up to current evidential requirements, but a few observations with exceptional participants are strongly suggestive of psi. The more recent meta-analyses support the notion that these two areas may be connected, although the effect of some variables (e.g., experimenter influences, hypnotizability levels) should be evaluated. Because high hypnotizables under a hypnotic context tend to have self-transcendent experiences, and the latter have been associated with successful performance in psi tasks, a possible mediating mechanism for psi performance may be a non-dualistic, transcendent type of cognition (Rosch, 2001).

With respect to spontaneous hypnotic phenomenology by high hypnotizables, events reported during very deep hypnosis (e.g., merging with a light, "being one with everything") are reminiscent of descriptions about mystical (e.g., Wulff, 2000), and near-death experiences (e.g., Greyson, 2000). Some reports were identical to those in a qualitative study of "deep states" of meditation (e.g., "There was no sense of my physical body ... no thought," "You've fallen into a hole that's so deep," "Utterly serene"; Gifford-May and Thompson, 1994), and with a study with meditators using the PCI that found significant changes in meaning, time sense, love, and state of awareness (Venkatesh, Raju, et al., 1997). The secular context of the research suggests, though, that these phenomena cannot be solely attributed to religious beliefs, expectations, neurophysiological challenges, or life-threatening circumstances. Rather, they suggest basic aspects of human experience that may then give rise to religious or other explanatory models (Wulff, 2000). Developmental psychology (Stern, 1985) suggests that a form of cognition somewhat similar to that expressed during deep hypnosis may be common during infancy, and could underlie ordinary consciousness (e.g., Marks, 2000; Wulff, 2000). The phenomena reported probably are not exclusive to a hypnosis context but rather support the notion that hypnotic virtuosos have a propensity to experience various anomalous experiences (Pekala and Cardeña, 2000), which differs from the experiences of medium and especially low hypnotizables (e.g., Kumar and Pekala, 1989). These experiences reflect common patterns of alterations of consciousness, probably share common neurological underpinnings (Newberg and D'Aquili, 2000), and may have evolutionary implications.

Although they were based on a linear numerical self-report scale, participants' reports indicate that different levels of hypnosis (e.g., light vs. very deep) should be better conceptualized as distinct modes of experiencing (Tart, 1975), than as variations in intensity (Singer, 1977). The non-linearity of certain phenomena (e.g., emotional intensity) and the emergence of occurrences (e.g. "merging with a light") only at a very deep level support this contention. The sequence of medium to deep hypnotic phenomena is consistent with phenomena of increasing absorption mentioned in the classical meditation literature (Holroyd, 2003), and with the content and sequence of going from simple images (e.g., geometric) to more complex narratives partly using those images found in studies of psychedelic-induced (Siegel, 1977) and other altered states of consciousness (Hunt, 1985).

The fact that significant alterations of consciousness occurred despite physical activity and even reports of arousal refutes Edmonston's (1991) and Rainville and Price (2003) mention of relaxation as an essential component of hypnosis. Consistent with Fellows and Richardson's (1993) study, quiescence was associated with reports of greater sense of disembodiment, depth and, more tentatively, imagery vividness. The "deeper" state might be explained by the initial greater body image and sensory alterations, especially floating, and disembodiment. This pattern is similar to the one shown in the cluster analyses of Winkelman (1992) on cross-cultural data on altered states of consciousness that revealed an association between immobility, a sense of floating out of one's body, and imagery. The somatic alterations mentioned may represent alternative body representations, associated with continued attention to subjective experience, and reduction of somatic feedback (Alvarado, 2000; Tart, 1975). The increase in visual imagery cannot be explained by the greater visual stimulation encountered when physically active, as Pope (1978) has proposed, because participants had their eyes closed during the sessions. Greater imagery could be explained either by stimulus generalization between lying down and dreaming (Morgan and Bakan, 1965), or by the hypothesis that the psychological resources not spent on movement may be deployed in facilitating greater imagery when quiescent. Although posture alone has not been seen to affect hypnotic responsiveness (Ruch and Morgan, 1971), lying down and inactivity were not separated in the present study, so further research is needed to elucidate this matter. The most important finding about physical activity, though, is that participants had intense alterations of consciousness even if they moved actively or passively, thus making links to the anthropological literature on ritually-based alterations of consciousness that include physical activity (Cardeña, 1996).

The diminished self-awareness in the motor activity condition suggests that repetitive activity does not have to be attended to (perhaps because of neural habituation) once the whole organism becomes attuned to a specific rhythm and then maintains residual, unreflective awareness. This result is also consistent with Winkelman's (1992) finding of an association between rhythmic drumming/dancing and amnesia in cross-cultural data. Finally, self-pedaling was deemed to be more arousing and dysphoric, and less conducive to hypnosis deepening. This last result is consistent with a previous study (Alarcón et al., 1999) in which people who do not habitually ride a bicycle preferred a simpler form of physical activity to a self-generated pedaling in a hypnotic context. Differences were obtained even with a relatively mild form of physical exertion; it may be that subjective experience in contexts of greater physical arousal and exertion will differ more from reports obtained from quiescence, as Winkelman's analysis (1992) suggests. In ritually induced altered states, social facilitation may also partly shape the interpretation of the phenomena and enhance the experience.

In summary, there is substantial evidence that different modalities of experience are consistently manifested according to self-assessed level of hypnotic depth. Although there were individual variations in the participants' experience, the similarity of many reports amongst themselves and with reports from other types of anomalous experiences suggest, if not universal, at least identifiable and common patterns of cognition. The first study also supports the importance of evaluating physical activity and embodiedness in alternate subjective experience. The positive aftereffects of participation suggest that, in addition to its theoretical and research import, the type of procedure described here may be beneficial in therapy and self-growth contexts.

Appendix: Participants' Expectations About the Deepest State

#1 Being as in a void, very relaxed, as in sleep; no body sensations.
#2 Complete separation of mind and body; mind independent of body; will follow suggestions much better.
#3 Being in a buffer between sleep and awareness; having a heavy body and being unaware of surroundings; being in another "plane of reality."
#4 Relaxed, at ease but not tired; clear; diminished awareness of environment; extraneous thoughts fade; increased suggestibility.
#5 Forget surroundings; a numb body; pleasant; no rational thought and entering into imaginary world; inspired to create artistically; remember anything I want; would not want to come out; would never be the same again if it occurred.
#6 Actions produced entirely by hypnotist; "freeing" the subconscious.
#7 Not expecting to have any control.
#8 Detach observing self from mind; no recall and greater freedom; greater awareness of thought processes and powers of the mind; relive memories.
#9 Reach different state of self-awareness and relation to the world.
#10 Relaxed body; unaware of surroundings; greater focus.
#11 The hypnotist will be in control; no recollection.
#12 Relive repressed situations that come out in dreams.

References

Aaronson, B. S. (1967). Mystic and schizophreniform states and the experience of depth. *Journal for the Scientific Study of Religion*, 6. 246–252.

Alarcón, A., A. Capafons, A. Bayot and E. Cardeña (1999). Preference between two methods of active-alert hypnosis: Not all techniques are created equal. *American Journal of Clinical Hypnosis*, 41. 269–276.

Alvarado, C. (2000). Out-of-body experiences. In E. Cardeña, S. J. Lynn, and S. Krippner (eds.), *Varieties of Anomalous Experience*. Washington, D.C.: American Psychological Association. 183–218.

Ås, A., and S. Ostvold (1968). Hypnosis as subjective experience. *Scandinavian Journal of Psychology*, 9. 33–38.

Banyai, E. I., and E. R. Hilgard (1976). A comparison of active-alert hypnotic induction with traditional relaxation induction. *Journal of Abnormal Psychology*, 85. 218–234.

Barabasz, A. F., and M. Barabasz (1992). Research designs and considerations. In E. Fromm and M. R. Nash (eds.), *Contemporary Hypnosis Research*. New York: Guilford. 173–200.

Braffman, W., and I. Kirsch (1999). Imaginative suggestibility and hypnotizability: An empirical analysis. *Journal of Personality and Social Psychology*, 77. 578–587.

Cardeña, E. (1996). "Just floating on the sky." A comparison of shamanic and hypnotic phenomenology. In R. Quekelbherge and D. Eigner (eds.), *6th Jahrbuch für Transkulturelle Medizin und Psychotherapie* [6th Yearbook of cross-cultural medicine and psychotherapy]. Berlin: Verlag für Wissenschaft und Bildung. 367–380.

Cardeña, E. (2005). The phenomenology of deep hypnosis: Quiescent and physically active. *International Journal of Clinical & Experimental Hypnosis*, 53. 37–59.

Cardeña, E. (in press). Consciousness and emotions as interpersonal and transpersonal systems. *Journal of Consciousness Studies*.

Cardeña, E., D. Lehmann, P. Jönsson, D. Terhune and P. Faber (2007). The neurophe-

nomenology of hypnosis. *Proceedings of the 50th Annual Convention of the Parapsychological Association.* 17–30.
Cardeña, E., S. J. Lynn and S. Krippner (eds.). (2000). Varieties of anomalous experience: Examining the scientific evidence. Washington, D.C.: American Psychological Association.
Cardeña, E. and D. Spiegel (1991). Suggestibility, absorption, and dissociation: An integrative model of hypnosis. In J. F. Schumaker (ed.), *Human Suggestibility: Advances in Theory, Research and Application.* 93–107. New York: Routledge.
Carpenter, J. C. (2004). Implicit measures of participant's experiences in the ganzfeld: Confirmation of previous relationships in a new sample. *Proceedings of the 47th Annual Convention of the Parapsychological Association.* 1–11.
Crawford, H. J. (1981). Hypnotic susceptibility as related to gestalt closure. *Journal of Personality and Social Psychology*, 40. 376–383.
Diamond, S. G., O. C. Davis and R. D. Howe (2008). Heat rate variability as a quantitative measure of hypnotic depth. *International Journal of Clinical & Experimental Hypnosis*, 56. 1–18.
Dingwall, E. J. (ed.) (1967–68). *Abnormal Hypnotic Phenomena: A Survey of Nineteenth-Century Cases.* 4 volumes. London: J & A Churchill.
Edmonston, W. (1991). Anesis. In S. J. Lynn and J. W. Rhue (eds.), *Theories of Hypnosis: Current Models and Perspectives.* New York: Guilford Press. 197–237.
Ellenberger, H. F. (1970). *The Discovery of the Unconscious.* New York: Basic Books.
Erickson, M. H. (1952). Deep hypnosis and its induction. In L. M. LeCron (ed.), *Experimental Hypnosis.* New York: Macmillan. 70–114.
Erickson, M. H. (1965). A special inquiry with Aldous Huxley into the nature and character of various altered states of consciousness. *American Journal of Clinical Hypnosis*, 8. 17–33.
Evans, F. J. (1963). *The Structure of Hypnosis: A Factor Analytic Investigation.* Unpublished doctoral dissertation. University of Sidney, Australia, 1963.
Evans F. J. (1964). Is there a general factor of hypnotizability. *Paper Read at the 35th Annual Meeting of the Eastern Psychological Association.*
Feldman, B. E. (1976). *A Phenomenological and Clinical Inquiry into Deep Hypnosis.* Unpublished doctoral dissertation, University of California, Berkeley, CA.
Fellows, B. J., and J. Richardson (1993). Relaxed and alert hypnosis: A experiential comparison. *Contemporary Hypnosis*, 10. 49–54.
Field, P. B. (1965). An inventory scale of hypnotic depth. *International Journal of Clinical and Experimental Hypnosis*, 13. 238–249.
Fromm, E., D. P. Brown, S. W. Hurt, J. Z. Oberlander, A. M. Boxer and G. Pfeifer (1981). The phenomena and characteristics of self-hypnosis. *International Journal of Clinical and Experimental Hypnosis*, 29. 189–246.
Gauld, A. (1992). *A History of Hypnotism.* Cambridge, UK: Cambridge University Press.
Gifford-May D. and N.L. Thompson (1994). "Deep states" of meditation: Phenomenological reports of experience. *Journal of Transpersonal Psychology*, 26. 117–138.
Gill, M., and M. Brenman (1959). *Hypnosis and Related States.* New York: International Universities Press.
Greyson, B. (2000). Near-death experiences. In E. Cardeña, S. J. Lynn, and S. Krippner (eds.), *Varieties of Anomalous Experience.* Washington, D.C.: American Psychological Association. 315–352.
Hilgard, E. R. (1968). *The Experience of Hypnosis.* New York: Harcourt, Brace & World.
Hilgard, E. R. (1986). *Divided Consciousness.* Expanded edition. New York: Wiley.
Hilgard, J. R. (1979). *Personality and Hypnosis. A Study of Imaginative Involvement.* Second edition. Chicago: University of Chicago Press.
Holroyd, J. (2003). The science of meditation and the state of hypnosis. *American Journal of Clinical Hypnosis.*
Honorton, C. (1977). Psi and internal attention states. In B. B. Wolman (ed.), *Handbook of Parapsychology.* New York: Van Nostrand Reinhold. 435–472.
Hunt, H. T. (1985) Relations between the phenomena of religious mysticism (altered states of consciousness) and the psychology of thought: A cognitive psychology of states of con-

sciousness and the necessity of subjective states for cognitive theory. *Perceptual and Motor Skills*, 61. 911–961.
Kelly, E. F., E. W. Kelly, A. Crabtree, A. Gauld, M. Grosso and B. Greyson (2007). *Irreducible Mind: Toward a Psychology for the 21st Century*. Lanham, MD: Rowan & Littlefield.
Kumar, V. K., and R. J. Pekala (1989). Variations in the phenomenological experience as a function of hypnosis and hypnotic susceptibility: A replication. *British Journal of Experimental & Clinical Hypnosis*, 6. 17–22.
Laurence, J. R., and C. Perry (1988). *Hypnosis, Will & Memory: A Psycholegal History*. New York: Guilford.
Ludwig, A. M. (1965). Alterations in consciousness produced by hypnosis. *Journal of Nervous and Mental Disease*, 140. 146–153.
Mallot, J. M. (1984). Active-alert hypnosis: Replication and extension of previous research. *Journal of Abnormal Psychology*, 93. 246–249.
Marks, L. E. (2000). Synesthesia. In E. Cardeña, S. J. Lynn, and S. Krippner (eds.), *Varieties of Anomalous Experience*. Washington, D.C.: American Psychological Association. 85–120.
Méheust, B. (2003). Un voyant prodigieux, Alexis Didier [A prodigious seer, Alexis Didier]. Paris: Les Empêcheurs de penser en rond-Le Seuil.
McConkey, K. M., and A. Barnier (2004). High hypnotizability: Unity and diversity in behavior and experience. In M. Heap., R. J. Brown, and D. A. Oakley (eds.), *The Highly Hypnotizable Person*. New York: Brunner-Routledge. 61–48.
Moreau, C., and R. Rogez (1977). Hypnose et parapsychology. *Revue de Parapsychologie*, 5. 5–29.
Morgan, R. F., and P. Bakan (1965). Sensory deprivation hallucinations and other sleep behavior as a function of position, method of report, and anxiety. *Perceptual & Motor Skills*, 20. 19–25.
Newberg, A. B., and E. G. D'Aquili (2000). The neuropsychology of religious and spiritual experience. *Journal of Consciousness Studies*, 7, 251–266.
Orne, M. T. (1959). The nature of hypnosis: Artifact and essence. *Journal of Abnormal and Social Psychology*, 58. 277–299.
Pekala, R. J. (1991). *Quantifying Consciousness: An Empirical Approach*. New York: Plenum.
Pekala, R. and E. Cardeña (2000). Methodological issues in the study of altered states of consciousness and anomalous experiences. In E. Cardeña, S.J. Lynn, and S. Krippner (eds.), *Varieties of Anomalous Experience: Examining the Scientific Experience*. Washington, D.C.: American Psychological Association. 47–82.
Pekala, R. J., V. K. Kumar, R. Maurer, N. C. Elliott-Carter and E. Moon (2006). "How deeply hypnotized did I get?": Predicting self-reported hypnotic depth from a phenomenological assessment instrument. *International Journal of Clinical and Experimental Hypnosis*, 54. 316–399.
Pope, K. S. (1978). How gender, solitude, and posture influence the stream of consciousness. In K. S. Pope and J. L. Singer (eds.), *The Stream of Consciousness*. New York: Plenum Press. 259–299.
Pontius, A. A. (1964). Comparison of phantoms and atavistic body schema experiences in a schizophrenic: A contribution to the study of hallucinations. *Perceptual and Motor Skills*, 19. 695–700.
Rainville, P., and D. D. Price (2003). Hypnosis phenomenology and the neurobiology of consciousness. *International Journal of Clinical and Experimental Hypnosis. Special Issue: University of Tennessee Conference on Brain Imaging and Hypnosis, Part I.* Vol. 51(2), April 2003: 105–129.
Rosch, E. (2001). "If you depict a bird, give it space to fly": Eastern psychologies, the arts, and self-knowledge. *SubStance*, 30. 236–253.
Rosenthal, R., and D. B. Rubin (1978). Interpersonal expectancy effects: The first 345 studies. *The Behavioral and Brain Sciences*, 1, 377–415.
Ruch, J. C., and A. H. Morgan (1971). Subject posture and hypnotic susceptibility: A comparison of standing, sitting, and lying down subjects. *International Journal of Clinical and Experimental Hypnosis*, 19. 100–108.
Sacerdote, P. (1977). Applications of hypnotically induced mystical states to the treatment of physical and emotional pain. *International Journal of Clinical and Experimental Hypnosis*, 25. 309–324.

Schechter, E. I. (1984). Hypnotic induction vs. control conditions: Illustrating an approach to the evaluation of replicability in parapsychological data. *Journal of the American Society for Psychical Research*, 78. 1–27.
Schlitz, M. (1992). Psychic unity: The meeting ground of anthropology and parapsychology. In B. Shapin and L. Coly (eds.), *Psychology, Depth Psychology, and Spontaneous Psi Research*. New York: Parapsychology Foundation Press.
Sherman, Spencer E. Very deep hypnosis: An experiential and electro-encephalographic investigation. Unpublished Doctoral Dissertation, Stanford University, 1971.
Siegel, R. K. (1977). Hallucinations. *Scientific American*, 237. 132–140.
Singer, J. L. (1977). Ongoing thought: The normative baseline of altered states of consciousness. In N. E. Zinberg (ed.), *Alternate States of Consciousness*. New York: Free University Press. 89–120.
Stanford, R. G. (1992). Experimental hypnosis–ESP literature: A review from the hypothesis-testing perspective. *Journal of Parapsychology*, 56. 39–56.
Stanford, R.G., and A.G. Stein (1994). A meta-analysis of ESP studies contrasting hypnosis and a comparison condition. *Journal of Parapsychology*, 58. 235–269.
Stern, D. N. (1985). *The Interpersonal World of the Infant*. New York: Basic Books.
Tart, C. T. (1970) Transpersonal potentialities of deep hypnosis. *Journal of Transpersonal Psychology*, 2. 27–40.
Tart, C. T., and E. R. Hilgard (1966). Responsiveness to suggestions under "hypnosis" and "waking-imagination" conditions: A methodological observation. *International Journal of Clinical & Experimental Hypnosis*, 14. 247–256.
Van de Castle, R. L. (1969). The facilitation of ESP through hypnosis. *American Journal of Clinical & Experimental Hypnosis*, 12. 37–56.
Venkatesh, S., T. R. Raju, Y. Shivani, G. Tompkins and B. L. Meti (1997). A study of structure of phenomenology of consciousness in meditative and non-meditative states. *Indian Journal of Physiological Pharmacology*, 41. 149–153.
Weitzenhoffer, A. M. (2000). *The Practice of Hypnotism*. Second edition. New York: Wiley.
Winkelman, M. (1992). *Shamans, Priests and Witches: A Cross-Cultural Study of Magico-Religious Practitioners*. Arizona State University Anthropological Research Papers #44.
Wulff, D. M. (2000). Mystical experiences. In E. Cardeña, S. J. Lynn, and S. Krippner (Eds.), *Varieties of Anomalous Experience*. 397–440. Washington, D.C.: American Psychological Association.

8
HAUNTING EXPERIENCES
An Integrative Approach
Ciarán O'Keeffe *and* Steve Parsons

Haunting experiences fit within the remit of parapsychology given that they are "apparent anomalies of ... experience that exist apart from currently known explanatory mechanisms that account for organism-environment ... and influence flow" (Parapsychological Association, 1989, pp. 394–395). There have, however, been attempts by parapsychologists and others to provide evidence for possible explanatory mechanisms. Several of these attempts, and approaches to studying haunting experiences, have been presented elsewhere (e.g., see Houran and Lange, 2001). In addition, there is a need to recognize the wealth of evidence that comes from anecdotal reports of haunting experiences. With the public's ever-growing interest in haunting investigations, an interest exacerbated by the media, there is a need to disseminate knowledge regarding the contribution of parapsychology to such field research. The educational and training background of many parapsychologists is in psychology, a science in which there is a basic knowledge of processes involved in visual perception, suggestion, group conformity and ethics. Additionally, some researchers have declared their interest in parapsychology to have been fuelled by spontaneous case research (e.g., O'Keeffe, Baker, Sherwood, Terhune and Parsons, 2008).

This chapter aims to highlight some unanswered questions regarding explanatory mechanisms that have been proposed for haunting experiences. We will draw attention to the potential problems conducting haunting experiences research whilst at the same time highlighting the importance of continuing such research. Whilst compelling experimental evidence may exist for certain alternative explanations, the authors acknowledge the need to be conservative in promoting one explanation as the overriding one. If anything, research into haunting experiences benefits from a more integrative approach, that where there is a natural explanation for such experiences, it consists of an interaction of influences (environmental and psychological) that may be at work. How those influences integrate and interact is, perhaps, the key to understanding haunting experiences.

Defining Haunting Experiences

Several explanations for haunting experiences are focused on particular phenomena (e.g., object movement, temperature changes) and so it would be worth clarifying what, as researchers, we are dealing with. Unfortunately, such a clarification is not an easy task. There are a multitude of terms associated with this particular paranormal phenomenon (e.g., apparition, poltergeist, spectre, ghost) and there is some disagreement regarding their definitions so it is beyond the scope of this chapter to define each and every term. It is important to note, however, that there is a generally accepted distinction between poltergeist and haunting experiences.

Haunting experiences are generally regarded as being location focused whereas poltergeist phenomena (often associated with haunted properties) are person focused. In addition, there is an established differentiation between the type of phenomena experienced, whether it is a haunting or poltergeist. Edge, Morris, Palmer and Rush (1987), for example, clearly distinguish between the two. They note that

> a haunting is characterized by subjective visions ("ghosts") and sometimes noises in a particular location, usually an old house. These phenomena typically recur sporadically for years.... Poltergeist manifestations usually are associated with a person rather than a place. They consist principally of noises and violent movements and breakage of objects, supplemented sometimes by intelligible communication through raps or mediumistic means. An outbreak typically begins abruptly and fades out in a few weeks or months [Edge, Morris, Palmer and Rush, 1987, p.25].

There is also a commonly held theory, originating with Fodor (1948), that the paranormal origin of poltergeist phenomena lies with the psychokinetic energy of one of the location's residents (referred to as the "agent" of the phenomena). This is reflected in the fact that poltergeist phenomena are sometimes referred to as "recurrent spontaneous psychokinesis" (RSPK).

Elsewhere there is less of an attempt to differentiate two distinct classes of phenomena and an admittance that some cases cannot be attributed to some sort of unconscious psychokinesis (PK) from a person but rather the action of a discarnate entity (e.g., Gauld and Cornell, 1979). Lange and Houran (1997) are also skeptical that a clear demarcation between hauntings and poltergeist phenomena can be made. Some researchers have even noted that a visual confirmation is necessary for others in order to designate a haunting: "the term 'haunting' usually applies to those cases where apparitions are reported as being seen, usually by more than one person, over a period of time" (Fontana, 2004, p. 55; although see also Alvarado and Zingrone, 1995). Despite these differences there is a clear consensus regarding the nature of the experiences. A haunting experience can be constituted by one, or more, of the following reports and experiences: apparitions; temperature changes; a sense of presence; unusual odors; noises (e.g., rapping, voices, moans, footsteps); and touching sensations (e.g., a pinch or "brushing" on skin). The definition of a haunting experience, for the purposes of this chapter, then, is taken from an adaptation of the term in Thalbourne's (2003) *Glossary of Terms Used in Parapsychology*: "A *sensory* experience in which there appears to be present a person or animal (deceased or living) who is in fact out of sensory range of the experient..." (Baker, 2002, p110). For the purposes of this review, to prevent confusion, haunting experiences will be the focus and any nuances in explanatory mechanisms that could be more attributable to poltergeist phenomena are omitted.

The Role of the Environment

Houran and Lange (2001) have argued that the belief a house is haunted may result from misinterpretation of environmental anomalies. Three such environmental anomalies are highlighted here.

TEMPERATURE CHANGE

A frequent characteristic associated with haunting experiences is that the experient reports a cold feeling (Tyrrell, 1953). In addition, sitters at séances, have since the earliest days of spiritualism, reported apparent drops in temperature (Randall, 2001). Rises in temperature have also been linked to hauntings. For example, Nickell (2001) recounts the eyewitness testimony of a naval captain who reported seeing a dark silhouette in a bedroom where "the room was insufferably hot" (Nickell, 2001, p. 216).

Parapsychologists have reported a correlation between unusual temperature experiences and allegedly haunted locations, often without verifying the hypothesized causes of such temperature changes (Wiseman, Watt, Stevens, Greening and O'Keeffe, 2003). Inevitably, perhaps, the majority of such reports from experients and researchers, are purely subjective and may point to expected physiological temperature changes, perceived and actual, in the experient as a result of being in a fearful situation. However, reports from spontaneous case investigations conducted using calibrated monitoring equipment suggest that a number are objective and represent highly unusual sudden changes in the ambient temperature (e.g., Turner, 1970). Despite evidence from fieldwork, no laboratory studies have attempted to demonstrate the same correlation. It should be noted, however, that there are reports elsewhere in experimental work on other anomalous experiences where participants report temperature drops (for example, see Chapter 11 for such work on séance room experiences).

Radin and Rebman (1996) constructed a psychomanteum* chamber to examine the relationship between a participant's mental state and changes in the local physical environment. Temperature was measured using a computerized thermometer with milli-degree sensitivity. The temperature sensor was positioned close to floor level behind the participant's chair with an output feed to a computer in an adjoining room. The majority of significant correlations between the environmental and physiological variables were due to temperature changes within the chamber. The temperature initially rose then began to drop. Radin and Rebman (1996) suggested the initial presence of an experimenter, participant and facilitator, prior to the session's commencement, would raise the temperature. The subsequent departure of the experimenter and facilitator would then cause the temperature to fall. The continued fall in the temperature throughout the session probably related to the participant's general calming. Due to this possibility that some of the significant ambient temperature and physiological correlations were artefacts of a common downward drift in temperature, Radin and Rebman (1996) excluded all ambient temperature cross-correlations from their subsequent data. The untested explanation given is one of a number of natural possibilities. For example, the lowering may simply be due to the floor level placement of the temperature sensor where it may be expected that cooler air collects after being displaced by warmer rising air that has been heated by the participant. Additionally, the data could represent a real correlation between the participant's mental state and a change within the physical environment.

ELECTROMAGNETIC AND GEOMAGNETIC FIELDS

An additional, perhaps more complex, environmental variable is concerned with brain sensitivity to electromagnetic (EM) and Geomagnetic (GM) fields. The theorized relationship between anomalous experiences and EMF stimulation of particular regions of the brain originates with Persinger (1985). He speculated that changes in geomagnetic fields created, for example, by tectonic stress in the earth's crust (something he termed transient geophysical fields) could stimulate a particular area of the brain and produce many of the subjective experiences associated with hauntings. Following this initial the-

---

A psychomanteum is a dimmed, quiet room in which the participant is comfortably seated, asked to relax and look into a mirror facing the wall above and behind them (Moody and Perry, 1994).

ory, researchers proposed that physical haunting phenomena (e.g., cold spots, popping sounds) may be caused by similar processes (e.g., Houran and Lange, 1998). A recent review of the link between phenomena (either subjective experiences or physical phenomena) reported some on-site investigations of alleged hauntings that found unusual local magnetic activity (Roll and Persinger, 2001; see also Persinger and Koren, 2001). Following initial research that examined large case collections of alleged hauntings and found significant relationships between the timing of experienced phenomena and sudden increases in global geomagnetic activity, Persinger was able to recreate in his lab similar variations in EMF and apply those to the brains of test subjects many of whom reported experiences that were similar to the experiences reported by witnesses in alleged paranormal cases (Persinger and Koren, 2001). Ultimately Persinger has concluded that the source for these EMF's are both natural in the form of variations within the Earth's geomagnetism (Persinger and Richards, 1995) or interactions with solar radiation and/or other sources such as electrical wiring and appliances.

Natural sources of electromagnetism are often referred to as Extremely Low Frequency EMF's. These "Geomagnetic Fields" are normally only measured by specialist equipment and are typically very low in frequency: 0—10Hz. Higher frequency sources typically those above 1kHz (1000Hz) are to be found in fluorescent lights and visual displays. These are capable of being measured by many readily available EMF meters although the actual value will normally be very different from the displayed value as the meter is calibrated or weighted for the much lower electricity supply frequency of 50 or 60Hz. Most amateur ghost investigators use an AC EMF meter of a type that is designed to measure frequencies around 50Hz or 60 Hz, which are, respectively, the domestic electricity supply frequencies for the UK and USA. Typically they will also measure EMF at frequencies above and below this calibration point although often with a greatly reduced accuracy and sensitivity as the frequency moves further from the 50/60Hz optimum. The S.I. unit, and thus the preferred unit of measurement, is the Tesla (typically micro Tesla, μT). EMFs are normally directional, surrounding the source such as a cable or appliance. The primary field strength is dependent upon the direction of current flow. The field strength also diminishes as the distance from the source is increased (for ease of visualization they may be likened to the ripples produced when a single pebble is dropped into a pond). The EMFs from several sources can interact with one another similar to the effect seen when two or more pebbles are dropped into the pond. This leads to areas where the strength may be much higher or significantly lower than would be expected from a single source.

Substantial research has now been undertaken that does strongly suggest that when some people are exposed to a powerful EMF or a less powerful but varying EMF they may report sensations that they may believe are paranormal in origin. These effects include a sense of presence, a sense of touch, offensive odors, unease, intense fear, and nausea. Exposure to electromagnetic fields when they are applied to particular regions of the brain can cause certain individuals to misinterpret the extra information from the EMF's. The resulting sensations may be perceived as paranormal in origin by some and may be one possible explanation in cases of haunting experiences (Persinger and Koren, 2001).

INFRASOUND

Infrasound is normally defined as acoustic energy with a frequency below that of normal human hearing, i.e., below 20Hz. Early psychical investigators recognized that sound vibrations were a component in some reported haunt and poltergeist cases (e.g., Fodor and Lodge, 1933). Whilst none of these early reports directly mention infrasound, the idea did gain scientific recognition in the 1940s. We now know that low frequency structural and airborne vibrations are produced by and also result from, infrasonic acoustic energy. The first direct claim of a possible causal link between infrasound exposure and reported anomalous experiences was made by Persinger (1974). He stated that although little public data have been available, weak infrasound energy from ambient sources could evoke vague responses and lead to reports of feelings of foreboding, depression of impending doom ahead of natural phenomena such as earthquakes.

Investigators did not begin to examine the role of infrasound in haunting experiences for many years, largely because of the technical difficulties associated with measuring it. Infrasound is now increasingly put forward as a contributing factor in the production of various physiological and psychological effects that are subsequently interpreted as a haunting experience (e.g., Fielding and O'Keeffe, 2006). Often such claims are not based upon empirical observations but instead draw upon similarities between witness reports and reported effects of exposure in laboratory studies. Recent interest in infrasound arose following the publication of a paper by Tandy and Lawrence (1998). Tandy traced an infrasound source to a defective fan within an allegedly haunted workplace. A key suggestion of this research was that infrasound, in addition to the psychological effects, may also be responsible at a specific frequency (18.98Hz) of causing eyeball vibration leading to visual effects that might be interpreted as apparitional encounters. Tandy later conducted a series of measurements in an allegedly haunted 14th century cellar (Tandy, 2000). The results seemed to confirm that infrasound close to 18Hz might be responsible for anomalous experiences. These two papers seem to have been the catalyst for the claims now being made for infrasound involvement in haunting cases.

Braithwaite and Townsend (2006) observe that there are no published studies that have found any implications for cognition or experience of infrasound as weak as the levels reported by Tandy (2000). This is also commented upon by Tandy (2000) who suggests that as haunting effects are rather less spectacular this may simply reflect the lower amplitudes found. Certainly the seminal work by Tandy and Lawrence (1998; Tandy, 2000) remains the only real basis for the assumption of an infrasonic involvement in personal experiences at haunted locations. Inevitably, such primary studies are flawed as there is little preceding data for the authors to make use of when developing arguments. There is also a lack of information about levels of ambient infrasound at haunted locations. The need for such baseline data was also highlighted by Braithwaite and Townsend (2006). Given that infrasound is produced by so many natural and artificial sources it is unlikely that infrasound on its own is the cause of people reporting paranormal-like experiences and, although further research is needed, it remains one of several possible environmental causal factors in the production of a range of psychophysical experiences that may lead to people reporting haunting experiences (Parsons, Winsper and O'Keeffe, 2008).

The Role of the Mind

There is a paucity of psychological research dealing exclusively with the role of the mind in haunted environments and yet there is also a vast array of concepts from psychology that are highly relevant. Almost a century of psychological research has demonstrated that factors as diverse as attention, arousal, context, belief, suggestion, expectancy, boredom, desire, fatigue, stress and even personality influence our perception of the environment.

BIAS AND BELIEF

As defined earlier, haunting experiences are ultimately about the perception of sensory experiences. It is therefore not surprising that each psychological factor mentioned above plays a significant role in such experiences. The environment in which haunting experiences tend to occur and the state of mind of those conducting investigations and reporting phenomena form conditions that are likely to heighten the role of psychological variables. Indeed there is support for a hypothesis that "the perceptions of ambiguous events should follow a predictable pattern that is consistent with the factors that govern human attention" (Lange and Houran, 2001, p. 287). The support shows that attentional bias is partly to blame for the interpretation of puzzling or ambiguous events as evidence of a haunting. It appears that bias, generally, is a powerful theme that runs throughout many of the potential psychological explanations for people's experiences, explanations that, on the face of it, seem internally based. One obvious external cue, however, is the widespread belief in ghosts and related entities and how this may bias experiences or a retelling of an experience. Like placebo effects, such internalized beliefs and expectations tend to induce and structure ambiguous experiences. The influence of beliefs and expectations is arguably greater on perceptual illusions. As noted by Baker (2002), the two main problems faced by researchers investigating cases of alleged haunting experiences are emotion and belief. Related to this are potential sources of bias that may be associated with fictional ghost stories. Irwin (2004) identifies two such concerns:

> First, some supposedly real-life cases initially may have been devised as a good story but then presented as authentic in the hope of enhancing their commercial potential. Second, fictional ghost stories (and folklore too) promote a particular stereotype of an apparitional experience and it is feasible that witnesses' accounts of their experience unwittingly are distorted to conform to these popular expectations. Parapsychologists therefore must be a little wary of accepting consistencies in spontaneous apparitions: in part these consistencies may reveal only the fictional conception of apparitions [p. 199].

SUGGESTION*

Two cognitive phenomena of critical importance to the incidence of haunting phenomena and the investigation thereof are suggestion, in which an implicit or explicit environmental cue, may induce congruent experiences, and contagion, in which one individual's experiences trigger similar reports in proximal individuals.

Suggestion and related constructs have been repeatedly found to play a critical role in the incidence of haunting phenomena. The reporting of anomalous experiences is associated with hypnotic and imaginative suggestibility (Kumar and Pekala, 2001) and the induction of hallucinatory experiences via suggestion is extensively documented (e.g., McConkey and Barnier, 2004). Haunting-type experiences have been induced by suggestion through different experimental techniques (Granqvist et al., 2005; Terhune and Smith, 2006). Haunt-specific suggestions have also been found to inflate the reporting of anomalous experiences in field experiments (Lange and Houran, 1997; Wiseman, Watt, Greening, Stevens, and O'Keeffe, 2002). Suggestion may

---

*This section is reproduced from Terhune's (2008) contribution to O'Keeffe, Baker, Sherwood, Terhune and Parsons (2008). We gratefully acknowledge Devin Terhune, the author of this section, for permission to include it in its entirety.

also facilitate the cessation of haunting phenomena (Roll, 1977; Terhune, 2004). In addition to triggering haunt phenomena, suggestion may inform the content and interpretation of anomalous experiences and may contribute to the occurrence of false memories of haunting episodes.

Research on the related phenomenon of contagion, though less studied than suggestion, indicates that under certain conditions, reports of anomalous experiences can trigger similar experiences in other individuals. This is in accordance with the finding that haunt phenomena are more likely to occur in sites with multiple individuals (McClenon, 2001). Finally, suggestion and contagion may function to determine the interpretation of ambiguous endogenous (e.g., somatic) and exogenous (e.g., unusual sounds) stimuli (Lange and Houran, 2001).

In addition to their role in the incidence of haunting experiences, suggestion and contagion need to be taken into account in field experiments and investigations of alleged haunts. In field experiments involving participant tours of allegedly haunted locations (Lange and Houran, 1997; Maher, 2000), investigators must be aware that identifying a particular site as a haunt can influence the perceptions reported by participants as well as experimenters. Some, but not all, of these effects can be circumvented in part through the use of double-blind experimental conditions and the inclusion of independent control sites in field experiments of alleged haunts (Houran and Brugger, 2000). However, the occurrence of contagion effects and the increase in suggestibility conferred by restricted environmental stimulation (Cardeña and Spiegel, 1991) may render common features of field experiments (e.g., multiple experimenter teams, night-time investigations) highly counterproductive.

Conclusion

There appears to be a strong case for haunting experiences being produced by a merging of psychological processes (Lange and Houran, 2001). Such processes include emotional, cognitive and motivational influences as well as certain environmental triggers and neurophysiological interactions. This chapter has highlighted some of the key psychological and environmental factors involved and does not propose that such factors are the answer to understanding all haunting experiences. Further research is needed to know whether it is the likely combination of factors (psychological and environmental) that induce haunting experiences, and whether in certain cases some factors are more intense than others.

References

Alvarado, C.S., and N.L. Zingrone (1995). Characteristics of hauntings with and without apparitions: An analysis of published cases. *Journal of the Society for Psychical Research*, 60. 385–397.
Ashby, R. H. (1972). *The Guidebook for the Study of Psychical Research.* London: Rider.
Baker, I. (2002). Do ghosts exist? A summary of parapsychological research into apparitional experiences. In Newton, J. (ed.), *Early Modern Ghosts.* Durham, UK: University of Durham.
Braithwaite, J., and Townsend, M. (2006). Good vibrations: The case for a specific effect of infrasound in instances of anomalous experience has yet to be empirically demonstrated. *Journal of the Society for Psychical Research*, 70. 211–225.
Cardeña, E., S. J. Lynn and S. Krippner (eds.). (2000). *Varieties of Anomalous Experience: Examining the Scientific Evidence.* Washington, D.C.: American Psychological Association.
Cardeña, E., and D. Spiegel (1991). Suggestibility, absorption and dissociation: An integrative model of hypnosis. In J. F. Schumaker (ed.), *Human Suggestibility: Advances in Theory, Research and Application.* New York: Routledge. 93–107.
Edge, H. L., R. L. Morris, J. Palmer and J. H. Rush (eds.). (1987). *Foundations of Parapsychology: Exploring the Boundaries of Human Capability.* London: Routledge & Kegan Paul.
Fielding Y., and C. O'Keeffe (2006). *Ghost Hunters: A Guide to Investigating the Paranormal.* London: Hodder & Stoughton.
Fodor, N. (1948). The poltergeist—psychoanalyzed. *Psychiatric Quarterly*, 22. 195–203.
Fodor, N., and O. Lodge (1933). *Encyclopedia of Psychic Science.* London: Arthurs Press.
Fontana, D. (2004). *Is There an Afterlife? A Comprehensive Overview of the Evidence.* Ropley, Hants: O Books.
Gauld, A., and T. Cornell (1979). *Poltergeists.* London: Routledge & Kegan Paul.
Granqvist, P., M. Fredrikson, P. Unge, A. Hagenfeldt, S. Valind, U. Larhammar and M. Larsson (2005). Sensed presence and mystical experiences are predicted by suggestibility, not by the application of transcranial weak complex magnetic fields. *Neuroscience Letters*, 379. 1–6.
Houran, J., and P. Brugger (2000). The need for independent control sites: A methodological suggestion with special reference to haunting and poltergeist field research. *European Journal of Parapsychology*, 15. 30–45.
Houran, J., and R. Lange (eds.). (2001). *Hauntings and Poltergeists: Multidisciplinary Perspectives.* Jefferson, NC: McFarland.
Irwin, H. J. (2004). *An Introduction to Parapsychology.* 4th Edition. Jefferson, NC: McFarland.
Kumar, V. K., and R. J. Pekala (2001). Relation of hypnosis-specific attitudes and behaviors to paranormal beliefs and experiences. In J. Houran and R. Lange (eds.), *Hauntings and Poltergeists: Multidisciplinary Perspectives.* Jefferson, NC: McFarland. 260–279.
Lange, R., and J. Houran (1997). Context-induced paranormal experiences: Support for Houran and Lange's model of haunting phenomena. *Perceptual and Motor Skills*, 84. 1455–1458.
Lange, R., and J. Houran (2001). Ambiguous stimuli brought to life: The psychological dynamics of hauntings and poltergeists. In J. Houran and R. Lange (eds.), *Hauntings and Poltergeists: Multidisciplinary Perspectives.* Jefferson, NC: McFarland. 280–306.
McClenon, J. (2001). The sociological investigation of haunting cases. In J. Houran and R. Lange (eds.), *Hauntings and Poltergeists: Multidisciplinary Perspectives.* Jefferson, NC: McFarland. 62–81.
McConkey, K. M., and A. J. Barnier (2004). High hypnotizability: Unity and diversity in behavior and experience. In M. Heap, R. J. Brown and D. A. Oakley (eds.), *The Highly Hypnotizable Person: Theoretical, Experimental and Clinical Issues.* New York: Routledge. 61–84.

Moody, R. A., and P. Perry (1994). *Reunions: Visionary Encounters with Departed Loved Ones.* New York: Random House.

Nickell, J. (2001). Phantoms, frauds, or fantasies? In J. Houran and R. Lange (eds.), *Hauntings and Poltergeists: Multidisciplinary Perspectives.* Jefferson, NC: McFarland. 214–224.

O'Keeffe, C., I. Baker, S. Sherwood, D. Terhune and S. Parsons (2008). Parapsychology and investigating haunting experiences. Panel Discussion Presented at the 51st Annual Parapsychological Association Convention, Winchester, UK.

Parapsychological Association. (1989). Terms and methods in parapsychological research. *Journal of Humanistic Psychology*, 29. 394–399.

Parsons, S., and C. O'Keeffe (2006). An initial exploration of ambient temperature fluctuations and anomalous experiences. Paper Presented at the 49th Annual Parapsychological Association Convention, Stockholm, Sweden.

Parsons, S., A. Winsper and C. O'Keeffe (2008). Was there something in the cellar? Paper Presented at the 32nd International Conference of the Society for Psychical Research, Winchester, UK.

Persinger, M. A. (1974). *The Paranormal: Part II Mechanisms & Models.* New York: MSS Information Corporation.

Persinger, M.A. (1985). Geophysical variables and behaviour: XXII. The Tectonogenic Strain Continuum of Unusual Events. *Perceptual and Motor Skills*, 60. 59–65.

Persinger, M. A., and S. A. Koren (2001). Predicting the characteristics of haunt phenomena from Geomagnetic factors and brain sensitivity: Evidence from field and experimental studies. In J. Houran and R. Lange (eds.), *Hauntings and Poltergeists: Multidisciplinary Perspectives.* Jefferson, NC: McFarland. 179–194.

Persinger, M. A., and P. M. Richards (1995). Vestibular experiences of humans during brief periods of partial sensory deprivation are enhanced when daily geomagnetic activity exceeds 15–20 nT. *Neuroscience Letters*, 2. 69–72.

Radin, D. I., and J. M. Rebman (1996). Are phantasms fact or fantasy? A preliminary investigation of apparitions evoked in the laboratory. *Journal of the Society for Psychical Research*, 61. 65–87.

Randall, J. L. (2001). The mediumship of Stella Cranshaw: a statistical investigation. *Journal of the Society for Psychical Research*, 65. 38–46.

Roll, W. G. (1977). Poltergeists. In B. B. Wolman (ed.), *Handbook of Parapsychology.* New York: Van Nostrand Reinhold. 382–413.

Roll, W. G., and M. A. Persinger (2001). Investigations of poltergeists and haunts: A review and interpretation. In J. Houran and R. Lange (eds.), *Hauntings and Poltergeists: Multidisciplinary Perspectives.* Jefferson, NC: McFarland. 123–163.

Tandy, V. (2000). Something in the cellar. *Journal of the Society for Psychical Research*, 64. 129–140.

Tandy, V., and T. Lawrence (1998). The ghost in the machine. *Journal of the Society for Psychical Research*, 62. 360–364.

Terhune, D.B. (2004). Investigation of reports of a recurrent sensed presence: Assessing recent conventional hypotheses. *Journal of the Society for Psychical Research*, 68. 153–167.

Terhune, D. B. (2008). Suggestion, contagion and haunting experiences. Brief Paper Presented as Part of C. O'Keeffe, I. Baker, S. Sherwood, D. Terhune and S. Parsons (2008). Parapsychology and investigating haunting experiences. Panel Discussion Presented at the 51st Annual Parapsychological Association Convention, Winchester, UK.

Terhune, D. B., and M. D. Smith (2006). The induction of anomalous experiences in a mirror-gazing facility: Suggestion, cognitive perceptual personality traits and phenomenological state effects. *Journal of Nervous and Mental Disease*, 194. 415–421.

Terhune, D. B., A. Ventola and J. Houran (2007). An analysis of contextual variables and the incidence of photographic anomalies at an alleged haunt and a control site. *Journal of Scientific Exploration*, 21. 99–120.

Thalbourne, M. A. (2003). *Glossary of Terms Used in Parapsychology.* Second edition. Charlottesville, VA: Puente Publications.

Turner, K. H. (1970) A South Yorkshire haunt. *Journal of the Society for Psychical Research*, 45. No. 745.
Tyrrell, G. N. M. (1953). *Apparitions*. London: Duckworth.
Wiseman, R., E. Greening and M. Smith (2003). Belief in the paranormal and suggestion in the séance room. *British Journal of Psychology*, 94. 285–297.
Wiseman, R., C. Watt, E. Greening, P. Stevens and C. O'Keeffe (2002). An investigation into the alleged haunting of Hampton Court Palace: Psychological variables and magnetic fields. *Journal of Parapsychology*, 66. 387–408.
Wiseman R., C. Watt, P. Stevens, E. Greening and C. O'Keeffe (2003). An investigation into alleged "hauntings." *British Journal of Psychology*, 94. 195–211.

9
APPARITIONS OF BLACK DOGS
Simon J. Sherwood

Apparitions have been investigated scientifically for over 100 years (e.g., Braithwaite, 2008; Gauld and Cornell, 1979; Green and McCreery, 1975/1989; Gurney, Myers, and Podmore, 1886; Haraldsson, 1991; Harte, Black, Hollishead, and Mitchell, 2001; Houran and Lange, 2001; Maher, 1999; Radin, 2001; Roll and Persinger, 2001; Schmeidler, 1966; Sidgwick, Johnson, Myers, Podmore, and Sidgwick, 1894; Tandy, 2000; Tyrrell, 1943/1973; Wiseman, Watt, Greening, Stevens, and O'Keeffe, 2003) but there has been relatively little development of theories to explain them over the last 50 years (Hart, 1956; Houran and Lange, 2001; McCue, 2002). Currently, a lot of attention is being paid to the possible relationship between reports of apparitional phenomena and environmental factors. Nevertheless, as yet, there is still no adequate explanation for all cases and for all features of reported apparitions.

According to parapsychologist Harvey Irwin (1999, p. 244), "The *apparitional experience* is perceptual-like and relates to a person or an animal that is not physically present, with physical means of communication being ruled out." In other words, people seem to encounter someone or something that isn't really there even though the "object" of the encounter might seem very real and the interaction proceeds as one might expect. The witness might not even realize that they have had an apparitional experience until later on (when they discover that the person or object could not have been there physically at the time) or until the apparition does something unexpected, such as vanish or move through a solid wall. Although we often talk about having "seen a ghost," it is not only the visual modality that is involved; such an experience can involve the auditory, tactile and olfactory modalities or even just a sense of presence (e.g., Green and McCreery, 1975/1989; Haraldsson, 1991; Sidgwick et al., 1894).

One of the big questions is whether apparitions are objective or subjective (Braude, 1991; Irwin, 1999) but such a question is possibly too simplistic and restrictive (Brown, 1958; MacKenzie, 1982; Osis, 1986; Price, 1938–1939); perhaps they are the result of complex interactions between physical, neurophysiological and psychological variables and only occur when a particular combination of circumstances is present (e.g., Houran and Lange, 1998; MacKenzie, 1982; Persinger, 1989; Radin, 2001; Williams, 2001).

There has been a growing number of calls for greater attention to be paid to the person(s) reporting apparitional phenomena as well as the circumstances and context in which they are reported (e.g., Alvarado and Zingrone, 1995; Cornell, 2002; Gauld, 1982; Haraldsson, 1991; Irwin, 2004). Nevertheless, this should not be at the expense of gaining a full appreciation of the range of features of different apparitional experiences. Parapsychologists have attempted to classify apparitions into a number of different types: experimental* (where a living person attempts to create an apparition of him/herself elsewhere), crisis (where an apparition appears within 12 hours of them experiencing some form of crisis), post-mortem (the apparition has been dead for at least 12 hours), ghosts/hauntings (the same apparition is seen in the same location repeatedly over time by the same or different people) (Gauld, 1977; Green and McCreery, 1975/1989, Irwin, 1999; Tyrrell, 1943/1973). With cases of hauntings, the phenomena tend to be recurrent but fairly unpredictable; they could occur repeatedly over the course of days or be only sporadic over the course of months, years or decades. The elusiveness and unpredictability of apparitional phenomena makes it a very challenging and difficult area to investigate scientifically in any controlled manner. This might be partly responsible for the slow progress in our understanding. Another type of apparition is the deathbed or "take-away" apparition (Gauld, 1977; Osis and Haraldsson, 1986). Inanimate types of apparition include ghostly objects—even cars, boats and planes—and luminous manifestations (Bayless, 1973; Gauld and Cornell, 1979; Green and McCreery, 1975/1989). According to the parapsychological literature, the vast majority of apparitions are of humans; animal apparitions are comparatively rare, and tend to be associated with domestic animals (e.g., Bayless, 1970, 1973; Green and McCreery, 1975/1989; O'Donnell, 1913; Sidgwick et al., 1894). This is probably why research has focused upon apparitions of humans but other forms of apparition that are less common or atypical provide a challenge to existing theories. One example of such an apparition is the "Black Dog"—well-known in folklore but not in parapsychology—which has been reported for centuries and still is being so. Although Black Dog apparitions are often associated with Great Britain, they are also found elsewhere in Europe and in North Amer-

---

*This is not the same as techniques designed to facilitate the appearance of apparitions before one's own self, such as the use of a psychomanteum (e.g., Moody with Perry, 1993; Radin, 2001).

ica and Latin America (e.g., Bord and Bord, 1985; Burchell, 2007; Harte, 2005a, 2005b; Sherwood, 2000; Trubshaw, 2005).

Not surprisingly, the term "Black Dog" is used to refer to an apparition that typically resembles a black dog, though it has also been used as a generic term for canine apparitions of other colors and types (e.g., Brown, 1978; Miller, 1984). The folklorist Theo Brown (1958) distinguished between three different types of Black Dog (see below) but noted that "obviously these three divisions exist for our convenience merely; there are many overlaps" (p.179). Unfortunately there has been no systematic analysis of the features contained in reports of Black Dog encounters and it is not clear whether there are different distinct types of experience and, if so, what features distinguish them:

> A. That which is generally known locally as the Barguest, Shuck, Black Shag, Trash, Skriker, Padfoot, Hooter, and other names. These are not the names of individuals but of an impersonal creature which is distributed over certain areas.... This type, which we may call the Barguest type, changes its shape, a thing that no true black dog ever does [p.176].
> B. That which is nearly always known as the Black Dog, is always black, and is always a dog and nothing else.... It is always associated with a definite place or "beat" on a road. It is always an individual. Sometimes it is associated with a person or a family.... Another personal association is that with witches [p.178].
> C. A third variety of Black Dog, which is rare, is that which appears in a certain locality in conjunction with a calendar cycle [p.179].

It would be helpful at this juncture to provide some examples of different Black Dog encounters that have been reported over the years, starting with some very old reports and finishing with some more modern ones. The most well-known case is probably the Black Dog of Bungay that is reported to have visited St. Mary's parish church in Bungay, Suffolk, on Sunday, 4 August 1577, during a thunderstorm (see Reeve, 1988). A clergyman called Abraham Fleming published a pamphlet entitled "A Straunge and Terrible Wunder wrought very late in the parish Church of Bungay" which included an account of the Black Dog's visit:

> Immediately hereupon, there appeared in a most horrible similitude and likenesse to the congregation then and there present a dog as they might discerne it, of a black color; at the site whereof, togither with the fearful flashes of fire which were then seene, moved such admiration in the minds of the assemblie, that they thought doomesday was already come. This black dog, or the divil in such a likenesse (God hee knoweth all who worketh all) running all along down the body of the church with great swiftnesse and incredible haste, among the people, in a visible fourm and shape, passed betweene two persons, as they were kneeling upon their knees, and occupied in prayer as it seemed, wrung the necks of them bothe at one instant clene backward, in so much that even at a moment where they kneeled, they strangely died.... There was at ye same time another wonder wrought; for the same black dog, still continuing and remaining in one and the self same shape, passing by another man of the congregation in the church, gave him such a gripe on the back,

that therewith all he was presently drawen togither and shrunk up, as it were a peece of lether scorched in a hot fire; or as the mouth of a purse or bag, drawen togither with string. The man albeit hee was in so strange a taking, dyed not, but as it is thought is yet alive: whiche thing is mervelous in the eyes of men, and offereth much matter of amasing the minde...

The same dog was apparently seen later at the Holy Trinity Church, Blythburgh, a few miles away. There three more people were allegedly killed and another burned by the dog. Local historian Christopher Reeve (1988) noted that although records of events at the Bungay and Blythburgh churches corroborate some aspects of Fleming's account, such as the terrible thunderstorm, they do not mention a dog.

A lane in Uplyme on the Devon-Dorset border has a history of Black Dog encounters (Brown, 1982; Sherwood, 2004). One such encounter happened in 1856 and is described in Chambers' *The Book of Days* (1879, vol. 2, p. 434):

> "As I was returning to Lyme," said she, "one night with my husband down Dog Lane, as we reached about the middle of it, I saw an animal about the size of a dog meeting us. 'What's that?' I said to my husband. 'What?' said he, 'I see nothing.' I was so frightened I could say no more then, for the animal was within two or three yards of us, and had become as large as a young calf, but had the appearance of a black shaggy dog with fiery eyes, just like the description I had heard of the 'black dog.' He passed close by me, and made the air cold and dank as he passed along. Though I was afraid to speak, I could not help turning round to look after him, and I saw him growing bigger and bigger as he went along, till he was as high as the trees by the roadside, and then seeming to swell into a large cloud, he vanished in the air. As soon as I could speak, I asked my husband to look at his watch, and it was then five minutes past twelve. My husband said he saw nothing but a vapour or cloud coming up from the sea."

The following case was collected by Miles (1908) during an investigation of strange animal apparitions that had been reported in a lane. The apparitions were believed to be the spirit of a local farmer who had hanged himself. One of the villagers gave the following account:

> In the beginning of January, 1905, about half-past seven in the evening, I was walking up from the Halfway [a local inn]. I suddenly saw an animal that seemed to be like a large, black dog appear quite suddenly out of the hedge and run across the road quite close in front of me ; I thought it was the dog belonging to the curate. I was just going to call it to send it home, when it suddenly changed its shape, and turned into a black donkey standing on its hind legs. This creature had two glowing eyes, which appeared to me to be almost as big as saucers. I looked at it in astonishment for a minute or so, when it suddenly vanished. After that I hurried home, for the sight of this creature with the large shining eyes gave me a shock. The evening was a light one for the time of year [Miles, 1908, p.259].

Below is an account of an experience that I had as a small child when I was living in Spalding, Lincolnshire. It was written when I was about 9 or 10 years of age.

> The year was about 1974. I had been in bed a couple of hours. I awoke to hear a patter of feet. I looked up thinking it was my dog, but to my terror I saw a massive black animal probably with horns, but perhaps ears, galloping along the landing towards my bedroom. I tried to scream but I found it impossible. The creatures eyes were bright yellow and as big as saucers. The animal got to my bedroom door and then vanished as quick as it has appeared. I then managed to scream and my mum came in to calm me down. She said it was a reflection of car headlights what I thought was a ghost. I believed this until a few years later when I was reading a local paper which had an article about a haunted council house which was inhabited by a poltergeist. A variety of objects were hurled at the family's baby child. The father claimed that a black dog rushed at him and then disappeared. He also claimed that a black goat had been seen running around the house. I also thought I saw a ghostly black goat on the landing of my old house. After reading this article I was convinced that what I thought had happened a few years back had most probably happened.

Here is a more recent case from my collection that occurred on 2 April 2005.

> I had an encounter with one in St Peter's church yard, Brackley, Northamptonshire. Until last night I had never heard of this phenomenon.... The time was 10 P.M. I left the house to make a phone call on my mobile due to receiving no phone signal inside. I was walking up Watery Lane whilst speaking on the phone when the signal got weak and so I turned and started walking back. As I walked towards St Peter's church yard I regained the signal and so strolled through the gates and along the path of the south graveyard towards the church. After walking only a few metres along the path I heard a loud panting and galloping of feet in front of me. I wasn't sure what was coming but didn't have time to think as within seconds a large black shaggy dog was running towards me. It appeared frantic and ran incredibly quickly. It was dark and so it was hard to tell but it either had large flapping ears or horns upon its head. It's eyes were not red or yellow but black and glinting in the light. It ran right up to me, within inches and then was enveloped in darkness and faded away. I was naturally very scared and had a very sleepless night.

Of particular interest is that, unlike many human and most animal apparitions, Black Dog apparitions tend not to be recognized as or appear similar to former living animals. What distinguishes Black Dog apparitions from normal dogs is often their size, their eyes, their body or their behaviour. They are often described as being bigger than an ordinary dog, often about the size of a calf. Their eyes are often described as glowing and as being rather large; one-eyed apparitions have also been reported. Sometimes these apparitions change in size or into a different animal or human form. Black dog apparitions are not always complete; for example, certain body parts might be missing or only certain body parts might be seen or, in a few cases, the "dog" has human or other animal body parts (e.g., Bord and Bord, 1985; Brown, 1958; Burchell, 2007; McEwan, 1986; Miles, 1908; Miller, 1984).

Sometimes the apparitions are silent but at other times the sound of their feet or panting or the sound of chains has been reported. Few Black Dogs bark or growl and rarer still are those that laugh or speak; the Lancashire Skriker is so-called because of its screams (Bord and Bord, 1985; Brown, 1958; McEwan, 1986; Rudkin, 1938).

Black Dogs are usually seen at night outside, often in lonely rural locations (Brown, 1978; Miller, 1984; Rudkin, 1938). Types of outdoor places associated with Black Dogs include roads, crossroads, bridges, gateways, boundaries, fields, hedges, treasure sites, churchyards and gallows, wells and trees. Black Dogs are often encountered near water too (Bord and Bord, 1985; Brown, 1958, 1978; Burchell, 2007). Types of indoor places where a Black Dog has been encountered include doorways, corridors, staircases, bedrooms and churches (Bord and Bord, 1985; Brown, 1978; McEwan, 1986; Miller, 1984).

Unlike many other types of apparition (Green and McCreery, 1975/1989; Irwin, 1999), during encounters with Black Dogs, witnesses are often physically active at the time and may be out walking, cycling or driving. In some cases, witnesses, who are driving at the time, believe that they have hit the dog or else it vanishes just before they do so (McEwan, 1986; Miller, 1986). Often a witness becomes aware of a dog walking or trotting along beside or just behind them; these tend to be more positive encounters. In more neutral cases, the dog may cross their path, seemingly unaware of their presence, and disappear through a wall, gateway or hedge (McEwan, 1986). In more frightening cases, the dog is reported to be walking or running towards the witness in a threatening manner or is sitting or standing in the middle of the road facing them. Some dogs are said to turn and look towards the witness or to stare at them (Bord and Bord, 1985). In one or two cases, witnesses have reported a dog seen flying through the air above the trees (McEwan, 1986). Most Black Dogs either vanish or gradually fade away or else they maneuver themselves out of sight. Sometimes the apparition may vanish if the witness's attention wanders or if attempts are made to touch it (e.g., Bord and Bord, 1985). A few appearances and disappearances of Black Dogs have also been accompanied by flashes of light and explosions (McEwan, 1986).

Sometimes more than one person present will experience an apparition — such cases are referred to as collective apparitions — though not everyone present will necessarily experience the apparition. Reactions to Black Dog apparitions vary from fear and aggression to acceptance and friendship (Miller, 1984). Sometimes people try to stroke the dog (presumably only if it appears friendly!) while at other times people have attempted to strike it (Bord and Bord, 1985). These reactions probably depend upon the witness, their circumstances, beliefs, expectations and knowledge of local folklore, as well as the behaviour and characteristics of the dog (Harte, 2005a, p. 16; Westwood, 2005). The appearance of a Black Dog has often been regarded as an omen of death, bad luck or bad weather (Bord and Bord, 1985; Burchell, 2007; Dale-Green, 1966, part III; Harte, 2005a; Miller, 1984; Reeve, 1988). However, Black dogs in Lincolnshire have been viewed more favorably and are often considered to be harmless and protective (Brown, 1958; Dale-Green, 1966, part III; Harte, 2005a; Miller, 1984; Rudkin, 1938). In some areas of Latin America, the Black Dog is viewed as a spirit that protects the drunk and the defenseless (Burchell, 2007).

Possible Explanations for Black Dog Apparitions*

So what explanations are there for Black Dog apparitions? Given the diversity of the features of Black Dog encounters, there may be more than one explanation for them. As the philosopher Braude (1991, p. 172) quite rightly points out, "Different sorts of apparitional phenomena may require different sorts of explanations." We might distinguish between "normal" versus "paranormal" or "supernatural" explanations for Black Dogs. In order to entertain a paranormal explanation one must first rule out all possible normal explanations, which can be easier said than done, so these will be considered first. Theories put forward to explain apparitions in general are applicable in this context (e.g., Gauld, 1982; Gauld and Cornell, 1979; Hart, 1956; Houran and Lange, 2001; MacKenzie, 1982; McCue, 2002; Tyrrell, 1943/1973).

POTENTIAL NORMAL EXPLANATIONS

Stories of Black Dogs might have been made up deliberately in the past to discourage grave-robbing or to prevent children from befriending rabid dogs or entering prohibited places (see Miller, 1984). Although plausible for some older cases, these specific reasons are not really applicable to more recent sightings. Whilst deliberate fraud is always possible, and might be difficult to rule out completely, the fact that many witnesses are reluctant to share their experiences suggests that many do not have attention-seeking desires that they wish to satisfy. Misinterpretation of normal experiences is another non-paranormal explanation that could involve misinterpretation of a real animal, not necessarily a dog, or some kind of misperception of the normal environment (e.g., Houran and Lange, 1996), a mixture of normal and hallucinatory experience (i.e., what Green and McCreery (1975/1989) refer to as a "metachoric experience") or an entirely hallucinatory experience. Such misinterpretation might be more likely if one has strong paranormal beliefs and/or existing knowledge of Black Dogs, especially if one expects a particular location to be haunted.

Archetypal imagery • Another theory is that the Black Dog might be some kind of archetypal image (see Dale-Green, 1966; Miller, 1984) shared

---

*This section is partly based upon Sherwood's (2005) chapter in Trubshaw's (2005) book Explore Phantom Black Dogs and I am grateful for the permission to include some of the material here.

by humans as a result of our long association and relationship with dogs in a domestic capacity. This theory is difficult to test. Also why do so few people have Black Dog experiences despite our continued association with dogs? If there is some truth to this theory then perhaps we might expect people who report Black Dog experiences to have a stronger link with dogs in general.

Cultural source and experiential source hypotheses • According to the "cultural source hypothesis" proposed by Hufford (1982, p. 14; see also McClenon, 1994b) for supernatural experiences, "The experiences are either fictitious products of tradition or imaginary subjective experiences shaped (or occasionally even caused) by tradition." Even if supernatural/paranormal beliefs do not actually cause related experiences directly, there is evidence to suggest that a person's beliefs (or knowledge) may shape their experience. For example, spontaneous case reports suggest that knowledge, beliefs and expectations may influence the content of hypnagogic/hypnopompic experiences (imagery of various sensory modalities experienced in the borderline states just as one is falling asleep (hypnagogic state) or just as one is waking from sleep (hypnopompic state)—see Mavromatis (1987) and Sherwood (2002). However, although strong cultural traditions and knowledge of Black Dogs in certain areas might well influence the characteristics and interpretations of reported experiences, I am less convinced that they could cause them.

The alternative to the cultural source hypothesis, the experiential source hypothesis (Hufford, 1982), predicts that certain phenomena have universal elements and will therefore occur in different cultures. If these experiences have universal characteristics, which might be deemed anomalous or supernatural, then similar experiences in different cultures should be associated with similar beliefs. The main idea is that "such experiences are instrumental in causing changes in belief, rather than merely being caused by belief" (McClenon, 1994b). This hypothesis allows for people with no apparent knowledge of a phenomenon, or traditions or beliefs associated with it, to still have such experiences whereas the cultural source hypothesis does not (Hufford, 1982). Certainly there are similarities in terms of Black Dog reports over time across different countries and cultures.

Evidence in support of the experiential source hypothesis has been obtained from cross-cultural surveys of anomalous experiences and there does indeed seem to be a great deal of uniformity in the features of anomalous experience and beliefs (see McClenon, 1994a, 1994b). My view is that some of the best evidence for the experiential source hypothesis comes from hypnagogic/hypnopompic experiences that have been associated with paranormal/supernatural interpretations and beliefs (see Sherwood, 2002). It is not necessarily a case of either-or when it comes to the cultural and experiential source hypotheses though; there could be an element of both involved. My view is that the experiential source would constitute the greater component in most cases though.

Brain-environment interaction • Another theory is that Black Dogs are connected with environmental phenomena, such as electromagnetic radiation, water, or "alternative" sources of energy (Bord and Bord, 1985; Miller, 1984). There has been a recent surge of interest in environmental variables in apparitional and poltergeist cases in general (see Houran and Lange, 2001; Williams, 2001). Persinger and Koren (2001, p. 179) make rather a bold claim about haunting apparitions:

> There is not a single case of haunt phenomena whose major characteristics cannot be accommodated by understanding the natural forces generated by the earth, the areas of the human brain that are stimulated by these energies, and the interpretation of these forces by normal psychological processes.

Williams (2001) provided a useful overview of evidence in support of the brain-environment interaction model of the apparitional experience but, quite rightly, noted that "this model is only applicable to certain types of apparitional experiences, while other seemingly more complex ones remain unaccounted for" (p. 364). There is an implicit assumption that it is the environmental influences on the brain, in particular, and also the body, and the interpretation of the resultant effects, which are the main causes of anomalous experiences. However, Radin (2001) has proposed more of a "three-way feedback cycle" involving the environment, the body and the mind. Radin's theory postulates that:

> Assuming the existence of complex interactions among mind, body and environment, we therefore suspect that at least some forms of apparitions may not be purely subjective (as in hallucinations) or purely objective (as in disembodied entities). Instead, we expect that some apparitions are—metaphorically speaking—short-term vortexes caused by short-term perturbations in a three-way equilibrium" [p. 175].

Such interactionist theories are not very good at explaining the specific features of the apparitions themselves, nor collective apparitions, but are quite good at explaining the feelings and sensations associated with witnessing them. Although these theories admit to being applicable only to certain types of apparitions, they do not clearly specify which types they do or do not apply to.

The main parts of the brain believed to be involved with reports of a variety of anomalous experiences are the temporal lobes. Functions of the temporal lobes include the integration of a variety of perceptual inputs and making sense of internal and external experiences (e.g., see reviews by Persinger, 1989; Neppe, 1990). The main types of environmental variables measured during field investigations of apparitions and haunting include: geomagnetic fields, magnetic fields, electric fields, background ionizing radiation, infrasound, ambient temperature, and lighting levels (e.g., Braithwaite, 2008; Harte et al., 2001;

Roll and Persinger, 2001; Tandy, 2000; Williams, 2001). Other contextual variables, such as the physical appearance of a location, demand characteristics and one's personal and social beliefs can also play a role (see Lange and Houran, 1997, 2001).

Research has discovered that reports of poltergeists and hauntings (Gearhart and Persinger, 1986; Wilkinson and Gauld, 1993), as well as epileptic seizures (Rajaram and Mitra, 1981), tend to be associated with periods during which the earth's geomagnetic field has increased. The hourly incidence of epileptic seizures and some psi experiences appear to be similar too with peaks between 2–4 A.M. and 9–11 P.M. (Persinger, 1989). Persinger and Koren (2001, p. 181) provide a list of experiences, reported by those who suffer from limbic epilepsy or complex partial seizures within the temporal lobes, that are similar to the subjective aspects of hauntings. However, a relationship between two variables does not necessarily mean that one causes the other. Nevertheless there is some experimental evidence indicating that the application of weak complex magnetic fields across the temporal and parietal lobes of the brain causes reports of a sense of presence and dancing lights (Cook and Persinger, 1997). Persinger and Koren (2001, p. 181) point out that the threshold for the induction of anomalous experiences using such stimulation is much lower within the temporal and limbic regions of the brain. Some people also have greater temporal lobe sensitivity than others, even if they are not epileptic (Persinger and Koren, 2001, p. 183).

A recent field investigation of Hampton Court Palace found that the average magnetic field strength was significantly higher than expected in certain areas of the "Haunted Gallery" (Wiseman et al., 2003). Other researchers have also recorded fluctuations in electromagnetic fields at allegedly haunted locations (Braithwaite and Townsend, 2005, 2008; Harte et al., 2001) though this is not always the case (e.g., Maher, 2000; see also cases reported in Roll and Persinger, 2001). The change in the geomagnetic/electromagnetic field strength or the level (see Roll and Persinger, 2001) might be important. Changes in the electromagnetic field can be caused by artificial sources, such as power sources and machinery (Williams, 2001), but also by accumulating tectonic strain (caused by changing stresses within the earth's crust) and thunderstorm activity. In some traditions, the Black Dog has been considered to be an omen of bad weather (Bord and Bord, 1985, p. 96), and indeed allegedly appeared during a thunderstorm in Bungay and Blythburgh churches (Reeve, 1988). Persinger and Koren (2001, p. 180) state,

> Areas that are prone to haunt phenomena cluster along fault lines or areas where tectonic strain accumulates. These localities are best discerned by geological maps but can be inferred by *the adjacency of small creeks or rivers* or indications of strain release [p. 180, italics added].

These findings are of interest given that many Black Dog encounters take place near water (Bord and Bord, 1985, p. 97; Rudkin, 1938). However, caution is advised: "Lest we seem to be accepting the black dog/water link too easily, we should also note that there are very few places in Britain where one is very far away from water..." (Bord and Bord, 1985, p. 98).

Infrasonic waves, generated naturally or artificially, might also account for features of some alleged apparitional experiences. For example, Tandy (2000, p. 360; Tandy and Lawrence, 1998) claimed that a 19 Hz standing air wave can create feelings of a sense of presence or of being watched, a sense of fear, or the perception of shadowy indescript figures, all of which might be misinterpreted. However, Braithwaite and Townsend (2006) reviewed the available evidence and concluded that "the case for specific effects due to infrasound *alone* has yet to be empirically demonstrated" (p. 211, italics added) and argued that in some circumstances the infrasound might only have an indirect effect by generating electromagnetic field variations in the local environment which are in turn responsible for affecting the brain and generating anomalous experiences.

Although such environmental variables might be associated with the occurrence of apparitional experiences, it is not certain whether the environmental variables cause them and, if so, how they can account for the entire specific and varying features of the apparitions.

POTENTIAL PARANORMAL EXPLANATIONS

Telepathy or psychokinesis • The various telepathic theories suggest that apparitions are subjective hallucinations that appear to be external to the witnesses and are the result of telepathic communication between the individual whose apparition is witnessed and the witness(es) (Braude, 1991, p. 193; Gurney et al., 1886; Hart, 1956; Tyrrell, 1943/1973). This type of theory was originally intended only to account for living and crisis apparitions. It is quite good at explaining selected features of some cases, such as veridical information being provided, the clothing worn by apparitions and the fact that some apparitions might appear as they are remembered rather than as they would have actually looked at the time (Gauld, 1977, p. 603) but the telepathy theory cannot easily account for the physical phenomena reported in some hauntings (McCue, 2002). The main difficulty with this theory is how it can explain collective apparitions witnessed by more than one person simultaneously and hauntings where the same deceased apparition is seen in the same location by different people over time, many of whom do not even recognize the apparition (Braude, 1991; Hart, 1956; Tyrrell, 1943/1973). However, if telepathy does exist, we do not yet know the limits of how it might operate so we cannot yet rule out collective telepathy (Braude, 1991).

A related objectivist explanation is H. H. Price's (1939) Psychic Ether hypothesis, which proposes that apparitions are mental images that, once created by a mind, are somehow able to persist independently in some kind of "psychic ether" and can be picked up by others in suitable circumstances (see Braude, 1991; Tyrrell, 1943/1973). Johnson (see Hart, 1956) expanded this Myers-Price theory and proposed that apparitions are formed as a result of sufficient chemical matter, able to reflect light, being condensed by telepathic thought-forms. There are obvious difficulties with the existence of such etheric material. In addition, how could this matter be transformed unless energy was exchanged with the environment? Also, as Braude (1991) points out, is there any evidence that mental images can exist outside of a brain/mind and are all images mentally created? If this were possible, why aren't there apparitions relating to people's dreams and day dreams? It is difficult to see how this theory can account for simultaneous collective apparitions.

A related possibility is that apparitions are caused by psychokinesis (PK) (Braude, 1991); in other words a person's mind can cause changes in the physical environment that, in this instance, result in the creation of an apparition. Such an objectivist theory could account for collective apparitions and haunting-related physical phenomena, but it might require PK from the mind of a deceased person. It should be noted that apparitions of Black Dogs have also been associated with reports of poltergeist phenomena (see Bord and Bord, 1985). Assuming PK does exist, Braude (1991) argues that, as with ESP, we do not yet understand its limits and thus cannot rule out PK as a potential explanation for apparitions at this stage. Related to the PK theory, is the trace or "stone-tape" theory which, although not well-documented, suggests that events can leave a trace in a particular location that certain people might pick up on (McCue, 2002). Although this might explain the repetitive, stereotypical behaviour of some haunting apparitions how would this trace be created, in what form would it be stored and what circumstances would be required for it to be detected? If this theory is true, an obvious question is why are so few locations haunted? (McCue, 2002).

In the case of apparitions of Black Dogs, what would be the source of the telepathic imagery and/or the psychokinesis? A real dog? If so, living or dead? Also, if it was a living dog what would be its motivation for appearing to humans, particularly strangers, and why are the characteristics of some Black Dog apparitions so very different from normal dogs? The idea that Black Dog apparitions might be created by the mental acts of living persons has also been suggested (see Jones, 2006, p. 53; Miller, 1984, p. 136) but clearly there are difficulties with the telepathy and psychokinetic theories in this context.

Spirit hypothesis • A traditional explanation for apparitions is that they are the spirit or soul of the observed person or animal but it is difficult to apply such an explanation to apparitions of inanimate objects (Green and McCreery, 1975/1989, chapter 35) and to explain why apparitions might appear to be appropriately dressed and carrying inanimate objects (Irwin, 1999). Some people believe that Black Dogs are apparitions of people or dogs that have suffered cruelty or violent deaths or are simply apparitions of working dogs (Miller, 1984). However, how would the veridicality of such information be established (Gauld, 1977) and how and why would an apparition of a dog-like creature be representing a human "spirit"?

The spirit explanation is an objectivist theory that proposes that "an apparition is a real, localized externalized entity, and not simply a subjective construct of the percipient" (Braude, 1991, p. 194). The fact that some apparitions seem able to adapt to their circumstances and have a sense of purpose has been taken as evidence in support of a spirit/survival-of-bodily-death explanation (Osis, 1986; Stevenson, 1982). The spirit theory is more parsimonious than telepathic theories and is better able to account for collective apparitions (Braude, 1991; Stevenson, 1982). The fact that some apparitions are seen repeatedly and independently by different people over time in the same location also supports the spirit theory (Braude, 1991). However, compelling evidence for the survival of a spirit/consciousness that is widely accepted remains elusive.

Supernatural • One supernatural theory of Black Dog apparitions is that they are real dogs possessed or controlled by the percipient (Brown, 1962, cited in Miller, 1984). This theory is difficult to test and it is hard to see how this explanation could account for some of the unusual features of Black Dogs' appearance and behaviour in many cases. The Black Dog has also been associated with the Devil or believed to be a form assumed by witches and/or their familiars (Dale-Green, 1966; McEwan, 1986; Miller, 1984); interestingly, in Latin America the Black Dog is only ever considered to be a human in dog form (possibly as a result of a curse or enchantment) or a manifestation of evil (Burchell, 2007, p. 34). Such supernatural theories are difficult to test and are really beyond the scope of this chapter.

Conclusion

Although parapsychologists have studied apparitions, their research has, perhaps understandably, concentrated upon human apparitions and there is very little mention of animal apparitions, even less so apparitions of Black Dogs. This is disappointing given that apparitions of Black Dogs are well-known in folklore, have been reported for centuries and still are being reported to this day. Although a variety of normal and paranormal explanations have been proposed to account for apparitions, some are good at explaining selected features but, as yet, none can satisfactorily explain all features nor can they accurately predict when and where they will appear, in what circumstances or to whom. Nevertheless, the psychological/parapsychological approach has a lot to offer and there is a resurgence of interest in apparitions. More attention needs to be paid to the psychology of those who report Black Dog experiences, the effects that such experiences can have on those concerned, and the interaction between relevant psychological, physiological and environmental variables.

Further information about Black Dog apparitions can be found on the author's website at http://www.blackshuck.info.

References

Alvarado, C. S., and N. L. Zingrone (1995). Characteristics of hauntings with or without apparitions. An analysis of published cases. *Journal of the Society for Psychical Research*, 60. 385–397.
Bayless, R. (1970). *Animal Ghosts*. New York: University Books.
Bayless, R. (1973). *Apparitions and Survival of Death*. New York: University Books.
Bord, J., and C. Bord (1985). *Alien Animals*. London: Panther Books.
Braithwaite, J. J. (2008). Putting magnetism in its place: A critical examination of the weak-intensity magnetic field account for anomalous haunt-type experiences. *Journal of the Society for Psychical Research*, 72. 34–50.
Braithwaite, J. J., and M. Townsend (2005). Sleeping with the entity: An investigation of an English castle's reputedly haunted bedroom. *European Journal of Parapsychology*, 20. 65–78.
Braithwaite, J. J., and M. Townsend (2006). Good vibrations: The case for a specific effect of infrasound in instances of anomalous experience has yet to be empirically demonstrated. *Journal of the Society for Psychical Research*, 70. 211–224.
Braithwaite, J. J., and M. Townsend (2008). Sleeping with the entity; part II—Temporally complex distortions in the magnetic field from human movement in a bed located in an English castle's reputedly haunted bedroom. *European Journal of Parapsychology*, 23. 90–126.
Braude, S. E. (1991). Apparitions. In S. E. Braude, *The Limits of Influence: Psychokinesis & the Philosophy of Science*. London: Routledge. 170–218.
Brown, T. (1958). The Black Dog. *Folklore*, 69. 175–192.
Brown, T. (1978). The Black Dog in English folklore. In J. R. Porter and W. M. S. Russell (eds.), *Animals in Folklore*. Totowa, NJ: Rowman & Littlefield. 45–58.
Brown, T. (1982). *Devon Ghosts*. Norwich: Jarrold.
Burchell, S. (2007). *Phantom Black Dogs in Latin America*. Wymeswold, UK: Heart of Albion Press.
Chambers, R. (Ed.) (1879). Spectre dogs. In *The Book of Days Vol. 2*. Philadelphia: J. P. Lippincott & Co. 433–436.
Cook, C. M., and M. A. Persinger (1997). Experimental induction of the "sensed presence" in normal subjects and an exceptional subject. *Perceptual and Motor Skills*, 85. 683–693.
Cornell, A. D. (2002). *Investigating the Paranormal*. New York: Helix Press.
Dale-Green, P. (1966). *Dog*. London: Rupert Hart-Davis.
Gauld, A. (1977). Discarnate survival. In B. B. Wolman (ed.), *Handbook of Parapsychology*. New York: Von Nostrand Reinhold. 577–630.
Gauld, A. (1982). *Mediumship and Survival: A Century of Investigations*. London: Heinemann.
Gauld, A., and A. D. Cornell (1979). *Poltergeists*. London: Routledge & Kegan Paul.
Gearhart, L., and M. A. Persinger (1986). Geophysical variables and behavior: XXXIII. Onsets of historical and contemporary poltergeist episodes occurred with sudden increases in geomagnetic activity. *Perceptual and Motor Skills*, 62. 463–466.
Green, C. E., and C. McCreery (1975/1989). *Apparitions*. London: Hamish Hamilton.

Gurney, E., F. W. H. Myers and F. Podmore (1886). *Phantasms of the Living*. London: Trubner & Co.
Haraldsson, E. (1991). Apparitions of the dead: Analyses of a new collection of 350 reports. *Proceedings of the 34th Parapsychological Association Convention.* 205–220.
Hart, H. (1956). Six theories about apparitions. *Proceedings of the Society for Psychical Research*, 50. 153–239.
Harte, J. (2005a). Black dog studies. In B. Trubshaw (ed.), *Explore Phantom Black Dogs*. Wymeswold, UK: Heart of Albion Press. 5–20.
Harte, J. (2005b). The black dog in England: A bibliography. In B. Trubshaw (Ed.), *Explore Phantom Black Dogs*. 98–128. Wymeswold, UK: Heart of Albion Press.
Harte, T. M., D. L. Black, M. T. Hollishead and D. Mitchell (2001). MESA: Multi-energy sensor array in a baseline vs. haunt site. *Proceedings of the 44th Parapsychological Association Convention.* 135–146.
Houran, J., and R. Lange (1996). Hauntings and poltergeist-like episodes as a confluence of conventional phenomena. *Perceptual and Motor Skills*, 83. 1307–1316.
Houran, J., and R. Lange (1998). Rationale and application of a multi-energy sensory array in the investigation of haunting and poltergeist cases. *Journal of the Society for Psychical Research*, 62. 324–336.
Houran, J., and R. Lange (eds.) (2001). *Hauntings and Poltergeists: Multidisciplinary Perspectives*. Jefferson, NC: McFarland.
Hufford, D. J. (1982). *The Terror That Comes in the Night: An Experience-Centered Study of Supernatural Assault Traditions*. Philadelphia: University of Pennsylvania Press.
Hufford, D. J. (2001). An experience-centered approach to hauntings. In J. Houran and R. Lange (eds.), *Hauntings and Poltergeists: Multidisciplinary Perspectives*. Jefferson, NC: McFarland. 18–40.
Irwin, H. J. (1994). The phenomenology of parapsychological experiences. In S. Krippner (ed.), *Advances in Parapsychological Research Volume 7*. Jefferson, NC: McFarland. 10–76.
Irwin, H. J. (1999). *An Introduction to Parapsychology*. Third edition. Jefferson, NC: McFarland.
Irwin, H. J., and C. A. Watt (2007). *An Introduction to Parapsychology*. Fifth edition. Jefferson, NC: McFarland.
Jones, S. (2006). Reviewing the Black Dog witch project. *Fortean Times*, 209. 53.
Lange, R., and J. Houran (1997). Context induced paranormal experiences: Support for Houran and Lange's model of haunting phenomena. *Perceptual and Motor Skills*, 84. 1455–1458.
Lange, R., and J. Houran (2001). Ambiguous stimuli brought to life: The psychological dynamics of hauntings and poltergeists. In J. Houran and R. Lange (eds.), *Hauntings and Poltergeists: Multidisciplinary Perspectives*. Jefferson, NC: McFarland. 280–306.
MacKenzie, A. (1982). *Hauntings and Apparitions*. London: Heinemann.
Maher, M. C. (1999). Riding the waves in search of the particles: A modern study of ghosts and apparitions. *Journal of Parapsychology*, 63. 47–80.
Maher, M. C. (2000). Quantitative investigation of the General Wayne Inn. *Journal of Parapsychology*, 64. 365–390.
Mavromatis, A. (1987). *Hypnagogia: The Unique State of Consciousness Between Wakefulness and Sleep*. London: Routledge & Kegan Paul.
McClenon, J. (1994a). Surveys of anomalous experience: A cross-cultural analysis. *Journal of the American Society for Psychical Research*, 88. 117–135.
McClenon, J. (1994b). *Wondrous Events: Foundations of Religious Belief*. Philadelphia: University of Pennsylvania Press.
McCue, P. (2002). Theories of haunting: A critical overview. *Journal of the Society for Psychical Research*, 66. 1–21.
McEwan, G. J. (1986). *Mystery Animals of Britain and Ireland*. London: Robert Hale.
Miles, C. (1908). Experiments in thought transference. *Journal of the Society for Psychical Research*. 243–262.
Miller, K. (1984). The Black Dog and other canine apparitions in Lincolnshire. In N. Field and A. White (eds.), *A Prospect of Lincolnshire*. Lincoln: Field & White. 130–137.
Moody, R. with P. Perry (1993). *Reunions: Visionary Encounters with Departed Loved Ones*. London: Little, Brown and Company.

Neppe, V. M. (1990). Anomalistic experience and the cerebral cortex. In S. Krippner (ed.), *Advances in Parapsychological Research Volume 6*. Jefferson, NC: McFarland. 168–183.
O'Donnell, E. (1913). *Animal Ghosts or Animal Hauntings and the Hereafter*. London: William Rider & Son.
Osis, K. (1986). Characteristics of purposeful action in an apparition case. *Journal of the American Society for Psychical Research*, 80. 175–193.
Osis, K., and E. Haraldsson (1986). Deathbed observations by physicians and nurses: A cross-cultural survey. *Journal of the American Society for Psychical Research*, 71. 237–259.
Persinger, M. A. (1989). Psi phenomena and temporal lobe activity: The geomagnetic factor. In L. A. Henkel and R. Berger (eds.), *Research in parapsychology 1988*. Metuchen, NJ: Scarecrow Press. 121–156.
Persinger, M. A., and S. A. Koren (2001). Predicting the characteristics of haunt phenomena from geomagnetic factors and brain sensitivity: Evidence from field and experimental studies. In J. Houran, and R. Lange (eds.), *Hauntings and Poltergeists: Multidisciplinary Perspectives*. Jefferson, NC: McFarland. 179–194.
Price, H. H. (1938–1939). Haunting and the "Psychic Ether" hypothesis; with some preliminary reflections on the present condition and possible future of psychical research. *Proceedings of the Society for Psychical Research*, 45. 307–343.
Radin, D. I. (2001). Seeking spirits in the laboratory. In J. Houran, and R. Lange (eds.), *Hauntings and Poltergeists: Multidisciplinary Perspectives*. Jefferson, NC: McFarland. 164–178.
Rajaram, M., and S. Mitra (1981). Correlations between convulsive seizures and geomagnetic activity. *Neuroscience Letters*, 24. 187–191.
Reeve, C. (1988). *A Straunge & Terrible Wunder*. Bungay, Suffolk: Morrow & Co.
Rogo, D. S. (1986). *Life After Death: The Case for Survival of Bodily Death*. London: Guild.
Roll, W. G., and M. A. Persinger (2001). Investigations of poltergeists and haunts: A review and interpretation. In J. Houran and R. Lange (eds.), *Hauntings and Poltergeists: Multidisciplinary Perspectives*. Jefferson, NC: McFarland. 123–163.
Rudkin, E. H. (1938). The Black Dog. *Folklore, XLIX*. 111–131.
Schmeidler, G. R. (1966). Quantitative investigation of a "haunted house." *Journal of the American Society for Psychical Research*, 60. 137–149.
Sherwood, S. J. (2000). Black Dog apparitions. *Journal of the American Society for Psychical Research*, 94. 151–164.
Sherwood, S.J. (2002). Relationship between the hypnagogic/hypnopompic states and reports of anomalous experiences. *Journal of Parapsychology*, 66. 127–150.
Sherwood, S. J. (2004). The Black Dog of Uplyme. *The Paranormal Review*, 32. 3–4.
Sherwood, S. J. (2005). A psychological approach to apparitions of Black Dogs. In B. Trubshaw (ed.), *Explore Phantom Black Dogs*. Wymeswold, UK: Heart of Albion Press. 21–35.
Sidgwick, H., A. Johnson, F. W. H. Myers, F. Podmore and E. M. Sidgwick (1894). Report on the Census of Hallucinations. *Proceedings of the Society for Psychical Research*, 10. 25–422.
Stevenson, I. (1982). The contribution of apparitions to the evidence for survival. *Journal of the American Society for Psychical Research*, 76. 341–358.
Tandy, V. (2000). Something in the cellar. *Journal of the Society for Psychical Research*, 64. 129–140.
Tandy, V., and T. R. Lawrence (1998). The ghost in the machine. *Journal of the Society for Psychical Research*, 62. 360–364.
Trubshaw, B. (ed.) (2005). *Explore Phantom Black Dogs*. Wymeswold, UK: Heart of Albion Press.
Tyrrell, G. N. M. (1943/1973). *Apparitions*. London: The Society for Psychical Research.
Westwood, J. (2005). Friend or foe? Norfolk traditions of Shuck. In B. Trubshaw (ed.), *Explore phantom Black Dogs*. Wymeswold, UK: Heart of Albion Press. 57–76.
Wilkinson, H. P., and A. Gauld (1993). Geomagnetism and anomalous experiences, 1868–1980. *Proceedings of the Society for Psychical Research*, 57. 275–310.
Williams, B. J. (2001). The ghost in the mind: A brain-environment interaction model of the apparitional experience. *Proceedings of the 44th Parapsychological Association Convention*. 364–376.
Wiseman, R., C. Watt, E. Greening, P. Stevens and C. O'Keeffe (2003). An investigation into alleged "hauntings." *British Journal of Psychology*, 94. 195–211.

10

PSYCHOLOGICAL ASPECTS OF THE ALIEN CONTACT EXPERIENCE*

Christopher C. French, Julia Santomauro,
Victoria Hamilton, Rachel Fox
and Michael Thalbourne†

Although it is hard to estimate just how many people have conscious memories of apparently being abducted by aliens (French, 2001), it is likely that the figure runs into at least several thousand worldwide. These memories often involve such elements as being taken on board spaceships and being subjected to medical examination. Several commentators have considered the psychological factors that may be relevant to understanding this phenomenon (e.g., Appelle, Lynn and Newman, 2000; Baker, 1992; Clancy, 2005; French, 2001; Holden and French, 2002; Newman and Baumeister, 1996; Spanos, 1996).

Clancy, McNally, Schacter, Lenzenweger and Pitman (2002) used a variant of the Deese/Roediger-McDermott (DRM) paradigm (Deese, 1959; Roediger and McDermott, 1995) to investigate this possibility. The paradigm involves the presentation of word lists to participants. Within each list, all of the words presented are associated with a single theme word, often referred to as the *critical lure*, that is itself not presented. For example, the list might include the words *sour, candy, bitter,* and *sugar,* all of which are strongly associated with the word *sweet*, although the word *sweet* would not itself be presented. On subsequent recall and recognition tests, a substantial proportion

---

*This chapter was published in a special issue of Cortex: French, C.C., Santomauro, J., Hamilton, V., Fox, R., and Thalbourne, M. "Psychological Aspects of the Alien Contact Experience," Cortex, 44, 1387–1395. Copyright © 2008 Elsevier.
†Thanks are due to the Bial Foundation for supporting this work and to all participants, especially to the experiencers for their courage and honesty in discussing their perplexing experiences with us.

of the participants are likely to report that the word *sweet* was in fact presented. Using this technique, Clancy et al. compared three groups. The first group consisted of people with conscious (allegedly "recovered") memories of having been abducted by aliens, the second consisted of people who believed they had been abducted by aliens but had no conscious memories of the event, and the third consisted of people who did not believe that they had ever been so abducted. The groups differed in terms of their propensity to falsely recognize lure words, with the first group showing the highest susceptibility and the third group the lowest.

A great deal of indirect evidence also supports the hypothesis that those reporting memories of alien contact ("experiencers") might be more susceptible to false memories. Many of the psychological variables that appear to be correlated with susceptibility to false memories are also correlated with paranormal belief and the tendency to report anomalous experiences, including claims of alien contact (French, 2003).

For example, a number of studies have reported that susceptibility to false memories appears to be correlated with dissociativity (e.g., Eisen and Carlson, 1998; Heaps and Nash, 1999; Wilson and French, 2006; Winograd, Peluso and Glover, 1998). Dissociation can be thought of as a lack of integration between conscious awareness and mental activity. Powers (1994) reported higher levels of dissociativity amongst experiencers than control samples.

Tellegen and Atkinson (1974) define the personality trait of absorption as "openness to absorbing and self-altering experiences, a trait related to hypnotic susceptibility." A number of studies have reported an association between susceptibility to false memories and absorption (e.g., Eisen and Carlson, 1998; Platt, Lacey, Iobst and Finkelman, 1998) and Clancy et al. (2002) reported that their experiencer samples had significantly higher absorption scores than the control sample.

The concept of fantasy proneness was first discussed by Wilson and Barber (1983). The fantasy prone personality has an extremely rich and vivid fantasy life, claiming that their fantasies are "as real as real." They admit that sometimes they confuse imagination and real events. They report vivid childhood memories, a wide range of ostensibly paranormal experiences, and intense religious experiences. They often believe that they themselves have strong psychic abilities, such as healing.

Differences in fantasy proneness between experiencers and non-experiencers have not previously been demonstrated using questionnaires (Rodeghier, Goodpaster and Blatterbauer, 1991; Spanos, Cross, Dickson and Dubreuil, 1993), although it should be noted that among participants reporting UFO-related experiences, the intensity of the experience was found to correlate with fantasy proneness by Spanos et al. (1993). Retrospective biographical analyses, on the other hand, have suggested that experiencers do demonstrate features of fantasy proneness (e.g., Bartholomew, Basterfield and Howard, 1991).

Dissociativity, absorption and fantasy proneness are overlapping concepts and all three inter-correlate significantly (e.g., Glicksohn and Barrett, 2003). The association between such variables and susceptibility to false memories is often discussed within the framework of models of reality monitoring (e.g., Johnson and Raye, 1981). Any factor which makes it more difficult to distinguish between past mental events that were internally generated (as a result of imagination, dreams, fantasy, and so on) and those which are based upon memories for objective events will heighten susceptibility to false memories. If a general problem in reality monitoring underlies this type of psychological profile, one would expect that similar problems would arise in the perceptual domain; that is to say, such individuals might also be expected to be more prone to hallucinations. This does indeed appear to be the case (e.g., Glicksohn and Barrett, 2003).

Recent systematic research by Basterfield and Thalbourne (2002) has confirmed anecdotal reports (e.g., Basterfield, 2001; Bullard, 1987; Druffel and Rogo, 1980; Evans, 1983, 1998; Gotlib, 1994; Mack, 1994; Randles, 1988; Schwarz, 1983; Spencer, 1994; Vallee, 1977) of higher levels of paranormal belief and reports of ostensibly paranormal experiences among those claiming alien contact. The current project attempted to replicate this basic finding.

Many commentators believe that the experience of sleep paralysis is one of the triggers that lead some people to develop the belief that they have been abducted by aliens (e.g., Holden and French, 2002; McNally and Clancy, 2005). Sleep paralysis is a common but frightening experience that takes place in the state between sleep and wakefulness (French and Santomauro, 2007). During sleep paralysis, sufferers become aware of the fact that they cannot move and the general cognitive state of the sufferer appears to be a blend of normal waking consciousness and dream mentation. Sleep paralysis is often associated with a strong sense of presence, visual and auditory hallucinations, intense fear, difficulty breathing, and anomalous sensations such as out-of-body experiences. It is a common belief among ufologists that these symptoms are indicators of probable alien abduction even though the sufferer may initially have no actual memories of aliens whatsoever. Anyone encountering such claims who had suffered from sleep paralysis would therefore run the risk of accepting this apparent explanation for their own puzzling experiences, possibly ultimately resulting in a detailed false memory of alien contact if techniques are employed, such as hypnosis or guided imagery, to "recover" the memory that the individual now feels must have been repressed.

A number of specific hypotheses were therefore tested in this project: (a) experiencers would be more susceptible to false memories than an age- and gender-matched control group in terms of false recall and false recognition on a version of the DRM task; (b) experiencers would have higher scores on various questionnaire measures assessing the psychological factors described above and (c) experiencers would report higher levels of the incidence of sleep paralysis.

Method

PARTICIPANTS

The experiencer category included anyone who claimed to have had extraterrestrial contact. These reported experiences included UFO sightings (repeatedly over many years in most cases), with the age of the first sighting varying from four years old or less to the late twenties. Most experiencers reported direct contact with a variety of alien life-forms as well as telepathic communication with aliens. Of the 19 experiencers who took part in the study, many reported experiences which reflect common themes in the UFO literature. For example, six reported believing that the aliens had implanted some device in their bodies, one believed that his terrestrial parents were not his real parents (his real parents being extraterrestrials), two reported finding marks on their bodies caused by the aliens, one reported "missing time" experiences, and three reported believing that aliens had removed fetuses from them or caused them to have miscarriages. A wide variety of other alien-related memories were also reported.

Participants were recruited via newspaper and radio publicity of the project, web site appeals and word of mouth. The experiencer and control groups were matched on age and gender and each consisted of 19 participants, 8 male and 11 female. The mean age of the experiencers was 45.0 years (SD = 13.7), ranging from 23 to 72 years. The mean age of the control group was 45.5 years (SD = 14.5), ranging from 21 to 74 years. Participants came from a wide range of backgrounds. They were tested either at Goldsmiths College, another educational institution, or in their own homes. They received traveling expenses and a small payment (typically £10) in return for their participation.

MATERIALS

Participants completed the following paper-based questionnaires:

Anomalous Experiences Inventory (AEI; Kumar, Pekala and Gallagher, 1994): This is a 70-item true-false inventory examining self-reports of beliefs and experiences of paranormal phenomena. It consists of various sub-scales: paranormal belief (Belief, 12 items, e.g., "I believe that mind can control matter"), anomalous/paranormal experiences (Experience, 29 items, e.g., "I often seem to become aware of events before they happen"), paranormal ability (Ability, 16 items, e.g., "I can influence or change an event by concentrating on that event"), fear of the paranormal (Fear, 6 items, e.g., "Hearing about the paranormal or psychic experiences is very scary"), and use of drugs and alcohol (Drugs, 7 items, e.g., "I have tried mind-altering substances"). The scale is acceptable in terms of its psychometric properties (Gallagher, Kumar and Pekala, 1994).

Wilson-Barber Inventory of Childhood Memories and Imaginings: Children's Form (ICMIC, Myers, 1983): This is a 48-item true-false inventory that examines memory for imaginative activities and fantasies from childhood and how childhood imaginings affect adult experiences or remain a part of adult functioning (e.g., "When I was younger, I enjoyed fairytales," "Now, I still live in a make-believe world some of the time"). It is the most widely used questionnaire measure of fantasy proneness and has satisfactory reliability and validity (Myers, 1983).

Launay-Slade Hallucination Scale (LSHS: Launay and Slade, 1981): This scale consists of 12 true-false items measuring predisposition to hallucinations. The items include questions about vivid or intrusive thoughts (e.g., "Sometimes a passing thought will seem so real that it frightens me"), vivid daydreams (e.g., "The sounds I hear in my daydreams are generally clear and distinct"), overt auditory hallucinations (e.g., "I often hear a voice speaking my thoughts aloud") and overt visual hallucinations ("On occasions I have seen a person's face in front of me when no-one was in fact there"). The scale has been shown to be reliable (e.g., Bentall and Slade, 1985) and valid (e.g., Serper, Dill, Chang, Kot and Elliot, 2005).

Tellegen's Absorption Scale (TAS; Tellegen and Atkinson, 1974): A 35-item true-false scale comprising measures of openness to experience cognitive-affective alterations across a range of situations, with good levels of validity and reliability (e.g., Glicksohn and Barrett, 2003).

Australian Sheep-Goat Scale (ASGS; Thalbourne, 1995): The 18-item true-false version of this scale measures various aspects of belief in and experience of the paranormal. Items relate to the three core concepts of the paranormal: extrasensory perception (e.g., "I believe in the existence of ESP"), psychokinesis (e.g., "I believe I have personally exerted PK on at least one occasion"), and life after death (e.g., "I believe in life after death"). The scale is widely used and has proven validity and reliability (Thalbourne, 1995; Thalbourne and Delin, 1993).

Curious Experiences Survey (CES; Goldberg, 1999): This 31-item measure is a revised version of the Dissociative Experiences Scale (Bernstein and Putnam, 1986) including three new items and a more user-friendly 5-option response format. Respondents are asked to indicate how often they have had various experiences (such as "found myself dressed in clothes I didn't remember putting on" and "felt like I was dreaming when I was awake"). Psychometric properties of the scale are satisfactory (Goldberg, 1999).

Nocturnal Experiences Questionnaire (NEC; French, Rose and Blackmore, 2002): This scale assesses the self-reported incidence of episodes of sleep paralysis as well as details of typical episodes. The only response analyzed for this report relates to self-reported incidence. Participants responded to the following question: "Have you ever had the experience as you were going to sleep, or perhaps as you were waking up, of feeling paralyzed, as if you could not move your arms or legs and could not speak or cry out?" Response options were "Never," "Once," "Two to five times" and "More than five times."

Procedure

Participants first completed the pencil-and-paper tests described above, without any imposed time limit (they typically took about 20 minutes). They then completed a computerized version of the Deese/Roediger-McDermott (DRM) task. The version used was based closely upon Experiment 1 of Robinson and Roediger's (1997) study. The twenty-four 15-word study lists and the accompanying critical lures that were used in Robinson and Roediger's Experiment 1, Clancy et al.'s (2002) experiment and Roediger and McDermott's (1995) Experiment 2 were modified for use in this experiment (e.g., by Anglicizing some of the more American words). Randomized word sequences were matched between participants in the control group and the experiencer group. Twenty lists were presented in total, four lists each of 3, 6, 9, 12 and 15 words. Participants studied the first 3, 6, 9, 12 or 15 words from each list as they appeared in the appendix of Roediger and McDermott (1995). The order in which the lists were presented was chosen randomly for each participant (but matched between groups). All words were presented on a computer screen in white on a black background.

Participants were instructed to pay close attention to the words presented to them because they would be asked to recall them later. The words from the first randomly chosen list were presented to the participant in a continuous sequence in the centre of the computer screen for 2 seconds each. Then a distracter task was given which consisted of four 2-digit addition sums that were presented on the screen and participants were instructed to complete these sums on paper. The participants had 30 seconds in which to do this.

Participants were asked to recall and write down on paper as many of the presented words as they could remember from the each list. They were asked not to guess any words. Robinson and Roediger (1997) reported that "casual observation revealed that most subjects completed recalling well before the end of the recall period" which in their experiment was 1.5 minutes. We chose to allow 6 seconds per word studied for the recall task. This procedure was repeated for all lists.

After all 20 of the lists of words had been presented a recognition task was given. This consisted of 80 words being presented one at a time on the computer screen with participants responding using the Y (yes) and N (no) keys on the keyboard. The 80 words comprised: the 24 critical lures, 8 unrelated filler items, 2 words each from the 20 presented lists (these 2 words were randomly selected from the first 3 words on each of the 20 lists) and 2 words each from each of the 4 lists that were not presented (again these 2 words were randomly selected from the first 3 words on each of the 4 lists).

Participants then completed some computerized tests of psychic functioning and finally a semi-structured interview about their experiences and general background (only the results of the pencil-and-paper tests and the memory tests will be reported here). All participants were fully debriefed following the completion of data collection.

RESULTS

Considering first the results of the computerized memory tests, separate ANOVAs were carried out on the false recall and false recognition data, each with list length (3, 6, 9, 12, and 15 semantic associates) as a repeated measures factor and participant group (experiencer vs. control) as a between-group factor (recognition data for one experiencer were lost due to technical problems). A summary of these data is presented in Table 1. List length was included as a factor in the analysis as previous research (e.g., Robinson and Roediger, 1997; Clancy et al., 2002) has shown that false recall and false recognition rates increase as a function of the number of semantic associates presented. These findings were replicated in the present study with significant main effects for list length with respect to both recall ($F(4, 144) = 22.03$, $p < .001$, partial ($\eta^2 = .38$) and recognition ($F(4, 140) = 8.86$, $p < .001$, partial ($\eta^2 = .20$). However, no significant effect of participant group was found ($F(1, 36) = .01$, partial ($\eta^2 = .00$, for recall; $F(1, 35) = 1.88$, partial ($\eta^2 = .05$, for recognition), despite the fact that the experiencer group showed higher levels of false recognition at all list lengths (see Table 1). The interaction between participant group and list length was also non-significant in both analyses ($F(4, 144) = .01$, partial ($\eta^2 = .01$, for recall; $F(4, 140) = .50$, partial ($\eta^2 = .01$, for recognition).

Table 1*

Number of Associates

	3	6	9	12	15	Overall
False Recall						
Experiencers (N = 19)						
Prop.	.03	.18	.38	.42	.32	.27
SD	(.08)	(.20)	(.26)	(.26)	(.25)	(.15)
Controls (N = 19)						
Prop.	.04	.22	.34	.38	.37	.27
SD	(.09)	(.22)	(.24)	(.28)	(.29)	(.13)
False Recognition						
Experiencers (N = 18)						
Prop.	.40	.56	.59	.67	.74	.59
SD	(.31)	(.28)	(.34)	(.28)	(.28)	(.24)
Controls (N = 19)						
Prop.	.33	.43	.58	.54	.58	.49
SD	(.28)	(.26)	(.34)	(.29)	(.35)	(.21)

*False recall and false recognition data for each group by list type

Questionnaire scores of the experiencer and control group participants were compared using unrelated t-tests (two-tailed). A summary of the results of these analyses is presented in Table 2. Significant differences were found between the groups for all measures except AEI (Fear), AEI (Drugs and Alcohol Use) and scores on the ICMIC, with the difference in scores on the latter approaching statistical significance. Non-parametric analysis of the single item relating to incidence of sleep paralysis from the Nocturnal Experiences Questionnaire (French et al., 2002) revealed that the self-reported incidence of sleep paralysis was higher in the experiencers than the control group (Mann Whitney U = 83, p = .002).

Correlations between the main psychometric measures used in this study across both participant groups combined are presented in Table 3. In line with previous studies, all of the main measures intercorrelate at a highly significant level. Table 4 presents the correlations between these measures and the total false recall and false recognition scores across all participants. No significant correlations were found for false recall scores, but false recognition scores correlated with absorption and tendency to hallucinate (although these correlations would not have remained significant had alpha levels been adjusted for multiple testing).

Table 2*

Scale	N in Each Group	Experiencer Mean (SD)	Control Mean (SD)	Mean Difference (SD)	95% CIs Lower	95% CIs Upper	t-value (df)	p	Omega-Squared
AEI: Experience	17	17.88 (5.60)	3.65 (4.78)	14.23 (1.79)	10.60	17.87	7.97 (32)	<.001	.65
AEI: Belief	18	9.89 (1.61)	4.28 (3.32)	5.61 (.87)	3.81	7.40	6.45 (24.52)	<.001	.60
AEI: Ability	18	6.72 (3.08)	1.33 (2.35)	5.39 (.91)	3.53	7.25	5.90 (34)	<.001	.48
AEI: Fear	18	1.22 (.88)	1.22 (1.35)	.00 (.38)	-.77	.77	.00 (34)	not sig.	.00
AEI: Drugs/Alcohol	18	2.44 (1.54)	2.33 (1.61)	.11 (.53)	-.96	1.18	.21 (34)	not sig.	.00
TAS	19	20.42 (7.38)	12.89 (6.02)	7.53 (2.19)	3.10	11.96	3.45 (36)	.001	.22
LSHS	19	4.16 (2.95)	2.26 (1.97)	1.90 (.81)	.25	3.54	2.33 (36)	.026	.10
ASGS	19	28.26 (4.47)	9.42 (8.81)	18.84 (2.27)	14.25	23.44	8.32 (26.70)	<.001	.70
ICMIC	19	19.00 (8.28)	13.21 (10.16)	5.79 (3.00)	-.31	11.89	1.93 (36)	not sig. (p = .062)	.07
CES	19	56.05 (18.42)	45.47 (7.72)	10.58 (4.58)	1.29	19.87	2.31 (36)	.027	.10

*Summary of unrelated t-test comparisons (two-tailed) between experiencers and control group on psychometric measures.

Key: AEI = Anomalous Experiences Inventory; TAS = Tellegen's Absorption Scale; LSHS = Launay-Slade Hallucinations Scale; ASGS = Australian Sheep-Goat Scale; ICMIC = Inventory of Childhood Memories and Imaginings: Children's Form; CES = Curious Experiences Survey.

Note: If Levene's test showed significantly different variances, degrees of freedom were adjusted accordingly. Occasionally, participants omitted to respond to one or more items from the administered scales. When this happened, both their score and that of their matched participant were omitted from the relevant analysis.

Table 3*

	AEI:B	AEI:A	TAS	LSHS	ASGS	ICMIC	CES
AEI: Experience	.833	.904	.782	.661	.861	.718	.675
AEI: Belief		.754	.562	.498[a]	.883	.656	.541[b]
AEI: Ability			.693	.622	.854	.602	.665
TAS				.759	.543	.776	.744
LSHS					.456[c]	.561	.449[d]
ASGS						.561	.449
ICMIC							.689

*Pearson intercorrelations between the main psychometric measures used in this study across both participant groups combined. N = 38, except for AEI: Belief and AEI: Ability (N = 37) and AEI: Experience (N = 35), due to missing data.

Note: All two-tailed p-values (not corrected for multiple tests) <.001 except those marked with superscripts, which had p-values as follows: a = .002, b = .001, c = .004, and d = .005. Key: As for Table 2.

Table 4*

	False Recall	False Recognition
AEI: Experience	.012	.260
N	36	35
AEI: Belief	-.043	.192
N	37	36
AEI: Ability	.015	.138
N	37	36
TAS	.002	.346[a]
N	38	37
LSHS	.173	.400[b]
N	38	37
ASGS	-.023	.198
N	38	37
ICMIC	.064	.283
N	38	37
CES	.071	.144
N	38	37

*Pearson Correlations Between the Main psychometric measures used in this study and total scores for false recall and false recognition across both participant groups combined (note that some N values, given in italics, are less than 38 due to missing data).

Note: All two-tailed p-values (not corrected for multiple tests) >.05 except those marked with superscripts, which had p-values as follows: a = .036 and b = .014.

Key: as for Table 2.

Discussion

Our results confirm that experiencers have a different psychological profile from non-experiencers in that they show higher levels of belief in and experience of the paranormal, self-reported paranormal abilities, tendency to hallucinate, absorption, dissociativity, and incidence of sleep paralysis. In considering the marginally significant difference between the groups on fantasy proneness, note that when these data were analyzed using either a related *t*-test or a one-tailed unrelated *t*-test, both of which would be justifiable, the difference between the groups is significant. It seems reasonable to conclude therefore that our results also show higher levels of fantasy proneness in experiencers than controls.

Much current theorizing and experimental work regarding susceptibility to both false memories and hallucinations is based upon the reality monitoring model proposed by Johnson and Raye (1981; see also Johnson, Nolde, Mather, Kounios, Schacter and Curran, 1993). This approach proposes that hallucinations arise as a consequence of a source monitoring error whereby internally generated imagery is misattributed to an external source. Similarly, false memories may arise if memories of internally generated events such as imaginings, fantasies and dreams are wrongly interpreted as memories for events which actually took place in objective reality (French, 2003). The decision as to whether a memory refers to an internally generated mental event or an external event is based partly upon the characteristics of the memory itself (e.g., the amount of perceptual detail, with memories for external events typically having more perceptual detail and clarity than mental events). Additionally, however, the criteria used to decide whether a memory is "real" or not also depends upon the criteria used to make this decision. Individuals may vary in the degree to which they are willing to accept, say, a fleeting image as a genuine memory fragment for an event which really took place.

The reality monitoring model provides a useful framework for understanding why the psychological profile of experiencers, and believers in the paranormal in general, may be susceptible to hallucinations and false memories which may form the basis for their reports of ostensibly paranormal experiences. With respect to hallucinations, it could either be the case that reports of hallucinatory experiences reflect particularly vivid imagery or the application of lax criteria in distinguishing imagination from perception. For example, absorption, dissociation and fantasy-proneness are all correlated with hypnotic suggestibility as assessed by standard scales. In this context, a number of investigators have used the "White Christmas" test to investigate susceptibility to hallucinations in both psychotic and normal samples (e.g., Barber and Calverley, 1964; Mintz and Alpert, 1972; Young, Bentall, Slade and Dewey, 1987). These studies generally involve asking participants to imagine hearing the Bing Crosby classic although the song itself is not actually played. A substantial majority of hallucinating schizophrenic patients report hearing a clear auditory image during the test, but so do a substantial minority of non-psychotic participants, especially those scoring high on the LSHS. Some participants report believing that the record was actually being played. Such findings have been interpreted as either reflecting hallucinatory reports based upon vivid imagery (e.g., Mintz and Alpert, 1972) or lax judgment criteria (e.g., Bentall and Slade, 1985). Merckelbach and van de Ven (2001) replicated the basic effect with a sample of student participants, showing that participants who reported hearing "White Christmas" against a white noise background scored more highly on the LSHS and a measure of fantasy proneness. They proposed that another possible explanation of this phenomenon might be the tendency on the part of fantasy prone participants to endorse odd items. Clearly, none of these explanations is mutually exclusive and further research is required. However, it is worth noting that a number of investigators have presented evidence suggesting more vivid self-reported imagery in believers in the paranormal than non-believers (e.g., Diamond and Taft, 1975; Finch, 2002; Greening, 2002).

The reality monitoring framework has also been useful in interpreting findings from investigations of the neural correlates of false memory using the DRM and similar paradigms (see Schacter and Slotnick, 2004, for a review). With respect to the DRM, it is assumed that strong activation of the critical lure words is a consequence of spreading semantic activation from the associated words that are presented, i.e., it is an internally generated mental event. However, memories of the words which are actually presented would be associated with a higher level of sensory reactivation than the lure words. Early neuroimaging studies (Schacter, Buckner, Koutstall, Dale and Rosen, 1997; Schacter, Reiman, Curran, Yun, Bandy, McDermott and Roediger, 1996) demonstrated that brain areas typically involved in episodic memory processing (including dorsolateral/anterior prefrontal, medial parietal, and medial temporal regions) were preferentially activated during both true and false recognition compared to a common baseline. Subsequent fMRI research by Cabeza, Rao, Wagner, Mayer and Schacter (2001), however, showed that if the perceptual processing of stimuli was increased at the encoding phase, differences between true and false recognition in terms of brain activation did emerge. Specifically, greater activation occurred for true recognition within two regions of the medial temporal lobe, i.e., the parahippocampal gyrus and the hippocampus, suggesting greater recovery of sensory or contextual information during true than false recognition. Okado and Stark (2003) used fMRI to study brain activation during true recognition of previously perceived events and false recognition of previously imagined events. A number of regions showed relatively greater activation during true recognition, including bilateral occipital cortices and right parahippocampal gyrus. This was once again interpreted as reflecting greater activation associated with the retrieval of perceptual information for true memories.

Recent research using fMRI has even begun to distinguish between different types of false memory. Garoff-Eaton, Slotnick and Schacter (2005) used the fMRI technique to investigate neural activity associated with true recognition of abstract shapes, false memory for related abstract shapes and false memory for unrelated abstract shapes. Greater activity in the prefrontal cortex, the parietal cortex and the medial temporal lobe were associated with both true recognition and related false recognition, whereas unrelated false recognition was associated with activity in language processing regions.

A similar picture emerges when we consider the recent history of event-related potential (ERP) studies of true and false recognition, which allow for greater temporal resolution of the neural processes involved at the expense of spatial precision. Early studies (Düzel, Yonelinas, Mangun, Heinze and Tulving, 1997; Johnson et al., 1997) suggested that brain activity was very similar for both types of recognition but more recent studies (e.g., Curran, Schacter, Johnson and Spinks, 2001; Fabiani, Stadler and Wessels, 2000) have revealed consistent differences between the two. Specifically, greater activation over the parietal area between 400 and 800 ms has been interpreted as a marker for sensory reactivation during true recognition.

The reality monitoring framework can also be applied to consideration of the differences in brain activation associated with false recognition in contrast to correct rejection. Gonsalves and Paller (2000) presented participants with words and instructed them to imagine the common objects to which they referred. On some trials, a photograph of the object was presented 1800 ms after the word. Recognition memory for the photographs was subsequently tested and participants sometimes indicated that a photograph had been presented when in fact the object had only been imagined. Posterior ERPs were more positive at encoding for words which subsequently produced false recognition of the associated photograph, consistent with the idea that more vivid imagery was associated with greater activation of sensory cortex at encoding. In a subsequent fMRI version of this investigation, Gonsalves, Reber, Gittelman, Parrish, Mesulam and Paller (2004) again found greater activation at encoding in areas associated with visual imagery and spatial attention, including precuneus and inferior parietal cortex, for false memories of imagined objects than for correct rejections. These findings support the idea that stronger visual imagery will produce more reality monitoring errors by making it more difficult to distinguish between memories for perceived and imagined events.

It is clear that our understanding of the neural underpinnings of false recognition is becoming clearer thanks to the application of modern neuroimaging techniques during performance on the DRM and similar tasks. However, no differences were found between our groups in terms of performance on the DRM task in the current study. Our failure to replicate the effects reported by Clancy et al. (2002) is puzzling. It should be noted that we used a different version of the DRM task to that used by Clancy and colleagues (e.g., we presented the word lists visually on a computer screen whereas they presented the lists on a tape recorder) but one would not anticipate that such changes in procedure would make much difference to the results if the findings reported by Clancy et al. reflected general differences between the groups in terms of susceptibility to false memories.

One possible reason for the apparent discrepancy between our results on the DRM task and those of Clancy et al. is the difference between our participant samples. Their study involved three different types of participant: those who had apparently "recovered" (typically as a result of hypnotic regression) once-forgotten memories of alien abduction, those who believed that they had been so abducted (typically based upon memories for sleep paralysis) but had no conscious memories of the event, and those who did not believe that they had been so abducted. The three groups all differed in their susceptibility to false memories as assessed by the DRM task. None of their participants, therefore, reported memories of alien contact that they claimed they had always been able to remember. In contrast, only six of our experiencers reported ever having been hypnotized. This does not, of course, indicate that their claims of alien contact reflected true memories as there are many ways in which false memories can occur other than the use of hypnotic regression and other so-called "memory recovery" techniques, such as the use of guided imagery. For example, it seems likely that people with an interest in UFOs would be likely to imagine what it would be like to experience alien contact as a result of media exposure to such accounts. It is well-established that simply imagining events that did not actually occur can lead susceptible individuals to believe that they did occur, an effect referred to as *imagination inflation* (e.g., Garry, Manning, Loftus and Sherman, 1996).

Given the psychological profile of our sample of experiencers, it seems plausible that a greater susceptibility to false memories might be demonstrated in such participants if a different technique were used to measure this susceptibility. Misremembering words from lists is intuitively quite different from reporting detailed false memories for entire episodes and it is by no means clear at this stage that identical psychological and neuronal processes underlie the two. One obvious candidate for an alternative technique to investigate possible differences between experiencers and controls in terms of susceptibility to false memories would be the imagination inflation method referred to above. A second possibility would be the use of the so-called "crashing memories" paradigm. This involves asking participants to recall where they were, who they were with, and what they were doing when they first saw the footage of memorable events in the news. Previous research has shown that sizeable minorities of respondents will report such details even for real events that were never actually caught on camera (e.g., the crashing of an El Al Boeing 747 into a block of flats in Amsterdam: Crombag, Wagenaar and van Koppen, 1996; the car crash in Paris in which Princess Diana and Dodi Fayed lost their lives: Ost, Vrij, Costall and Bull, 2002). Wilson and French (2006) recently employed this technique and demonstrated that those participants reporting false memories of non-existent footage of a bombing in a Bali nightclub scored higher than other respondents on various measures on paranormal belief and experience.

Although much has been learned regarding the patterns of brain activation associated with false recognition, considerably less research has been directed at activation patterns associated with false recall. This is mainly due to the fact that there are many experimental techniques, such as the DRM, that are suitable for use in neuroimaging studies, which require sufficient numbers of time-locked trials of different types to allow for the separation of signal from noise. Such paradigms do not currently exist with respect to the formation of false memories for entire episodes and may, arguably, be impossible to develop. However, suitable techniques that focused on other aspects of false recall might be developed for use in future neuroimaging studies. Neuroimaging approaches have great potential in terms of improving various aspects of our understanding of the neuropsychology of susceptibility to false memories such as whether individual differences reflect strength of imagery or the adoption of lax criteria.

The psychological profile of the experiencers who took part in this study appears to be simply an extreme version of the psychological profile of believers in the paranormal in general and that profile appears to be one that would be associated with greater susceptibility to hallucinations and false memories. This supports the argument that at least some reports of ostensibly paranormal experiences are likely to be based upon hallucinations and false memories (French, 2003; French and Wilson, 2006). It should be borne in mind, however, that direct personal experience of ostensibly paranormal events is only one of the factors that underlie paranormal belief. Others include acceptance of such reports from trusted others and positive media coverage of such claims. Future researchers should pay greater attention to the distinction between those who claim direct personal experience of the paranormal and those who believe for other reasons. It is only the former that we would expect to demonstrate similar (if possibly less extreme) psychological profiles to the experiencers in the current study.

References

Appelle, S., S. J. Lynn and L. Newman (2000). Alien abduction experiences. In E. Cardeña, S.J. Lynn and S. Krippner (eds.), *Varieties of Anomalous Experience: Examining the Scientific Evidence.* Washington, D.C.: American Psychological Association. Chapter 8.
Baker, R. A. (1992). *Hidden Memories: Voices and Visions from Within.* Buffalo: Prometheus.
Barber, T. X., and D. S. Calverley (1964). An experimental study of "hypnotic" (auditory and visual) hallucinations. *Journal of Abnormal and Social Psychology*, 68. 13–20.
Bartholomew, R. E., K. Basterfield and G. S. Howard (1991). UFO abductees and contactees: Psychopathology or fantasy proneness? *Professional Psychology: Research and Practice*, 22. 215–222.
Basterfield, K. (2001). Paranormal aspects of the UFO phenomenon: 1975–1999. *Australian Journal of Parapsychology*, 1. 30–55.
Basterfield, K., and M. A. Thalbourne (2002). Belief in, and alleged experience of, the paranormal in ostensible UFO abductees. *Australian Journal of Parapsychology*, 2. 2–18.

Bentall, R. P., and P. D. Slade (1985). Reliability of a scale measuring predisposition towards hallucinations: A brief report. *Personality and Individual Differences*, 6. 527–529.
Bernstein, E. M., and F. W. Putnam (1987). Development, reliability, and validity of a dissociation scale. *Journal of Nervous and Mental Disease*, 174. 727–735.
Bullard, T. E. (1987). *UFO Abductions: The Measure of a Mystery*. Mount Rainier, MD: Fund for UFO Research.
Cabeza, R., S. M. Rao, A. D. Wagner, A. R. Mayer and D. L. Schacter (2001). Can medial temporal lobe regions distinguish true from false? An event-related functional MRI study of veridical and illusory recognition memory. *Proceedings of the National Academy of Science, USA*, 98. 4805–4810.
Clancy, S. A. (2005). *Abducted: How People Come to Believe They Were Kidnapped by Aliens*. Cambridge: Harvard University Press.
Clancy, S. A., R. J. McNally, D. L. Schacter, M. F. Lenzenweger and R. K. Pitman (2002). Memory distortion in people reporting abduction by aliens. *Journal of Abnormal Psychology*, 111. 455–461.
Crombag, H. F. M., W. A. Wagenaar and P. J. van Koppen (1996). Crashing memories and the problem of "source monitoring." *Applied Cognitive Psychology*, 10. 95–104, 1996.
Curran, T., D. L. Schacter, M. K. Johnson and R. Spinks (2001). Brain potentials reflect behavioral differences in true and false recognition. *Journal of Cognitive Neuroscience*, 13. 201–216.
Deese, J. (1959). On the prediction of occurrence of particular verbal intrusions in immediate recall. *Journal of Experimental Psychology*, 58. 17–22, 1959.
Diamond, M. J., and R. Taft (1975). The role played by ego-permissiveness and imagery in hypnotic responsivity. *International Journal of Clinical and Experimental Hypnosis*, 23. 130–138, 1975.
Druffel, A., and D. S. Rogo (1980). *The Tujunga Canyon Contacts*. Englewood Cliffs, NJ: Prentice Hall.
Düzel, E., A. P. Yonelinas, G. R. Mangun, H. J. Heinze and E. Tulving (1997). Event-related brain potential correlates of two states of conscious awareness in memory. *Proceedings of the National Academy of Science, USA*, 94. 5973–5978.
Eisen, M. L., and E. B. Carlson (1998). Individual differences in suggestibility: Examining the influence of dissociation, absorption, and a history of childhood abuse. *Applied Cognitive Psychology*, 12. 47–61.
Evans, H. (1983). *The Evidence for UFOs*. Wellingborough: Aquarian.
Evans, H. (1998). *From Other Worlds: The Truth About Aliens, Abductions, UFOs and the Paranormal*. London: Carlton.
Fabiani, M., M.A. Stadler and P. M. Wessels (2000). True but not false memories produce a sensory signature in human lateralized brain potentials. *Journal of Cognitive Neuroscience*, 12. 941–949.
Finch, S. E. (2002). *Daydream Believers? Fantasy-Proneness, Transliminality, and Reality Monitoring: A Search for Vulnerability Factors in False Memory Creation*. Unpublished Ph.D. thesis, Goldsmiths College, University of London.
French, C. C. (2001). Alien abductions. In R. Roberts and D. Groome (eds.), *Parapsychology: The Science of Unusual Experience*. London: Arnold. Chapter 8.
French, C. C. (2003). Fantastic memories: The relevance of research into eyewitness testimony and false memories for reports of anomalous experiences. *Journal of Consciousness Studies*, 10. 153–174.
French, C. C., N. J. Rose and S. J. Blackmore (2002). *Paranormal belief and interpretations of sleep paralysis*. Paper presented at the 45th Annual Convention of the Parapsychological Association, Paris.
French, C. C., and J. Santomauro (2007). Something wicked this way comes: Causes and interpretations of sleep paralysis. In S. S. Della (ed.), *Tall Tales: Popular Myths About the Mind and Brain*. Oxford: Oxford University Press. Chapter 23.
French, C. C., and K. Wilson (2006). Incredible memories: How accurate are reports of anomalous events? *European Journal of Parapsychology*, 21.2. 166–181.
Gallagher, C., V. K. Kumar and R. J. Pekala (1994). The Anomalous Experiences Inventory: Reliability and validity. *Journal of Parapsychology*, 58. 402–428.

Garoff-Eaton, R. J., S. D. Slotnick and D. L. Schacter (2005). Not all false memories are created equal: The neural basis of false recognition. *Cerebral Cortex*, 16. 1645–1652.

Garry, M., C. G. Manning, E. F. Loftus and S. J. Sherman (1996). Imagination inflation: Imagining a childhood event inflates confidence that it occurred. *Psychological Bulletin and Review*, 3. 208–214.

Glicksohn, J., and T. R. Barrett (2003). Absorption and hallucinatory experience. *Applied Cognitive Psychology*, 17. 833–849.

Goldberg, L. R. (1999). The Curious Experiences Survey, a revised version of the Dissociative Experiences Scale: Factor structure, reliability, and relations to demographic and personality variables. *Psychological Assessment*, 11. 134–145.

Gonsalves, B., and K. A. Paller (2000). Neural events that underlie something that never happened. *Nature Neuroscience*, 3. 1316–1321.

Gonsalves, B., P. J. Reber, D. R. Gittelman, T. B. Parrish, M.-M. Mesulam and K. A. Paller (2002). Neural evidence that vivid imagining can lead to false remembering. *Psychological Science*, 15. 655–660.

Gotlib, D. (1994). Comments, questions on Keith Basterfield's talk "Abductions: The paranormal connection." In A. Pritchard, D. E. Pritchard, J. E. Mack, P. Casey and C. Yapp (eds.), *Alien Discussions: Proceedings of the Abduction Study Conference Held at MIT*. Cambridge, MA: North Cambridge Press.

Greening, E. K. (2002). *The Relationship Between False Memory and Paranormal Belief*. Unpublished Ph.D. thesis, University of Hertfordshire.

Heaps, C., and M. Nash (1999). Individual differences in imagination inflation. *Psychonomic Bulletin & Review*, 6. 313–318.

Holden, K. J., and C. C. French (2002). Alien abduction experiences: Clues from neuropsychology and neuropsychiatry. *Cognitive Neuropsychiatry*, 7. 163–178.

Johnson, M. K., and C. Raye (1981). Reality monitoring. *Psychological Review*, 8. 67–85.

Johnson, M. K., S. Hashtroudi and D. S. Lindsay (1993). Source monitoring. *Psychological Bulletin*, 114. 3–28.

Johnson, M. K., S. F. Nolde, M. Mather, J. Kounios, D. L. Schacter and T. Curran (1997). The similarity of brain activity associated with true and false recognition memory depends on test format. *Psychological Science*, 8. 250–257.

Kumar, V. K., R. J. Pekala and C. Gallagher (1994). The Anomalous Experiences Inventory (AEI). Unpublished psychological test. West Chester: West Chester University of Pennsylvania.

Launay, G., and P. Slade (1981). The measurement of hallucinatory predisposition in male and female prisoners. *Personality and Individual Differences*, 2. 221–234.

Mack, J. (1994). *Abduction: Human Encounters with Aliens*. New York: Scribner's.

McNally, R. J., and S. A. Clancy (2005). Sleep paralysis, sexual abuse, and space alien abduction. *Transcultural Psychiatry*, 4. 113–122.

Merckelbach, H., and V. van de Ven (2001). Another White Christmas: fantasy proneness and reports of "hallucinatory experiences" in undergraduate students. *Journal of Behavior Therapy and Experimental Psychiatry*, 32. 137–144.

Mintz, S., and M. Alpert (1972). Imagery vividness, reality testing, and schizophrenic hallucinations. *Journal of Abnormal Psychology*, 79. 310–316.

Myers, S. A. (1983). The Wilson-Barber Inventory of Childhood Memories and Imaginings: Children's form and norms for 1337 children and adolescents. *Journal of Mental Imagery*, 7. 83–94.

Newman, L. S., and R. F. Baumeister (1996). Toward an explanation of the UFO abduction phenomenon: Hypnotic elaboration, extraterrestrial sadomasochism, and spurious memories. *Psychological Inquiry*, 7. 99–126.

Okado, Y., and C. Stark (2003). Neural processing associated with true and false retrieval. *Cognitive, Affective, and Behavioral Neuroscience*, 3. 323–334.

Ost, J., A. Vrij, A. Costall and R. Bull (2002). Crashing memories and reality monitoring: Distinguishing between perceptions, imaginings and false memories. *Applied Cognitive Psychology*, 16. 125–134.

Platt, R. D., S. C. Lacey, A. D. Iobst and D. Finkelman (1998). Absorption, dissociation,

fantasy-proneness as predictors of memory distortion in autobiographical and laboratory-generated memories. *Applied Cognitive Psychology*, 12. 77–89.
Powers, S. M. (1994). Dissociation in alleged extraterrestrial abductees, *Dissociation*, 7. 44–50.
Randles, J. (1988). *Abduction*. London: Robert Hale.
Robinson, K. B., and H. L. Roediger, III. (1997). Associative processes in false recall and false recognition. *Psychological Science*, 8. 231–237.
Rodeghier, M., J. Goodpaster and S. Blatterbauer (1991). Psychosocial characteristics of abductees: Results from the CUFOS abduction project. *Journal of UFO Studies*, 3. 59–90.
Roediger, H. L., III, and K. B. McDermott (1995). Creating false memories? Remembering words not presented in lists. *Journal of Experimental Psychology: Learning, Memory, and Cognition*, 21. 803–814.
Schacter, D. L., R. L. Buckner, W. Koutstall, A. M. Dale and B. R. Rosen (1997). Late onset of anterior prefrontal activity during true and false recognition: an event-related MRI study. *Neuroimage*, 6. 259–269.
Schacter, D. L., E. Reiman, T. Curran, L. S. Yun, D. Bandy, K. B. McDermott and H.L. Roediger, III. (1996). Neuroanatomical correlates of veridical and illusory recognition memory: evidence from positron emission tomography. *Neuron*, 17. 267–274.
Schacter, D. L., and S. D. Slotnick (2004). The cognitive neuroscience of memory distortion. *Neuron*, 44. 149–160.
Schwarz, B. E. (1983). *UFO dynamics*. Moore Haven, FL: Rainbow Books.
Serper, M., C.A. Dill, N. Chang, T. Kot and J. Elliot (2005). Factorial structure of the hallucinatory experience: Continuity of experience in psychotic and normal individuals. *Journal of Nervous and Mental Disease*, 193. 265–272.
Spanos, N. P. (1996). *Multiple Identities and False Memories: A Sociocognitive Perspective*. Washington, D.C.: American Psychological Association.
Spanos, N. P., P. A. Cross, K. Dickson and S. C. DuBreuil (1993). Close encounters: An examination of UFO experiences. *Journal of Abnormal Psychology*, 102. 624–632.
Spencer, J. (1994). *Gifts of the Gods?* London: Virgin.
Tellegen, A., and G. Atkinson (1974). Openness to absorbing and self-altering experiences ("absorption"), a trait related to hypnotic susceptibility. *Journal of Abnormal Psychology*, 83. 268–277.
Thalbourne, M. A. (1995). Further studies of the measurement and correlates of belief in the paranormal. *Journal of the American Society for Psychical Research*, 89. 235–247.
Thalbourne, M. A., and P. S. Delin (1994). A new instrument for measuring the sheep-goat variable: Its psychometric properties and factor structure. *Journal of the Society for Psychical Research*, 59. 172–186.
Vallee, J. (1977). *UFOs: The Psychic Solution*. St. Albans: Panther.
Wilson, K., and C. C. French (2006). The relationship between susceptibility to false memories, dissociativity, and paranormal belief and experience. *Personality and Individual Differences*, 41. 1493–1502.
Wilson, S. C., and T. X. Barber (1983). The fantasy-prone personality: Implications for understanding imagery, hypnosis, and parapsychological phenomena. In Sheikh A. A. (ed.), *Imagery: Current Theory, Research and Application*. New York: John Wiley. 340–387.
Winograd, E., J. P. Peluso and T. A. Glover (1998). Individual differences in susceptibility to memory illusions. *Applied Cognitive Psychology*, 12. S5–27.
Young, H. F., R. P. Bentall, P. D. Slade and M. E. Dewey (1987). The role of brief instructions and suggestibility in the elicitation of auditory and visual hallucinations in normal and psychiatric subjects. *Journal of Nervous and Mental Disease*, 175. 41–48.

11

OBSERVING THE IMPOSSIBLE
Eyewitness Testimony for Darkroom Séances
Richard Wiseman

Some people seem to be able to perform the impossible. Alleged psychics appear to bend metal with the power of their minds. Faith healers seem to reach deep inside people's bodies and remove diseased tissue. Mediums claim to be able to channel spirit entities or have them move luminous objects in darkened séance rooms.

Many people report seeing amazing phenomena during such demonstrations, and their testimony is often taken as evidence in support of the paranormal. But just how reliable are their accounts? And what are the factors that influence the perception and recall of seemingly impossible phenomena? This paper tackles these issues within the context of just one type of demonstration—namely, the darkroom séance.

Background

For over a century people have held séances in an attempt to contact the dead. In a typical séance, a group of people (referred to as "sitters") sit around a table with a medium, turn out the lights, hold hands and attempt to communicate with the spirit world. In some "physical" séances, most popular during the Victorian period, objects that have been treated with luminous paint are placed in the centre of the table, and the spirits apparently cause these objects to levitate and move.

Many writers have questioned the reliability of testimony for séance phenomena, arguing that witnesses may have been the victims of trickery and self-deception (see, e.g., Lewis, 1886, Fraser-Harris, 1935; West, 1982). A small number of researchers have also carried out studies demonstrating how sitters can be fooled by fake mediums, and the difficulties involved in accurately observing and remembering the events that take place during a séance. Hodgson and Davey (1887) held fake séances for unsuspecting sitters and asked them to write a description of the séance. They reported that many sitters omitted important events, recalled others in an incorrect order and often believed that they had witnessed genuine paranormal phenomena. Likewise, Besterman (1932) had sitters attend a mock séance and then answer questions relating to various phenomena that had occurred. Besterman reported that sitters had a tendency to underestimate the number of persons present in the séance room, failed to report major disturbances that took place (e.g., the experimenter leaving the séance room) and experienced the illusory movement of objects.

This paper describes three experiments, conducted by the author, that have further examined the reliability of testimony for darkroom séances.

Experiment One

In this first study, three fake séances were faked, with approximately twenty-five people attending each séance (for further details, see Wiseman, Smith and Wiseman, 1995). Everyone was first asked to complete a short questionnaire, noting their age, gender and whether they believed that genuine paranormal phenomena might sometimes take place during séances. A séance room had been prepared. All of the windows and doors in the room had been blacked out, and twenty-five chairs had been arranged in a large circle. Three objects—a book, a slate and a bell—had been treated with luminous paint and placed onto three of the chairs. A small table, the edges of which were also luminous, was situated in the middle of the circle. Two luminous maracas rested on the table.

Following a brief talk on the aims of the project, the participants were led into the darkened séance room. I played the part of the medium. With the help of a torch, I showed each person to a chair and, where appropriate, asked the person to pick up the book, slate or bell. Next, I drew participants' attention to the table and maracas. Those participants who had picked up the other luminous objects were asked to make themselves known, and the "medium" collected the objects one by one and placed them on the table.

I then pointed out the presence of a small luminous ball, approximately 5cm in diameter, which was suspended on a piece of rope from the ceiling. Finally, I took my place in the circle, extinguished the torch and asked everybody to join hands.

I first asked the participants to concentrate on trying to move the luminous ball, and then to try the same with the objects on the table. Finally, the participants were asked to concentrate on moving the table itself. The séance lasted approximately ten minutes. Clearly, it was important that some phenomena occurred to provide an opportunity for us to assess the reliability of eyewitness testimony. The maracas were therefore "gimmicked" to ensure their movement during the séance. In the third séance the table was also similarly moved by trickery. We also used trickery to create a few strange noises at the end of each séance.

After leaving the séance room, the participants completed a short questionnaire that asked them about their experience of the séance. Would participants remember which objects had been handled before the start of the séance? As the maracas were "gimmicked," we had to ensure that they were not examined or handled by anyone. Nevertheless, one in five participants stated that they had been. This was an important inaccuracy, as observers are likely to judge the movement of an object more impressive if they think that the item has been scrutinized beforehand.

This type of misconception was not confined to the maracas. In the first two séances, the slate, bell, book and table remained stationary. Despite this, 27 percent of participants reported movement of at least one of these. In the third séance the table was gimmicked so that it shifted four inches towards the medium, but participants' testimony was again unreliable, this time with one in four people reporting no movement at all.

An interesting pattern developed when the results were analyzed by separating the participants by belief (there were 44 people classified as believers and 22 as disbelievers). The ball, suspended from the ceiling, did not move at any time. Seventy-six percent of disbelievers were certain that it hadn't moved. In contrast, the same certainty among believers was only 54 percent. In addition, 40 percent of believers thought that at least one other object had moved, compared to just 14 percent of disbelievers. The answers to the question "Do you believe you have witnessed any genuine paranormal phenomena?" perhaps provide the most conclusive result for the believer/disbeliever divide. One in five believers stated that they thought they had seen genuine phenomena. None of the disbelievers thought so.

The results clearly show that it is difficult to obtain reliable testimony about the séance. Indeed, our study probably underestimated the extent of this unreliability as the séance only lasted ten minutes and participants were asked to remember what had happened immediately afterwards. Also, all participants were fully debriefed after the séance. Although a minority of participants believed that they had observed genuine paranormal phenomena, it doesn't seem unreasonable to assume that these individuals might be the most likely to tell others about their experience. Our results suggest that many of their reports would be fraught with inaccuracies and it might only take a few of the more distorted accounts to circulate before news that "genuine" paranormal phenomena had occurred became widespread.

Experiment Two

A few years later I decided to carry out a second study in the area (for further details see Wiseman, Greening and Smith, 2003). Magicians and fraudulent mediums have written extensively about how they often attempt to use suggestion to deceive sitters into believing, for example, that the séance room has suddenly become cold, that stationary objects are moving, and that there is an unusual sense of presence in the room. This experiment examined the impact that such suggestions have on the reliability of eyewitness testimony for séance phenomena.

We held eight séances and again had approximately twenty-five people attend each one. The séances took place in a large, dark room. Before the start of each séance, everyone completed a short form to establish whether they believed in the existence of genuine paranormal phenomena. The participants then sat around a small table containing a hand bell, a maraca and wicker ball. Beforehand we had treated the table and all of the objects with luminous paint, and had gimmicked the ball to move during the séance.

Andy Nyman (a professional actor and magician) kindly agreed to play the part of the medium, and followed a set script for all of the séances. Initially, the participants were asked to join hands. All of the lights were then extinguished and the objects on the table became visible from their luminous glow. The group was first asked to concentrate on the ball. It slowly rose approximately 12 inches into the air, moved around the séance room and gently returned to the table. Andy then asked everyone to concentrate on moving the table. The table remained completely stationary, but Andy suggested that it was levitating with comments like "That's good, lift the table up, that's good, keep concentrating, keep the table in the air."

Two weeks later, everyone was sent a questionnaire about their experiences during the séance. We first asked people whether they thought that any of the phenomena they had experienced were actually paranormal. Not all participants returned the questionnaire but, as with our first experiment, participants' belief in the paranormal affected how they interpreted what they had seen, with 40 percent of believers stating that the séance was genuine, compared with only 2.6 percent of disbelievers (in this experiment, 36 people were classified as believers and 39 as disbelievers).

A second question examined whether the verbal suggestion had been effective. 34 percent of people stated that they had actually seen the table levitate. Again, participants' belief in the paranormal played a key role, with 51 percent of disbelievers correctly stating that the table didn't move, versus just 31 percent of believers.

Our questionnaire also asked people whether they had had any unusual experiences during the séance. Almost one in five people said that they had, and reported various strange feelings including; cold shivers when concentrating on the objects, a strong sense of energy flowing through the circle and a presence in center of the room near table. Interestingly, 30 percent of believers reported these experiences compared to just 8 percent of disbelievers. Once again, all participants were fully debriefed after the séance.

Experiment Three

I decided to build upon the previous study by examining the degree to which the effectiveness of the suggestion depended upon whether it was consistent with participants' prior belief in the paranormal (for further details, see Wiseman, Greening and Smith, 2003).

In the previous experiment, believers may have been influenced by the actor's suggestions, in part, because his comments (i.e., that the table was levitating) were consistent with their belief in paranormal phenomena. Our third experiment examined this issue by having the actor make two different types of suggestion. In one part of the séance, referred to as the "pro-paranormal" condition, the actor suggested that a stationary object (a handbell) was moving. In another part of the séance, referred to as the "anti-paranormal" condition, he suggested that a moving object (a slate) was stationary.

Believers may be more susceptible to suggestion than disbelievers regardless of whether the actor's suggestions are consistent or inconsistent with their belief in the paranormal. If so, we would predict a significant relationship between participants' prior belief in the paranormal and the reported movement of objects in both conditions. Alternatively, participants may only be influenced by suggestions that are consistent with their belief in the paranormal. If this were the case, a greater percentage of believers than disbelievers would report that the hand-bell had moved in the pro-paranormal condition, whilst a greater percentage of disbelievers than believers would report that the slate had remained stationary in the anti-paranormal condition. Finally, it is possible that believers would only be influenced by suggestions that are consistent with their belief in the paranormal, whilst disbelievers would not be influenced by the suggestions in either condition. In this were the case, the findings would show a significant relationship between prior belief and reported movement in the pro-paranormal condition, with a greater percentage of believers than disbelievers reporting movement of the hand-bell. There would, however, be a non-significant relationship between prior belief and the reported movement of the slate in the anti-paranormal condition.

Almost 200 people attended one of twelve séances, with up to 25 people attending each fake séance. Once again the séances took place in a large, dark room, and before the start of each séance, everyone completed a short form to establish whether they believed in the existence of genuine paranormal phenomena (in this experiment, 37 people were classified as believers and 32 as disbelievers). During the séance I played the role of the medium. I asked the group to concentrate on the hand-bell. Although the hand-bell remained stationary, I suggested that it was moving by using phrases such as "That's good, the bell is moving now, lift the bell up, that's good," etc. Participants were then asked to observe the slate. The slate moved approximately two inches, however, I suggested that it was not moving by using phrases such as "it's not working, not to worry, don't be disappointed" etc.

Two weeks later, all participants were sent a questionnaire about their experiences during the séance. Eleven percent of participants incorrectly reported that the hand-bell had moved during the séance. There was a significant relationship between participants' belief in the paranormal and the reported movement of the hand-bell, with a greater percentage of disbelievers than believers reporting that the hand-bell had not moved (76 percent vs 59 percent). Eighty-six percent of participants incorrectly reported that the slate had remained stationary during the séance. There was a non-significant relationship between participants' prior belief in the paranormal and the reported movement of the slate. One again, all participants were fully debriefed.

Conclusion

For over a century people have attended physical séances and reported witnessing seemingly inexplicable phenomena. Experiments conducted around the turn of the last century revealed that many of these accounts were unreliable. The experiments reported here have shown that modern day witnesses also produce inaccurate testimony of séance phenomena. In addition, these experiments represent the first attempt to systematically examine verbal suggestion within the context of the séance. They have demonstrated that such suggestions have the potential to cause sitters to incorrectly report that stationary objects were moving, and that moving objects were stationary. The studies have also produced strong evidence that within the context of a séance, believers are significantly more susceptible to verbal suggestion than disbelievers, but only when the suggestion is consistent with the existence of paranormal phenomena.

It is difficult to know the extent to which these findings will generalize to other groups of participants and other settings. The participants in these experiments were self-selecting individuals attending a convention about strange phenomena. As such, their responses may not be typical of a wider, and more representative, cross-section of the general public. In addition, there were several major differences between the séances held during these experiments and most "genuine" séances. Many sitters at "genuine" séances may be far more motivated to believe that they are witnessing genuine paranormal phenomena than the participants in our experiments because, for example, they may have recently suffered a bereavement and want to see evidence that the spirit of their friend or relative has survived bodily death. Also, during our fake séances, participants were not told that the séance would contain genuine paranormal phenomena, nor did the person leading the séance claim to be a medium. In a "genuine" séance, sitters are explicitly told that the séance will involve contact with the spirit world, and that the person in charge of the séance has genuine mediumistic abilities. Finally, "genuine" séances often last for many hours, whereas our fake séances only lasted approximately fifteen minutes. It is highly likely that the conditions associated with a "genuine" séance could greatly enhance many of the psychological effects obtained in the fake séances, thus resulting in even more unreliable and inaccurate testimony.

In the same way that other types of magic tricks have provided interesting insights into attentional, perceptual and memorial processes (see, e.g., Lamont and Wiseman, 1999), so these experiments have demonstrated how the séance room can provide psychologists with a naturalistic way of examining verbal suggestion, thus overcoming the concerns of those researchers who have questioned the ecological validity of laboratory based studies involving only students and relatively unrealistic stimulus material, such as slides and videotapes. It is hoped that the findings will encourage other investigators to venture out of their laboratories and into the séance room.

References

Besterman, T. (1932). The psychology of testimony in relation to paraphysical phenomena: Report of an experiment. *Proceedings of the Society for Psychical Research*, 40. 363-387.
Fraser-Harris, D. F. (1935). Is seeing believing? *Discovery*, May. 138-141.
Hodgson, R., and S. J. Davey (1887). The possibilities of mal-observation and lapse of memory from a practical point of view. *Proceedings of the Society for Psychical Research*, 4. 381-495.
Lamont, P., and R. Wiseman (1999). *Magic In Theory*. Hatfield: University of Hertfordshire Press.
Lewis, A. J. (1886). How and what to observe in relation to slate-writing phenomena. *Journal of the Society for Psychical Research*. 362-375.
West, D. J. (1982). Thoughts on testimony to the paranormal. *Parapsychology Review*, 13(5). 1-8.
Wiseman, R., M. Smith and J. Wiseman (1995). Eyewitness testimony and the paranormal. *Skeptical Inquirer*, November/December. 29-32.
Wiseman, R., E. Greening and M. Smith (2003). Belief in the paranormal and suggestion in the séance room. *British Journal of Psychology*, 94. 285-297.

12

Developing a Dissociational Account of Out-of-Body Experiences

Craig D. Murray*

A key topic in the parapsychological literature has been the phenomenon of the Out-of-Body Experience (OBE), in which the person who has an OBE has an experience in which their self or consciousness and their body are spatially separated. Alvarado (1992) notes that the key features of an OBE often include a sensation of floating, seeing one's own physical body from outside, and an experience of travel to a place remote from one's actual physical-body location.

Despite the OBE being reported by a large proportion of the population (12 percent in a random British sample studied by Blackmore, 1984a), mainstream psychology has largely overlooked OBEs. Nevertheless, parapsychologists have developed psychological explanations of the OBE, and at present there are three main psychological theories of OBEs which emerge from this work. In this chapter I will present a brief overview of these psychological theories of the OBE before describing my own recent work in which a dissociational account of the OBE has been elaborated.

---

*This research was funded by the Bial Foundation, as part of the projects "The Flexibility of Body Boundaries and Its Relationship to Out-of-Body Experiences" (number 124/02) and "Investigating the Multidimensional Nature of Body Image, Sensorial Representation, and Phenomenology in Relation to Different Forms of Out-of-Body Experience" (number 134/04).

Psychological Theories of the Out-of-body Experience

PALMER'S PSYCHOANALYTIC THEORY

Palmer (1978) presented a psychological theory of the OBE that centred on the body image of the experient (OBEer). He argued that a reduction of proprioceptive information from the body resulted in changes to the "body concept" which (in some instances) in turn "triggered" the OBE. Drawing on Freudian theory, Palmer argued that the person's change in body concept threatened their self-concept or sense of individual identity. As a result of this threat, unconscious processes are activated in an attempt to re-establish the person's sense of individual identity. An example given by Palmer (1978) is one of "deathbed experiences" in which he argued that an OBE is more likely to occur when the experient first has had a prolonged confinement to bed in a weakened condition (which is likely to encourage changes in body image) and they have a "psychological set" of death (irrespective of whether they accept it or not) which involves the separation of the soul from the body. With the re-establishment of the normal body concept the OBE ends.

It is important to note that Palmer views changes in the body image as necessary but not sufficient for an OBE to occur; it is the Freudian "primary process" attempt at reintegration which in some cases results in an OBE. Palmer refers to "psychological conditions that predispose one to OBEs" (Palmer, 1978; p.21) but does not elucidate beyond some general circumstances that surround the occurrence of OBEs "such as when in sleep, on the verge of sleep, or in a relaxed state" and in a minority of cases "under conditions of physical or psychological stress" (Palmer, 1978; p.20). Therefore Palmer's theory does not account for why some people appear more prone to having an OBE.

BLACKMORE'S COGNITIVE THEORY

A second psychological theory of OBEs is that provided by Blackmore (1984b), who proposed a cognitive explanation for the occurrence and phenomenology of OBEs. She argued that one of the key functions of the brain is the construction of models of the self within the environment. These may be short-term models (such as those created through perception) or long-term models (such as those formed through memory) and each may influence the other. One of these models that Blackmore (1984b, p.203) identifies is that of the body image, which she states is the sum of "somatosensory information, visual, and other sensory input and memory."

Rather than modeling what is "really" there, Blackmore (1984b) points out that we "build" models of reality. Moreover, we are continually engaged in multiple model-making processes: a model of the activity we are currently engaged in, a model of a remembered event, a model of an imagined state of affairs, and so on. Central to Blackmore's theory is the proposal that at any given time only one model is taken to represent "reality." For most people at most times this "reality" model will be taken to be that which is most complex, stable and coherent. This model would usually be that generated in most part through sensory input. However, at times sensory input may be reduced, as in sensory isolation experiments, resulting in impoverished sensory models. This may result in an over-reliance on information from memory in order to achieve stability. Therefore for an OBE to occur at least two things are needed: the failure of the somatosensory input-controlled model, and the substitution of an imagery-based one built-up from memory. The required incapacitation of the input model leads Blackmore (1984b) to argue that her theory explains why such experiences as sensory deprivation, relaxation, illness, and certain drugs frequently occasion OBEs.

If OBEs are in part an imaginal experience, then OBErs might be expected to have better visual imagery skills than non–OBErs. Certainly Blackmore (1984b) has proposed that this is the case, although the research on this issue provides a mixed picture (Alvarado, 2000). Irwin (1980) found no evidence to suggest that OBErs were any more habitual "visualizers" or "imagers" than the normal population. OBErs also scored lower than the norms for that group would predict on a questionnaire assessing vividness of visual imagery. Blackmore (1983a) found no differences between OBErs and non–OBErs on a vividness of imagery scale, and no differences between a second OBE and non–OBE sample on Gordon's (1949) Control of Imagery Questionnaire. She also found no differences between OBErs and non–OBErs when combining the scores of two questionnaire items assessing vividness of visual imagery, and concluded that "in general vividness of imagery does not seem to be a good predictor of the people who have these [OBE] experiences" (Blackmore, 1983a; p.242).

Some supporting evidence for Blackmore's (1984b) thesis is available. Alvarado and Zingrone (1994) did find that vividness of mental imagery was positively correlated with the OBE. Further evidence in support of better imagery skills in OBErs includes Blackmore's (1983a) finding that experients were better able to switch viewpoints in imaginary scenes, although they did not remember scenes any more frequently from above than at eye-level. Cook and Irwin (1983) found that OBErs were better at judging how an object would appear from different perspectives, but found no relationship between having an OBE and performance on the Necker Cube Fluctuation Test of imagery.

A finding by Blackmore (1983b) that OBErs report more hypnagogic imagery than non–OBErs is sometimes cited as evidence for better imagery skills in experients. However the question used to assess this ("Have you ever experienced very vivid and realistic images just before going to sleep?")

addresses experiences rather than measuring any specific imagery skill. It also presents problems of interpretation as many people who have an OBE might equate that experience with the one posed in the question. Both Irwin (1986) and Blackmore (1987) have found that people who dream as though they were spectators have more OBEs though there were no differences in the waking use of different viewpoints. Hunt, Gervais, Shearing-Johns, and Travis (1992) found a relationship between the OBE and performance of block design and embedded figures tests. Blackmore (1994) cites the findings of Irwin (1986) and herself (Blackmore, 1987) as generally confirming the predictions from her psychological theory of the OBE (Blackmore, 1984b), although this glosses over the failure of an appreciable number of her own and other studies to find differences in the visual imagery skills of OBErs and non–OBErs.

Irwin's Dissociational Theory

Whilst Palmer's and Blackmore's psychological theories of the OBE have a strong emphasis on the role of body image in the occurrence of OBEs, there has been little attention beyond this of the experience of the body in relation to OBEs. However, one exception to this is a study by Irwin (2000) who has built upon his initial synesthetic theory of the OBE (Irwin, 1985) to examine the experience of somatic symptoms and OBEs and to develop a dissociational model (Irwin, 2000). Irwin's (1985) psychological theory of the OBE initially sought to explain some of the phenomenology of the OBE as due to dissociation between somatic inputs in which cross-modal processing (synesthesia) took place. With a lack of somatic processing the assumption of the perceiving self as inside the physical body is undermined and through an abstract perception of a disembodied consciousness a cognitive representation of a static floating self is generated. Through a process of synesthesia this somaesthetic image may be transformed into a visual image.

More recently, Irwin (2000) has elaborated upon this model to propose his dissociational theory of the OBE. Drawing upon the work of Nijenhuis and colleagues (e.g. Nijenhuis, Spinhoven, van Dyke, van der Hart and Vanderlinden, 1996) into dissociative states, Irwin argues that OBEs are in part the result of somatoform dissociation in which there can be a "deficit symptom" such as numbness in a part of the body, or "positive symptom" in which psychosomatic pain or tics are experienced. Irwin's rationale for studying somatoform dissociation in OBEs is that "at a phenomenological level the OBE appears to entail a dissociation between sensory processing of somatic (somaesthetic and kinaesthetic) events and the sense of self or identity" (Irwin, 2000, p.265). In his study involving 113 psychology students, with an OBE incidence rate of 38.9 percent, Irwin (2000) administered the Somatoform Dissociation Questionnaire. This was found to be the only predictor variable (from a logistic regression analysis which included participants' data for dissociative experiences, absorption, gender and age) able to independently discriminate between people with and without a prior OBE, as well as the only independent variable which contributed significantly in predicting OBE frequency.

Irwin (2000) therefore provides a third theory for the occurrence of the OBE, namely that it is the result of the convergence of a number of dissociative factors. This includes high levels of "absorption" (a psychological state in which the person is in a high state of engrossment in experience), as well as a simultaneous occurrence of dissociation from somatic input. This theory includes a reformulation of Irwin's earlier account (1985) based upon his findings that people with prior OBEs exhibit a high capacity for psychological absorption, whilst people with high levels of psychological absorption were more susceptible to experimentally induced OBEs. These changes are posited to undermine the socially conditioned assumption that the body is the container of the self, and as a result to promote the feeling that the person's consciousness is no longer in the spatial confines of the body. In turn, this abstract perception of a disembodied self is cognitively processed "into a passive, generalized somaesthetic image of a static floating self" (Irwin, 2000, p.272) and into an experience of an OBE. Through the process of synesthesia, and providing the experient has a basic visuospatial ability, the somaesthetic image may be translated into a visual image. Irwin (2000) argues that strong absorption during the above state is responsible for the experienced realism of the OBE.

Again, there are similarities between Irwin's (2000) OBE theory and those of Palmer (1978) and Blackmore (1984b). A breakdown between sensory input and experience of this input is central to all three theories. However, Irwin's (2000) findings are indicative of a new line of inquiry in relation to OBEs. Whilst both Palmer and Blackmore concur that a change in body image precipitates the occurrence of an OBE, Irwin's findings are suggestive of pre-existing, possibly long-term differences between the bodily experiences of people who have (or who are likely to have) OBEs and those who have not (and are unlikely to do so in the future).

Bodily Experience and the OBE: Building Upon Irwin's Dissociational Theory

Prior research has found that people who report having had an OBE are more likely to have had multiple rather than single OBEs (Palmer, 1979; see also Alvarado (1986) for a meta-analysis of 19 studies). Alvarado and Zingrone (1999) found 65 percent of their participants were multiple OBErs. Whilst Palmer's (1978) theory includes suggestions for the circumstances which may precipitate an OBE it does not explain individual differences or make predictions about the characteristics of people who will be more prone to an OBE. Blackmore's (1984b) theory predicts that people with better visual imagery skills will be more prone to OBEs than others, although as reviewed earlier the evidence for this is mixed. In contrast, Irwin's (2000) empirical work suggests some people with certain bodily experience are more likely to have an OBE.

The occurrence of an OBE has been found to correlate positively with dissociation (Richards, 1991; Alvarado and Zingrone, 1997; Zingrone and Alvarado, 1994) and absorption (e.g. Dalton, Zingrone, and Alvarado, 1999; Glicksohn, 1990; and Irwin, 1980), both of which are dissociational processes. Furthermore, rather than OBEs occurring only in the absence or reduction of sensory information, the association between somatoform dissociation (which includes items that measure "positive symptoms" or the *amplification* (rather than just the reduction or absence) of some sensory experiences, such as pain) in Irwin's (2000) study indicates that the relationship between bodily experience and OBEs is more complex than that outlined in Palmer's (1978) and Blackmore's (1984) theories.

Recently I and colleagues have begun to build upon Irwin's (2000) work to argue that OBEs are more likely to occur in people who usually have a *weak* sense of embodiment, characterized by a generalized dissociation between their self and body which can be measured on a number of body experience dimensions (Murray and Fox, 2004; 2005a; 2005b). Whereas Palmer's (1978) and Blackmore's (1984) theories posit body image change or disturbance as an immediate precursor to the occurrence of OBEs, I have argued that there is a qualitative difference in the everyday bodily experience of people who do and do not have OBEs. This is not to challenge the central premise of these theories, namely that a "change" in body image precipitates OBEs, but rather to complement these theories by suggesting that OBErs have pre-existing differences in their body experience compared to non–OBErs, and that these pre-existing differences are possibly exacerbated in the moments in which an OBE occurs.

All three psychological theories of the OBE presented earlier appear to share the central idea that it occurs following a lack of sensory input or processing, but they diverge in important ways thereafter. Palmer's (1978) theory, with its focus on unconscious threats to identity, has the drawback of being difficult to test empirically (see Alvarado, 2000). In contrast, both Blackmore's (1984b) and Irwin's theories appear more open to hypothesis testing. As reviewed earlier, Blackmore's (1984b) argument for better visual imagery skills in OBErs has received some but not strong support. Irwin's (1985, 2000) theory proposes that OBErs need only a "basic visuo-spatial ability." Furthermore, OBErs have been found consistently to differ on measures of dissociation and absorption, both of which are considered dissociational processes.

The finding by Irwin (2000) that the OBE also correlates with somatoform dissociation further supports the interpretation of the OBE as the result of a number of converging dissociational processes.

Whilst the theories of Palmer, Blackmore and Irwin, are informative exceptions to the lack of consideration given to bodily experience in the OBE research literature, they have a very narrow focus on perceptual aspects of this experience. For instance, Palmer's and Blackmore's theories posit changes in the "body concept" or "body image" where these terms would seem to refer to conscious or unconscious changes in the sensorial topography of the body, such as might occur with a lack of somatosensory input. Irwin's study goes a little further in that it considers not just a lack of sensory input (negative symptoms) but amplified sensory inputs (such as pain, or "positive" symptoms). However, what are overlooked in these studies are other ways of experiencing the body.

Within psychology, studies of body image can be divided into research areas which address people's perceptual experience of their bodies (such as body size estimation (e.g. Cappon and Banks, 1968), and sometimes referred to as the "body percept"), their own subjective feelings towards their bodies (such as weight and body shape satisfaction, and sometimes referred to as the "body concept") (Slade, Dewey, Newton, Brodie and Kiemle, 1990), and their beliefs about others' responses to their bodies (e.g., Hart, Leary, Rejeski, 1989). Whilst these approaches differ in significant ways they share a concern with elaborating the relationship between the body and the self. Given that the phenomenological description of the OBE includes that of a dissociation, or separation, between the physical body and the self, my own work has explored if the person who experiences an OBE has a different relationship between their physical body and sense of self than do people without such experiences.

In the remainder of this chapter I summarize the findings from my recent work in which I have extended the work of Irwin to explore the OBE as a dissociational process which can be examined across a number of dimensions of bodily related experience. This approach has been in accordance with, and informed by, Irwin's (2000) dissociational theory of the OBE. I have postulated that the nature of this bodily experience is a generalized dissociation (as compared with non–OBErs) between their self and body that can be assessed on a number of levels: perceptual, affective and social.

STUDY 1: BODY SATISFACTION, SELF-CONSCIOUSNESS AND PHYSICAL SELF-PRESENTATION BY OBERS

In the first study several measures of body image were employed in order to compare these experiences in an OBE and non–OBE sample (Murray and Fox, 2004; 2005a). It was hypothesized that the daily bodily experiences of people with and without a prior OBE would differ along a number of dimensions. In order to test this, an online questionnaire study on "body experience" using an in-house sample of academic staff and students was conducted. Of all respondents (n=243), 62 (25.5 percent) reported a previous OBE and 49 (79 percent) of these reported having had two or more OBEs. In a review of the literature Alvarado (2000) reports an average OBE prevalence of 10 percent in the general population and 25 percent in student populations. Given that many of the respondents in this study were or had been students the percentage of respondents reporting an OBE is comparable to Alvarado's provided student average. In line with other research which has not found gender differences in relation to the occurrence of an OBE (e.g. Blackmore, 1984a), there was an almost identical incidence of OBEs in men (26 percent) and women (24 percent).

A number of hypotheses were made concerning the body experiences of those respondents reporting OBEs compared to those who did not. As in Irwin's (2000) study, respondents reporting a previous out-of-body experience (OBE) were found to score higher on a measure of somatoform dissociation, indicative of a dissociation between their perceptual body and self. On first inspection this finding would appear to support the psychological theories of OBEs advanced by Palmer (1978) and Blackmore (1984b) in which the loss of somatosensory information from the body precipitates an OBE. However, the Somatoform Dissociation Questionnaire used in both Irwin's and this study also includes items which refer to amplified somatosensory experiences which are more difficult to explain by reference to these theories alone. In order to confirm the contention that these amplified or "positive" symptoms contributed significantly to a relationship between somatoform dissociation and out-of-body experiences analysis was conducted on five of the 20 SDQ items which qualify in this regard (items 5, 12, 14, 15 and 17) (some other items refer to both or are difficult to place in either "deficit" or "positive" categories). The mean score for OBErs on all these items was significantly higher than the non–OBE group.

In addition OBErs were found to have a heightened self-awareness or self-consciousness. This had been expected due to the theorized dissociation between the self and body that this sample was expected to have. In their development of the Self-Consciousness Scale, Fenigstein, Scheier, and Buss (1975) suggested people who scored highly on this measure would be better able to take part in meditation. Whereas I expected people without this psychological and phenomenological separation of self and body to have a stronger sense of embodiment, the OBE sample was expected to have a weak sense of embodiment in part characterized by an increased focus on the private or inner self. Indeed, when analyses were carried out on the sub-scales of the Self-Consciousness Scale, namely the Private Self-Consciousness, Public Self-Consciousness and Social Anxiety sub-scales, only the first of these remained statistically significant, that is the OBE group was higher in Private Self-Consciousness.

OBErs were also found to be more dissatisfied with their bodies, and to have lower confidence in the presentation of their physical skills. However, the hypotheses that they would have a reduced belief in their physical ability (Ryckman, Robbins, Thornton and Cantrell, 1982), an objectified view of their bodies (McKinley and Hyde, 1996), and be more anxious at the prospect of having their physique evaluated by others (Hart et al., 1989) were not supported. The higher levels of body dissatisfaction in the OBE sample had also been expected; body dissatisfaction could be seen as a contributory cause, or reflective of, dissociation from the body. No differences were found between OBErs and non–OBErs on the Public Self-Consciousness and Social Anxiety sub-scales on the Self-Consciousness Scale, or the Social Physique Anxiety Scale, suggesting that as well as having no differences in social anxiety in relation to their physique, these groups did not differ in regards to public self-consciousness and social anxiety in general.

Study 2: Self-Concept and Body Investment in OBErs

In the general population people who score higher on measures of body dissatisfaction tend to score higher on measures of social anxiety also. However, although scoring higher on body dissatisfaction, the OBE sample in Study 1 did not score any higher on social anxiety or social physique anxiety than non–OBErs. The findings arising from Study 1 led me to argue that a future avenue of research would be to examine OBErs' and non–OBErs' levels of "self-satisfaction," as well as looking at body dissatisfaction (Murray, Fox and Wilde 2006a). For instance, measures which examine people's sense of personal worth apart from their body or social relationships would help in this regard. The inclusion of such a measure would allow the examination of an expected difference between body and self satisfaction which may contribute to dissociation between the body and the self. It was also hypothesized that OBErs may not have as much psychological investment in their bodies as non–OBErs, and that this may account in part for why they do not demonstrate any social anxiety about their body dissatisfaction.

A total of 59 participants (19 OBErs) completed a questionnaire comprised of the Tennessee Self-concept Scale (Fitts, 1965), the Body Investment Scale (Orbach and Mikulincer, 1998), and Palmer's (1979) item for assessing the prior occurrence of an OBE. It was hypothesized that OBErs would score significantly higher on measures of Moral-Ethical and Personal Self-concept, and lower on measures of body investment. As predicted OBErs scored higher on the "Moral-Ethical Self" and the "Personal Self" subscales of the Tennessee Self-concept Scale, but there were no differences between on the Body Investment Scale or any of its subscales.

These findings lend support to the argument that although OBErs score higher on a measure of body dissatisfaction (Murray and Fox, 2004; 2005a), they maintain a positive self-image. Whereas for people in general scoring high in body dissatisfaction is usually accompanied by increased feelings of social anxiety and social physique anxiety, this relationship does not generally appear to be the case for OBErs (though see Study 3). However, it had been expected OBErs to score lower on body investment, based upon theorizing that a lack of body investment would help explain why OBErs score higher than non–OBErs on body dissatisfaction but do not differ on measures of social anxiety. In fact, although there were no significant differences between OBE and non–OBE participants on the complete scale or its subscales, the OBE sample scored higher on all of these scales.

Study 3: OBErs' Awareness of Body Boundaries

The third study was concerned both with the broad body image experience of OBE and non–OBErs, and with to the degree to which the perceptual experience of OBErs' bodies could be manipulated (Murray and Fox, 2005b). The experimental procedure in this research involved the measurement of a number of dimensions of participants' body image and the use of an immersive virtual reality (IVR) system. IVR systems have previously been found to distort persons' perceptions of their bodies (e.g. Murray and Gordon, 2001), and it was hypothesized that OBErs would be more susceptible to procedures, such as this, which may undermine perception of body boundaries.

It was hypothesized that, in comparison to non–OBErs, OBErs would score significantly higher on body dissatisfaction; lower on Physical Self-Efficacy, and on its subscales Perceived Physical Ability, and Physical Self-Presentation (Ryckman, et al., 1982); higher on Social Physique Anxiety (Hart, et al., 1989); higher on Somatoform Dissociation (Nijenhuis et al., 1996); and higher on Perceptual Body Awareness (where high scores indicate reduced body awareness) (Murray and Gordon, 2001).

A total of 64 people (34 OBErs) took part in the study. As predicted, OBErs and non–OBErs differed along a number of dimensions of body image. The OBE group scored significantly higher on the Perceptual Body Awareness Questionnaire, which indicated a reduced awareness of the body following these participants use of an immersive virtual reality system. OBErs were significantly more dissatisfied with their bodies than non–OBErs, and scored significantly lower on Physical Self-Presentation. As in Irwin's (2000) study and Murray and Fox (2004), OBErs were also found to score significantly higher on Somatoform Dissociation.

In contrast to Study 1, OBErs also reported more Social Physique Anxiety. Unlike Study 1, these findings lent support to a social dimension of body image being implicated in the occurrence of OBEs that has not been previously reported. This is difficult to account for. However, one possible explanation relates to the different forms of participation each study required. In Study 1 the stated study focus was on "body experience" and participation was anonymous, involving the completion of an online questionnaire. In Study 3, participation was in person and participants knew that whether they had had an OBE or not was of research interest. The study involved the use of an immersive virtual reality system, and anecdotally it was noticed that some participants appeared self-conscious about being watched by the experimenter who they themselves could not see while immersed. It may be that these aspects of the studies are responsible for molding and making available different sample frame characteristics and responses. However it is more difficult to explain why this would result in differences between OBE and non–OBE samples in one study and not the other.

The findings of this study further challenge current psychological theories of OBEs that focus solely on perceptual dissociation as underpinning the occurrence of an OBE, and suggests that OBErs may be characterized by a more general dissociation between their bodies and selves that includes affective and social dimensions of body image. OBErs then, seem to have both a qualitatively different form of perceptual embodiment as well as being more susceptible to procedures designed to manipulate or artificially reduce their perception of their perceptual and body boundary experience.

STUDY 4: OBERS' BEHAVIORAL EMBODIMENT

In the fourth study another dimension of body image, "behavioural embodiment" (Murray and Fox, 2006b), was hypothesized as informative in the study of OBEs. It was suggested that under conditions where persons are not required to behave in an embodied manner (that is, in a manner which is constrained by normal embodied capacities), some persons will be more likely to continue to do so, and some persons less likely to do so. Some evidence is available to support this hypothesis. For instance, both Blackmore (1987) and Irwin (1986) have found that OBErs more frequently dream using disembodied perspectives than do non–OBErs. The dream can be considered one circumstance or condition in which persons are not required to behave in an embodied manner, given the dream is an imaginal rather than a "real" experience. However, in the "real" physical world, if one was to try and behave in this manner then the physical impossibility of some feats achieved in dreams (e.g. rising off the floor and flying), or the real consequence of some actions performed in dreams (e.g. jumping off a building and attempting to fly), would quickly be realized.

For Study 4 consideration was given to another circumstance when people are not necessarily required to behave in an embodied manner, but a circumstance that is available when awake. This referred specifically to some desktop virtual reality (DVR) and immersive virtual reality (IVR) systems in which persons explore virtual environments. For example, Murray, Bowers, West, Pettifer and Gibson (2000) found that when placed in a virtual city, although not required to do so, some persons continued to act in an embodied manner, such as "walking" on paved areas rather than roads, staying at ground level, traveling around buildings, and so on. In contrast, others exploited the lack of physical laws in such an environment, "flying" in the air to obtain a bird's-eye-view of the environment, and traveling through buildings and other objects. Despite these latter "transgressions," Murray et al. (2000) argued that for the most part virtual environments modeled on real-world forms draw upon peoples everyday understandings and expectations, therefore presenting users with certain affordances whilst by-and-large obscuring up other possibilities.

Such computer-generated environments in the present context offered the possibility to explore the behavioral embodiment of people who do and do not report a previous OBE. Based upon the general hypothesis that OBErs have a more distanced relationship between their bodies and selves it was hypothesized that this group would exhibit more of the latter kind of behaviors described above, in contrast to non–OBErs who we hypothesized would exhibit more of the former type of behaviors.

The study used two measures of Behavioral Embodiment whilst immersed in a virtual reality system. For the first, the proportion of time that each participant spent at an elevated level in the virtual environment was calculated as a proportion (percent) of the total time spent immersed. For the second, the number of collisions that participants had with virtual objects (e.g. buildings, trees, lampposts) during the trial period was tallied. No significant differences were found on these measures between OBErs and non–OBErs. However, for participants reporting a prior OBE a significant correlation was found between the number of reported prior OBEs and the amount of time participants spent at an elevated level. Significant differences were also found between OBE and non–OBE participants on measures of Somatoform Dissociation, Absorption and Dissociation.

The finding that the more frequently a person has had an OBE is positively correlated to the amount of time they spend navigating an immersive virtual environment at an elevated level suggests that examining the frequency with which (and perhaps a related issue of how recently) a person has an OBE in relation to behavioral embodiment may be a useful avenue of future research. However, unlike for the differences found between OBErs and non–OBErs on measures of Somatoform Dissociation, Absorption and Dissociation in this study, the hypothesis that OBErs would differ in terms of behavioral embodiment did not receive strong support.

STUDY 5: BODY IMAGE AND DIFFERENCES BETWEEN OBERS AND NEAR-DEATH EXPERIENTS

One problem identified in the earlier studies (Murray and Fox, 2004; 2005a,b) was that the use of Palmer's (1979) item to assess whether an OBE had been experienced allowed only a broad delineation between those who responded "yes" or "no," and it was recommended that future research employing the same or similar measures should be accompanied by a more fine-grained analysis of the circumstances surrounding the OBE and the form which it took. This included a suggestion to look at the OBE as part of the related phenomenon of near-death experiences. It was argued that such analyses might reveal certain body image qualities to be more characteristic of particular types of OBE. Therefore Study 5 was designed to examine differences in body image between people reporting near-death and spontaneous out-of-body experiences (Murray and Fox, 2006b).

The study was implemented as a web-based questionnaire, incorporating many of the same measures used in Study 1. It was advertised to Internet newsgroups bulletin boards, and subscription groups dedicated to the topics of out-of-body and near-death experiences. As with Study 1 it was designed to test a number of hypotheses concerning the body experiences of those respondents reporting spontaneous OBEs and OBEs as part of a near-death experience (NDE). The theory which underpins this work would suggest that a wide variety of dissociational body experiences found in OBErs would be more typical of those who have a spontaneous OBE (defined here as one which is does not occur under the influence of alcohol or drugs or traumatic stress) and which tend to occur when the person is on the verge of being awake (hypnapompic states) and being asleep (hypnagogic states). In contrast, OBEs which form part of an NDE usually occur in particularly stressful circumstances, such as a serious accident, illness or perceived life-threatening event (see Irwin 1999), and NDE experients were therefore hypothesized not to have the same pattern of dissociational body experiences.

In line with the predictions of the study, spontaneous OBErs were found to have a heightened self-awareness or self-consciousness, and to be more dissatisfied with their bodies. However, they were not found to be more anxious at the prospect of having their physique evaluated by others, to have a reduced belief in their physical ability and in providing an acceptable physical self-presentation, or to experience higher levels of dissociation between their perceptual body and self. These findings provide support to the argument that people who have spontaneous OBEs not only have qualitatively different bodily experiences than people who do not, but differ in respect to OBEs experienced in other circumstances, such as near-death experiences.

Drawing the Studies Together: Implications for a Dissociational Theory of the OBE

For a long time the body, an implicit referential point in the OBE, has been overlooked in the composition of the phenomenon itself. Just as the phenomenology of the OBE is of a dualist distinction between body and self, OBE researchers have addressed it in a dualist fashion, and have for too long focused on the self of the experient in isolation from the body. In contrast, the present work has built upon the relatively recent insight of Irwin (2000) that OBErs seem to have a qualitatively different experience of their body than non–OBErs.

Taken together the studies reported here have found that, in comparison to non–OBErs, OBErs tend to report higher levels of body dissatisfaction and somatoform dissociation, a heightened self-awareness or self-consciousness, lower confidence in physical self-presentation, a more positive self-concept, and to be more susceptible to procedures designed to undermine body boundary awareness. They also tend to behave in a more "disembodied manner" in virtual environments as the number of OBEs they have had increases. There is mixed evidence about whether OBErs have higher levels of social physique anxiety or not, with the larger anonymous survey detailed here finding no differences, while the virtual reality study, where participants were physically present, found higher levels. In addition, in comparison to NDErs, OBErs were found to have a heightened self-consciousness and to be more dissatisfied with their bodies.

Although further work is needed in this area, the findings presented here are indicative of pre-existing differences in the body image of OBErs and non–OBErs, which become exacerbated in the moments which precede an OBE, and which help to explain why some people are more prone to OBEs than others. Work has begun to examine these issues for different forms of OBEs and have found indicative differences between OBErs and NDErs. This work has demonstrated how the psychological study of out-of-body experiences can be broadened from a narrow focus on perceptual aspects of OBErs body image to include a consideration of affective and social dimensions of body experience and as a consequence contribute to a dissociational theory of the OBE.

References

Alvarado, C. S. (1986). Research on spontaneous out-of-body experiences: a review of modern developments, 1960–1984. In B. Shapin and L. Coly (eds.), *Current Trends in Psi Research*. New York: Parapsychology Foundation. 140–167.

Alvarado, C.S. (1992). The psychological approach to out-of-body experiences: a review of early and modern developments. *Journal of Psychology*, 126(3). 237–240.

Alvarado, C. S. (2000). Out-of-body experiences. In E. Cardena, S. J. Lynn and S. Krippner (eds.), *Varieties of Anomalous Experience: Examining the Scientific Evidence.* Washington, D.C.: American Psychological Association. 183–218.

Alvarado, C. S., and N. Zingrone (1994). Individual differences in aura vision: relationships to visual imagery and imaginative-fantasy experiences. *European Journal of Parapsychology*, 10. 1–30.

Alvarado, C. S., and N. L. Zingrone (1997). Out-of-body experiences and dissociation. Paper presented at the 40th Annual Convention of the Parapsychological Association, Brighton, England.

Alvarado, C. S., and N. L. Zingrone (1999). Out-of-body experiences among readers of a Spanish new age magazine. *Journal of the Society for Psychical Research*, 63. 65–85.

Blackmore, S. J. (1982). Out-of-body experiences, lucid dreams, and imagery: Two surveys. *The Journal of the American Society for Psychical Research*, 76(4). 301–317.

Blackmore, S. J. (1983a). Imagery and the OBE. In W. G. Roll, J. Beloff and R. A. White (eds.), *Research in Parapsychology 1982.* Metuchen, NJ: Scarecrow Press. 231–232.

Blackmore, S. J. (1983b). Birth and the OBE: An unhelpful analogy. *Journal of the American Society for Psychical Research*, 77. 229–238.

Blackmore, S. J. (1984a). A postal survey of OBEs and other experiences. *Journal of the American Society for Psychical Research*, 52. 225–244.

Blackmore, S. J. (1984b). A psychological theory of the Out-of-body Experience. *Journal of Parapsychology*, 48. 201–218.

Blackmore, S. J. (1987). Where am I? Perspectives in imagery and the out-of-body experience. *Journal of Mental Imagery*, 11. 53–66.

Blackmore, S. J. (1994). Out-of-body experiences and confusion-ism: A response to Woodhouse. *New Ideas in Psychology*, 12. 27–30.

Cappon, D., and R. Banks (1968). Distorted body perception in obesity. *Journal of Nervous and Mental Disorders*, 46. 465–467.

Cook, A. M., and H. J. Irwin (1983). Visuospatial skills and the out-of-body experience. *Journal of Parapsychology*, 47. 23–35.

Dalton, K., N. L. Zingrone and C. S. Alvarado (1999). Exploring out-of-body experiences, dissociation, and alteration of consciousness in the ganzfeld with a creative population. *Paper Presented at the 42nd Annual Convention of the Parapsychological Association, Stanford University, Palo Alto, CA.*

Devinsky, O., E. Feldmann, K. Burrowes and E. Bromfield (1989). Autoscopic phenomena with seizures. *Archives of Neurology*, 46. 1080–10888.

Fenigstein, A., M. F. Scheier and A. H. Buss (1975). Public and private self-consciousness: Assessment and theory. *Journal of Consulting and Clinical Psychology*, 43. 522–527.

Fitts, W. H. (1965). *Tennessee Self Concept Scale Manual.* Nashville: Counselor Recordings and Tests.

Gabbard, G. O., and S. W. Twemlow (1984). *With the Eyes of the Mind.* New York: Praeger.

Glickson, J. (1990). Belief in the paranormal and subjective paranormal experience. *Personality and Individual Differences*, 11. 675–683.

Gordon, R. (1949). An investigation into some of the factors that favour the formation of stereotyped images. *British Journal of Psychology*, 64, 17–24.

Graham, M. A., C. Eich, B. Kephart and D. Peterson (2000). Relationship among body image, sex, and popularity of high school students. *Perceptual & Motor Skills*, 90 (3), Pt.2: 1187–1193.

Hart, E. A., M. R. Leary and W. J. Rejeski (1989). The measurement of social physique anxiety. *Journal of Sport and Exercise Psychology*, 11. 94–104.

Hunt, H. T., A. Gervais, S. Shearing-Johns and F. Travis (1992). Transpersonal experiences in childhood: An exploratory empirical study of selected adult groups. *Perceptual and Motor Skills*, 75. 1135–1153.

Irwin, H. J. (1980). Out of the body down under: Some cognitive characteristics of Australian students reporting OBEs. *Journal of the Society for Psychical Research*, 50. 448–459.

Irwin, H. J. (1985). *Flight of Mind: A Psychological Study of the Out-of-Body Experience.* Metuchen, NJ: Scarecrow Press.

Irwin, H. J. (1986). Perceptual perspectives of visual imagery in OBEs, dreams and reminiscence. *Journal of the Society for Psychical Research*, 53. 210–217.

Irwin, H. J. (2000). The disembodied self: an empirical study of dissociation and the out-of-body experience. *Journal of Parapsychology*, 64(3). 261–276.

McKinley, N. M., and J. S. Hyde (1996). The objectified body consciousness scale. *Psychology of Women Quarterly*, 20. 181–215.

Murray, C. D., and M. Gordon (2001). Changes in bodily awareness induced by immersive virtual reality. *CyberPsychology and Behavior*, 4(3). 365–372.

Murray, C. D., and J. Fox (2004). Body image in respondents with and without out-of-body experiences. In S. Schmidt (ed.), *Proceedings of the Parapsychological Association, 47th Annual Convention*. 145–156.

Murray, C. D., and J. Fox (2005a). Body image in persons with and without prior out-of-body-experiences. *British Journal of Psychology*, 96(4). 441–456.

Murray, C. D., and J. Fox (2005b). The out-of-body experience and body image: Differences between experients and non-experients. *Journal of Nervous and Mental Disease*, 193(1). 70–72.

Murray, C. D., and J. Fox (2006). From dreams to (virtual) reality: exploring behavioural embodiment in out-of-body experients. *Australian Journal of Parapsychology*, 6(2). 125–134.

Murray, C. D., and J. Fox (2006). Differences in body image between people reporting near-death and spontaneous out-of-body-experiences. *Journal of the Society for Psychical Research*, 70(2). 98–109.

Murray, C. D., J. Fox and D. Wilde (2006). Self-concept and body investment in out-of-body experients. *European Journal of Parapsychology*, 21(1). 27–37.

Murray, C. D., J. Bowers, A. West, S. Pettifer and S. Gibson (2000). Navigation, wayfinding and place experience within a virtual city. *Presence: Teleoperators and Virtual Environments*, 9(5). 438–451.

Nijenhuis, E. R. S., P. Spinhoven, R. van Dyke, O. van der Hart and J. Vanderlinden (1996). The development and psychometric characteristics of the somatoform dissociation questionnaire. *The Journal of Nervous and Mental Disease*, 184(11). 688–694.

Orbach, I., and M. Mikulincer (1998). The body investment scale: construction and validation of a body experience scale. *Psychological Assessment*, 10(4). 415–425.

Palmer, J. (1978). The out-of-body experience: a psychological theory. *Parapsychology Review*, 9(5). 19–22.

Palmer, J. (1979). A community mail survey of psychic experiences. *Journal of the American Society for Psychical Research*, 73. 221–251.

Ryckman, R. M., M. A. Robbins, B. Thornton and P. Cantrell (1982). Development and validation of a physical self-efficacy scale. *Journal of Personality and Social Psychology*, 42. 891–900.

Richards, D. G. (1991). A study of the correlation between subjective psychic experiences and dissociative experiences. *Dissociation*, 4. 83–91.

Slade, P. D., M. E. Dewey, T. Newton, D. Brodie and G. Kiemle (1990). Development of the body satisfaction scale (BSS). *Psychology and Health*, 4. 213–226.

Zingrone, N. L., and C. S. Alvarado (1994). Psychic and dissociative experiences: A preliminary report. Paper Presented at the 37th Annual Convention of the Parapsychological Association, Amsterdam.

13

ANOMALOUS EXPERIENCES AND BOUNDARY THINNESS IN THE MIND AND BRAIN

Christine Simmonds-Moore

Boundaries in the brain and mind reflect how connected versus separate a neural structure or cognitive process is to other structures or processes. Weak or thin boundaries imply many connections between structures and processes in the neurological and cognitive systems, while firm or thick boundaries implies fewer connections between such structures and processes. Boundaries can also be viewed in terms of the extent to which inhibitory processes* are active in the system; less inhibition allows for the inclusion of more neurological structures and more cognitive processes, which have an impact on what is available to conscious awareness. As such, less inhibition implies more availability of the right hemisphere to the usually dominant left hemisphere, more availability of the sub-cortical processes to the left hemisphere, and a "looser" associational thinking style. These features reflect the tendency to find associations between events and to perceive or apply meaning (locally as creative thinking, and globally as seeing meaningful signals where there is randomness). It follows from having a system with fewer restrictions that boundary thinness also reflects the level of "permeability" in the threshold for mental imagery and processes that are usually subliminal to reach conscious awareness, such that in some people dreams are more likely to be remembered, and subliminally presented information is processed very efficiently. The concept of boundaries can also be applied to the extent to which states of conscious-

---

*Much of the neurological system functions as a result of a balance between excitatory and inhibitory connections between neurons and neuronal pathways. We are wired such that many of our nerve cells and neuronal pathways connect with one another, but are not all activated due to the execution of inhibitory controls. Less inhibition means that the pathways that do already exist are more "used."

ness are distinct, i.e., those with thin boundaries are more likely to experience dream and sleep like states during wakefulness. Interpersonal boundaries reflect a tendency for those with thinner boundaries to become very psychologically close to other human beings and subjectively feel states of empathy and connection. At the opposite end of the spectrum, a thick boundaried system reflects one that is less connected, more inhibited and more focused in terms of thinking. In terms of permeability, such individuals would have less awareness of subliminal information. Someone displaying a thick boundary profile would be less likely to find connections between events and less likely to apply meaning. States of consciousness, emotional states and the sense of self would also be experienced as firmly distinct from others.

It has been suggested recently (Hansen, 2001) that extrasensory perception (ESP) and psychokinesis (PK) are *by definition* associated with crossing boundaries. Hansen notes that barriers between mind and mind are crossed in cases of telepathy; barriers between mind and matter are crossed in cases of clairvoyance and PK; the usual limits of time are crossed in the case of precognition and the normal boundaries of life and death are crossed in the cases of spirit mediumship, ghosts and reincarnation (p. 29).

Boundaries are not a new idea in psychology or parapsychology. Indeed, the concept of thresholds and boundaries in the mind were explored over a century ago by Frederick Myers (1902/2002) and William James (e.g., 2003) and are also apparent in the thinking of Bergson in terms of *filter* theories of psi (e.g., 1913) — the idea that psi is present within the cognitive system, but filtered out of conscious awareness by attentional mechanisms alongside other non-relevant information in any given moment. I suggest here that most anomalous experiences can be understood in terms of increased permeability of boundaries and barriers in the mind.

Louisa Rhine (1953) suggested that psi expression might be a function of the "ease of transmission" from unconscious to conscious levels in the mind. At the time, this idea was rejected because dreaming is traditionally associated with the expression of unconscious material into consciousness and subjective paranormal experiences occur as often in waking life as they do in dreams. As thinner psychological boundaries are associated with less distinct states of consciousness, and in particular, "sleep-like" thinking whilst awake (see Hartmann, 1991, and later section in this chapter), it may be that dream like phenomena (and by extension, anomalous experiences) do occur during the waking state. In this chapter, I take the perspective that psi and subjective anomalous phenomena may be experienced as a function of the ease of transmission, due to individual differences in boundary thinness (trait boundary thinness). Boundary thinness may also be considered to be a state of consciousness (state boundary thinness). As such, this allows for a parsimonious explanation for anomalous experiences as all experiences may be associated with a similar "state," but some individuals might be more readily in that state during wakefulness (and sleep) than are others. This chapter will firstly explore thin boundaried personality, and later move on to discuss state boundary thinness, possible control of boundaries and their implications for mental health and ESP.

Personality Types Associated with Boundary Thinness

Boundaries have been explored explicitly and psychometrically in recent years by two main researchers, Thalbourne in his construct of Transliminality (e.g. Thalbourne and Houran, 2000) and Hartmann in his construct of Boundary Thinness (e.g. Hartmann, 1991). A third route of understanding derives from the literature on positive schizotypy (e.g., see Claridge, 1997) and related variables (e.g., Persinger's Temporal lobe lability, Persinger and Makarec, 1987). These personality variables are all associated with increased reporting of subjective paranormal experiences and seem to share neurological and cognitive attributes. Indeed, Positive schizotypy, temporal lobe lability, boundary thinness and transliminality are considered by this author to be associated with greater connections (reduced inhibitory processes) in the brain and mind, which results in a range of "thinner boundaries" (to be explored in more detail later in this chapter. See also Simmonds, 2003).

POSITIVE SCHIZOTYPY

Schizotypy is a term derived from "schizophrenic genotype" and indicates a greater disposition toward schizophrenia (Claridge, 1997). Some authors (e.g., the Chapmans, e.g., see Claridge and Beech, 1995) consider that *any* presence of "schizotypal traits" are indicative of psychopathology, and therefore take a quasi-dimensional view on schizotypy. Other authors (in particular, Claridge, e.g., 1997) consider schizotypy to be a fully dimensional personality construct. As such, the cognitive and perceptual anomalies associated with schizophrenia are considered to be normally distributed among the general population, with only extreme levels *potentially* resulting in psychotic breakdown. At one end there is very little manifestation of the traits, while the majority of people would exhibit the traits to a certain extent. This implicates a useful role for watered down schizotypal traits; indeed, there is some evidence for the idea of the high scoring "happy" or "benign" schizotype (e.g., Goulding, 2004, 2005; Holt, Simmonds-Moore and Moore, 2008; Jackson, 1997) who is psychologically healthy and exhibits adaptive traits such as creativity (e.g., Brod, 1997; Holt, Simmonds-Moore and Moore, 2008). The competing perspectives on schizotypy continue to co-exist despite considerable evidence for the better explanatory value of the personality explanation over that of the psychopathological "taxon" (e.g., Rawlings, Williams, Haslam, and Claridge, 2008). The perspective of this author is that schizotypy reflects a personality continuum ranging from low scorers through normals to high scorers who may be more prone to schizophrenic breakdown.

Schizotypy is a multidimensional variable, which is comprised of four factors (Claridge and Beech, 1995). These are positive schizotypy; cognitive disorganization (attentional difficulties); negative schizotypy or introvertive anhedonia (preference for solitude, lack of enjoyment from social sources); and impulsive nonconformity* (impulse ridden, reckless behaviors). The traits associated with positive schizotypy are those most associated with anomalous phenomena. These include magical thinking, hallucinations and altered perceptual experiences. This variable relates to subjective anomalous and paranormal experiences and beliefs (e.g., Simmonds and Roe, 2000; Wolfradt, Oubaid, Straube, Bischoff and Mischo, 1999). Several authors have also found that Magical Ideation (as a measure of positive schizotypy) is a predictor of above chance ESP scoring in the ganzfeld (Lawrence and Woodley, 1998; Parker, 2000; Parker, Grams and Pettersson, 1998; Parker and Westerlund, 1998). However, work using other measures of positive schizotypy (e.g., unusual experiences subscale of the OLIFE, Mason, Claridge, and Jackson, 1995) has found no significant relationship with ESP (Simmonds, 2003; Simmonds-Moore and Holt, 2007). However, a recent assessment of clusters or types of schizotypy scorers indicated that those who score high on positive schizotypy but low on the other 3 scales did better at an ESP test addressing psi as the unattended stimulus (Holt and Simmonds-Moore, 2008). Other work by Simmonds (e.g., Simmonds, 2003; Simmonds and Holt, 2007; Simmonds and Fox, 2004; Holt and Simmonds-Moore, 2008) has also addressed schizotypy and ESP from a multidimensional perspective. The only significant relationship with ESP, when each scale was individually correlated with the psi measure was a negative relationship with impulsive nonconformity (Simmonds and Fox, 2004).

Temporal Lobe Lability

Temporal lobe lability may also be considered to reflect a personality continuum from normals through to epileptics in the general population (Persinger and Makarec, 1987). This reflects a continuum of electrical activity in the temporal lobes—effectively indicating how interconnected temporal lobe structures are with the rest of the brain. Lability can also change as a result of meditation, hypoglycemia (prolonged fasting), fatigue, hypoxia, alterations in vascu-

---

Impulsive nonconformity is however a controversial factor considered by some to reflect more manic tendencies (e.g., Loughland and Williams, 1997).

lar flow associated with drugs and the biochemical effects caused by personal crises (Persinger and Makarec, 1987; Persinger, 1989).*

Normal people with heightened lability of their temporal lobes, may experience a benign or sub-clinical variety of "seizure," which may be associated with anomalous experiences (c.f. Persinger and Makarec, 1993). Those who score higher on this scale are indeed particularly likely to report paranormal beliefs (e.g., Persinger and Richards, 1991), subjective paranormal experiences (e.g., Persinger and Valliant, 1985) and anomalous experiences (e.g., Kennedy, Kanthamani and Palmer, 1994). High scorers are also prone to finding great meaning or significance in events, and are more likely to be creative and suggestible (Persinger and Makarec, 1993). Meaning and significance are associated with the functioning of the amygdala, (housed within the temporal lobes) which is effectively more available to the rest of the brain in those who score high on this scale.

HARTMANN'S BOUNDARY QUESTIONNAIRE

Hartmann's (1991) personality construct of psychological boundaries refers to a continuum of boundary thinness in the mind and brain. *Thin* boundaries refer to a relative connectedness of psychological processes, which is reflected in a thinking style of "shades of grey." *Thick* boundaries in the mind, on the other hand, refer to a relative separateness of psychological processes, which is reflected in a thinking style of "black and white" (Hartmann, Rosen and Rand, 1998). These concepts reflect structural boundaries, e.g., how connected neural structures are to one another; representational boundaries, e.g., how related representations and concepts are to one another, and boundaries in how one thinks or processes information, e.g. is thinking focused or unfocused. Hartmann (1991) suggests that boundaries should be seen as one broad dimension of personality, although he considers that there are 12 types of boundary assessed by the Hartmann Boundary Questionnaire (BQ) (Hartmann, 1991), see Table 1.

Table 1: Examples of Boundary Types from the Hartmann Boundary Questionnaire (1991)

Type of Boundary	*Example of a Question Addressing This Form of Boundary*
Sleep/wake/dream	When I awake in the morning, I am not sure whether I am really awake for a few minutes.
Unusual experiences	I have had déjà vu experiences.
Thoughts, feelings, moods	Sometimes I don't know whether I am thinking or feeling.

*The idea that boundary thinness is a state as well as a trait is revisited later in this chapter.

Childhood, adolescent, adulthood	I am very close to my childhood feelings.
Interpersonal	When I get involved with someone, we sometimes get too close.
Sensitivity	I am very sensitive to other peoples' feelings.
Neat, exact, precise	I keep my desk or work table neat and well organized.
Edges, lines, clothing	I like houses with flexible spaces, where you can shift things around and make different uses of the room.
Opinions about children and others	I think a good teacher must remain in part a child.
Opinions about organizations	In an organization, everyone should have a definite place and a specific role.
Opinions about people, nations, groups	There are no sharp dividing lines between normal people, people with problems and people who are considered psychotic or crazy.
Opinions about beauty and truth	Either you are telling the truth or you are lying; that's all there is to it.

Boundary thinness has been associated with subjective success at a psi task (Richards, 1996) and is higher among those who consider themselves to be psychic (Krippner, Wickramasekera and Tartz, 2001). Richards (1991) found that only four boundaries relate to perceived success at an interpersonal psi task. These relate to the experiential and emotional types of boundary and were sleep, unusual experiences, thoughts and feelings and sensitivity. A recent study found that overall thinner boundaries related to biological PK where PK was located in the data set (Palmer, Simmonds-Moore and Baumann, 2006) and sensitivity and childishness subscales of a short form of the BQ correlated directly with PK performance (unpublished findings from the dataset of Palmer, Simmonds-Moore and Baumann, 2006).

THALBOURNE'S TRANSLIMINALITY

The Transliminality variable reflects "the hypothesized tendency for psychological material to cross thresholds into or out of consciousness" (Thalbourne and Houran, 2000, p. 861). It was originally derived from a factor analysis of several variables including paranormal belief, magical ideation, manic like experience, depressive experience, creative personality and mystical experience. These clustered on a single factor (Thalbourne and Delin, 1994).

The transliminality construct, as it is currently defined, is comprised of absorption, fantasy proneness, magical ideation, paranormal belief, mystical experience, hyperesthesia, (this is a "hypersensitivity to environmental stimulation," Thalbourne, 1998, p. 403), creative personality, manic experience and attitude to dream interpretation, it is currently measured employing a 17-item scale (Lange, Houran, and Storm, 2000). There is some evidence that transliminality is associated with increased psi performance in the laboratory (see Sanders, Thalbourne and Delin, 2000; Storm and Thalbourne, 2001) although results are mixed overall, and several studies addressing transliminality have found chance scoring (c.f., Simmonds, 2003).

How Do These Variables Inter-Relate?

Although no previous study has addressed *all* of these variables simultaneously, previous work does indicate that they are highly correlated. Temporal lobe lability shares considerable variance with schizotypy, (e.g., Brugger and Graves, 1997; Simmonds, 2003) and with the Transliminality scale (Thalbourne, Crawley and Houran, 2003). Transliminality also correlates positively and significantly with schizotypy (Thalbourne, 1998). Thalbourne (1999) has suggested that "schizotypy represents what is probably the closest conceptually and empirically to transliminality" (p. 20). Transliminality has also been found to correlate positively with boundary thinness (Houran, Thalbourne, and Hartmann, 2003). Until recently, boundary thinness had not been directly compared to schizotypy, however, those with schizotypal personality were found to score "thinner" (Hartmann, 1991).

These variables also correlate with the same other variables, in particular creativity, absorption and dissociation; all of which relate independently with psi performance and subjective paranormal experiences. Creativity is high among those scoring high on positive schizotypy (e.g., Brod, 1997) and transliminality (Thalbourne, 2000). Absorption correlates with both schizotypy (Parker, 1999) and temporal lobe lability (Kennedy, Kanthamani and Palmer, 1994). Williams (1997) found a common factor between schizotypy variables of Magical Ideation, Perceptual Aberration and Hypomania alongside absorption and paranormal experiences. He suggests that "an imaginative cognitive style seems to underlie both paranormal experience and schizotypy" (Williams, 1997, p.109). This looks similar to transliminality. Dissociation correlates with temporal lobe lability (Persinger and Makarec, 1993), positive schizotypy (Merckelbach, Rassin, and Muris, 2000) and transliminality (Thalbourne, 1998) and is itself related to subjective paranormal experiences (Pekala, Kumar, and Marcano, 1995). Overall, then, these variables look like they represent an anomaly-prone personality type, characterized by thinner psychological boundaries.

Simmonds (2005) examined the relationship between boundary thinness, schizotypy, temporal lobe lability, transliminality and anomalous experiences (alongside other variables). Transliminality and temporal lobe lability showed the strongest correlations, followed by schizotypy, then boundary thinness. For the purpose of the current paper, a principal component analysis was undertaken on these data. One component, which I have labeled Boundary Thinness was extracted which supports the idea of a boundary related understanding to anomalous experiences. The component matrix is illustrated in Table 2.

Table 2: Component Matrix from a Principal Components Analysis of Boundary-Related Variables

Variable	Component
Transliminality	.883
Schizotypy	.828
Personal philosophy inventory	.889
anomalous experience inventory	.825
boundary questionnaire	.707

A cluster analysis was also undertaken which indicates the existence of two types of scorer in the data set (it was pre-specified that two clusters should be derived from the analysis), and supports the idea of a boundary basis for anomalies, see Table 3. These indicate that cluster one has very high scores on temporal lobe lability, transliminality, anomalous experiences and schizotypy, moderately high scoring on boundary thinness and marginally reduced sleep patterns. Cluster two had lower scoring on all boundary related questionnaires and anomalous experiences alongside average sleep quality.

Table 3: Cluster Analysis of Z-Scores of Personality and Sleep Variables

Variable	Cluster One	Cluster Two
Quality of sleep	-.11	.07
Transliminality	.8	-.6
Schizotypy	.75	-.6
Personal philosophy inventory	.86	-.7
Anomalous experience inventory	.78	-.6
Boundary questionnaire	.55	-.45

An exploratory regression path analysis from Simmonds (2005) is reproduced in Figure 1.

These results indicate that the boundary-related variables have slightly different relationships with anomalous experiences and have slightly different variables as their own predictors. These variables may all be measuring aspects of *boundary thinness* but some are more directly important when considering the etiology of anomalous experiences than others. This also indicates that there are other moderators of boundary thinness, in particular sleep and handedness. The following section explores the nature and type of boundaries and considers *how* boundaries might relate to paranormal experiences.

A Hierarchical Perspective on Boundaries

I consider that boundaries are important at all levels in the cognitive-perceptual system in terms of gaining insight into anomalous experiences. This section will take a hierarchical approach toward boundaries in the body/brain/mind and observe how beliefs and experiences result from physiological and

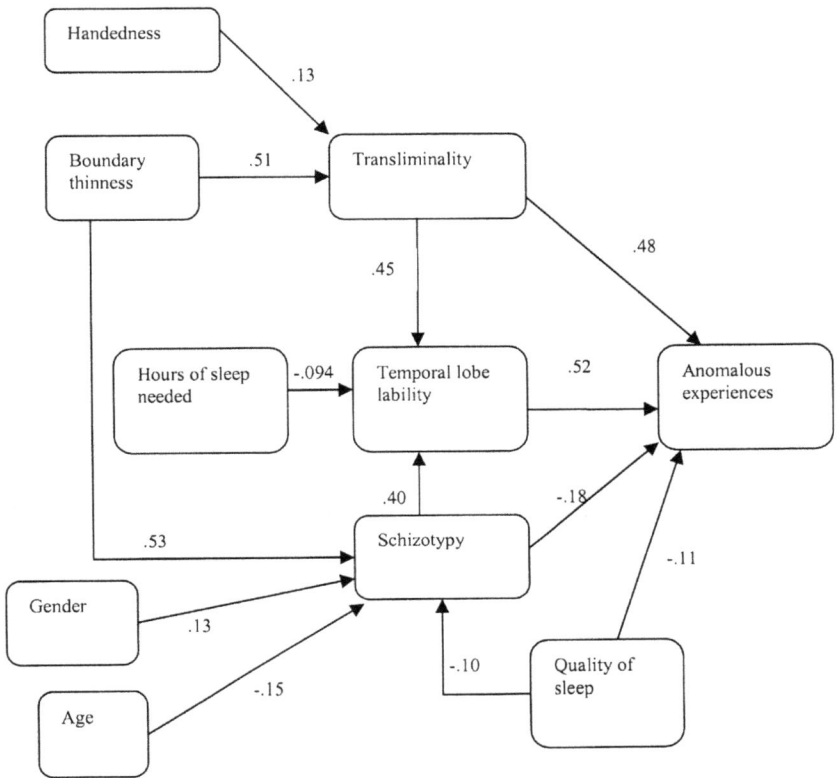

Figure 1: Path model of personality, sleep related and demographic variables predicting anomalous experiences (with beta weights as annotations).

cognitive biases that are more likely among these personality types. A discussion will be presented on the nature of the cognitive-perceptual system of these individuals, which exhibits a reduction in cognitive inhibition, increased proneness to borderline states of consciousness, more connectivity between brain areas, and more influence of sub-cortical processes on cortical processes, which results in more conscious availability of information that is associated with lower levels of processing. This effectively allows information that is usually outside the focus of attention and in the subliminal mind to be consciously perceived, or more available to bias behaviour (consciously or unconsciously). This information may or may not allow for more psi to reach conscious awareness. However, more "non-psi" will also reach conscious awareness. For example, Myers (1902/2002) noted that "hidden in the deep of our being is a rubbish heap as well as a treasurehouse; degenerations and insanities as well as beginnings of higher development" (p. 48).

In line with the pseudo psi interpretation, cognitive aspects of boundaries are associated with an increased likelihood to see meaningful shapes amid noise, to see associations between events, and overall to have a greater propensity for the allocation of meaning (often where there are no such associations present). There is also a tendency to generate more hypotheses but test less of them and conclude rapidly that a perception is both real and external.

The metaphor of boundaries can be applied at all levels, in the mind and brain, and beyond the mind and brain, reflected at the level of consciousness and interpersonal and social behavior. I suggest that some may be more valuable in understanding anomalous and paranormal phenomena than others.

More Physiological Lability

If psi exists, it may function like a weak stimulus, which registers in the body. The idea that psi works more efficiently at an unconscious level has been suggested by several authors (e.g., Beloff, 1974) and there is evidence that physiological and implicit measures of ESP are superior to conscious measures. For example, Stanford's PMIR model (1974a; 1974b) indicates that there are unconscious biases on behavior indicative of ESP and PK. More recent work in this area has explored the presentiment effect, whereby there is a small peak in autonomic activity prior to the presentation of emotional stimuli (Radin, 1997). Other work has found that ERPs measured in the gamma range distinguish future targets from non targets, whilst conscious guessing has been at chance (e.g., Don, McDonough, and Warren, 1998).

Braud proposed that free variability or "lability" of the brain or mind is important in the psi process (Braud, Shafer and Mulgrew, 1993, p. 193). If this is the case, those who are physically more reactive may also be more reactive to remote stimuli (psi). There is a greater physiological reactivity among those with thinner boundaries than those with thicker boundaries. Due to the altered arousal levels in the nervous systems of schizotypes, positive schizotypes, those with hypomanic personality and cognitive disorganization demonstrate an increased lability in their nervous systems, while introvertive anhedonics have *reduced* lability (Claridge, 1967). The construct of temporal lobe lability is inherently labile. The autonomic nervous system is regulated by the amygdala (housed within the temporal lobes of the brain), which serves as a vigilance system to emotional events in the world. It also has projections to cortical regions of the brain, and primes the cortex in the processing of information that is biologically relevant to the organism. Those with greater neural connections/reduced inhibition may also experience more influence from [emotional] perceptions in the body (or lower levels of the brain). At times, these could coincide with events in the real world, which seem psychic but are actually coincidental.

CONNECTIONS IN THE BRAIN

The thin boundaried brain is more interconnected with itself. This refers to the brain structure considered from several perspectives. At the neuronal level, there are "more complex or multiple connections in the cortex (for thin boundaries) versus relatively simple straightforward or specific connections (for thick boundaries)" (Hartmann, 1991, p. 241–242). The normal nervous system has *fine-tuned* itself, whilst the thin-boundaried system exhibits connections that have grown (or not been neurally "pruned"). A conceptual diagram of thin and thick-boundaried thinking in the brain may be observed in Figure 2 (after Hartmann, 1991). Hartmann (1991) suggests that the "thick boundary brain is relatively finished, all grown up, solidified, no longer developing, in comparison to the thin boundary brain which is still changing or growing, still somewhat childish" (p. 246). This is of interest given a recent (and currently unpublished) finding in the dataset of Palmer, Simmonds-Moore and Baumann (2006) who found that the subscale of *childishness* correlated moderately with performance at a biological PK task.

The role of subcortical processes and "vertical" connectivity • Boundary thin personalities and states of consciousness may be associated with increased connections between lower and higher brain structures. Thalbourne, for instance, has suggested that the physiological nature of transliminality may be conceptualized as the interconnectedness of various distinct parts of the brain. Thalbourne (1999) cites Houran (personal communication) who suggests "transliminality is a by-product of the extreme sensitivity of the neocortex to information from both the R-Complex [the so called reptilian brain] and Limbic system" (p. 21). Thus, there is an increased communication between higher and lower parts of the brain. A similar theory is suggested by Hartmann (1991) in terms of boundary thinness.

The description of the physiological nature of transliminality (which correlates with both unusual experiences and impulsive nonconformity) suggested an increased sensitivity of the cortex to limbic processes in the brain (Thalbourne, 1999). This implies a greater connection with lower structures and awareness of lower level processes in the brain and a relative reduction in overall cortical arousal, which was suggested to be psi-conducive. In his discussion of QiGong, Hong Xiong (2000) discusses the possibility that the cortex usually functions as the effective attentional filter and suggests that psi may not often reach conscious awareness, because it is associated with lower areas of the brain such as the limbic system. It is of interest that increased psi ability has been claimed to be associated with the Chinese/Japanese meditative practice of QiGong. There is also an association between states of consciousness associated with a dominance of alpha and theta EEG rhythms (which reflect more influence of sub-cortical structures on the cortex) and extrasensory perception (see Alvarado, 1998). This is also associated with the hypnagogic state of consciousness, which will be discussed later in this chapter when boundary *states* are explored.

The right hemisphere and "lateral" connectivity • Among those with positive schizotypy, there is greater connection between the right and left hemispheres, and right hemispheric associative thinking is likely to intrude into the left hemisphere (see Simmonds, 2003). Brugger (e.g., Brigger, Gamma, Muri, Shafer and Taylor, 1993) has noted that associational processing, which is one characteristic of those with thinner boundaries, is a right hemispheric process, and that those with positive schizotypy have a right hemispheric bias in processing information. Simmonds (2005) found that handedness (which could function as an indirect measure of laterality) related indirectly to anomalous experiences via Transliminality (see Figure 1). Specifically, ambidextrous individuals reported more subjective paranormal experiences, which implicates the deployment of *both* left and right hemispheric processes (Simmonds, 2005). This finding fits with previous work which found that those possessing a complimentary thinking style, including both rational and intuitive thinking styles, tend to be more likely to believe in paranormal phenomena than those with only intuitive or rational thinking styles (Wolfradt, Oubaid, Straube, Bischoff and Mischo, 1999; Genovese, 2005). The expression of *two* thinking styles simultaneously related to paranormal belief, experience and ability, and was associated with schizotypy. They suggest the combination of the two modes results from the brain's attempted psychological regulation of the two very different types of thought. This may imply that processes associated with both right and left hemispheres are more involved in such experiences, which suggests increased hemispheric connection (or communication) and ability to entertain two different ways of approaching the world simultaneously. However, Irwin and Young (2001) did not find the combination pattern in their later study, and note that Wolfradt et al. failed to find it in a replication of their 1999 study. In fact, Irwin and Young found that paranormal beliefs were more related to an intuitive (and not rational) thinking style. However, there was a trend toward a relationship between a combination of rational and intuitive thinking and new age beliefs.

The right hemisphere is considered to be important in the psi process (e.g., Braud, 1975). There has been some empirical support for the role of the right hemisphere in psi processing (Broughton, 1983), but recent work has not supported a difference between those with a preference for the right or left hemisphere on a psi task (Alexander and Broughton, 1999). It may well be that a contribution of *both* hemispheres might be more informative when considering the psi process, and subjective paranormal experiences.

These ideas are revisited in the final section of this chapter where the idea that healthy boundary thinness reflects a combination with some thicker boundaried processes is explored.

ATTENTIONAL WIDENING

Boundaries may be considered *cognitively* in terms of the wideness of the attentional "spotlight." From this perspective, psi might be considered as the unattended stimulus, which usually falls outside of this spotlight. The idea of a filter in the mind that sifts incoming information dates back to Bergson (e.g., 1913), Broadbent (cited in Roney-Dougal, 1986) and Myers (1902/2002). Roney-Dougal (1986) suggests that selection filters in the normal mind prevent our experiencing this sort of overload, and that we would go mad if we were aware of everything at once. The result of a breakdown in attentional mechanisms is that filtering cannot function properly, resulting in too much information in the cognitive system, which may or may not include the psi signal, or any "real" signal. Roney-Dougal (1986) cites Price who suggested that mental barriers are needed, else we might experience too much psi in conjunction with a deluge of other seemingly irrelevant information. The implication is that a thinner filter in a healthier individual would allow more information, including psi, to reach conscious awareness.

In the normal nervous system, two arousal systems function in equilibrium to maintain homeostasis in the central nervous system and to filter overall sensory input into the system (Claridge, 1967). These are *tonic arousal*, which ranges from low to high anxiety, and *homeostatic arousal*, which reflects the arousal profiles of extraverts and introverts. These become partially dissociated in positive schizotypy, which results in the inhibitory mechanisms in the central and autonomic nervous systems being weakened (McCreery and Claridge, 1996). The nervous system is generally more relaxed and open to incoming and lower levels of information as there are fewer inhibitory processes functioning; it has been described as an "open nervous system ... where excitatory mechanisms are high and inhibitory processes low" (McCreery and Claridge, 1996, p. 756).

A widening of attention and increased association due to reduced inhibition has been demonstrated in the better performance of positive and impulsive schizotypes on several cognitive paradigms (cf. Simmonds, 2003), which have been referred to as "superior performance paradigms" (Claridge and Beech, 1995). These are the negative priming paradigm, the latent inhibition paradigm and semantic activation without conscious identification paradigm.

Recent work has explored the idea that ESP might work like the unattended stimulus, which is usually filtered out of conscious awareness by employing a latent inhibition paradigm (Holt, Simmonds-Moore and Moore, 2007). Latent inhibition addresses the fate of an initially inconsequential masked stimulus (in this study, a triangle) that later becomes important in learning a rule. Normally, there are two conditions, pre-exposure versus non-pre-exposure. We added two psi pre-exposure conditions (one in addition to the existing psi stimulus and the second where there was no normal pre-exposure of the stimulus). The initial stimulus is usually inhibited from entering into cognitive associations in the rule learning part of the study, as such, there is a corresponding slowing of rule learning where one is "pre-exposed." This work found that where a psi stimulus was masked and sent during a first stage, there was an equivalent slowing of rule learning. This implies that psi is processed in a similar way to how the mind treats the normal unattended stimulus.

Further work by the author has explored the idea that attentional widening in schizotypy and transliminality might relate to ESP (e.g., Holt, Simmonds-Moore and Moore, 2008). It was found that creativity, belief in the paranormal and unusual experiences (which may function as the transliminality variable) correlated with the attention based psi effect, but schizotypy (as measured as a unidimensional scale) did not.* This work should be replicated to further understand and disseminate the role of attention and personality for the psi process.

Bullen, Hemsley and Dixon (1987) explored the relationship between attention and anomalous experiences from a mainstream perspective. Anomalies of attention allow more automatic or preconscious processing to become conscious. This may be associated with experiential and perceptual anomalies, which presumably may seem to be psychic, perhaps due to coincidence with events in the external world.

Subliminal information is more available • "Subliminal" information refers to stimuli presented below the normal perceptual threshold for conscious awareness. There is evidence that subliminal information is more available to conscious awareness among those with thinner boundaries. This may be mediated by lax attentional processing and a general lowering of inhibitory processes in the mind-brain, which would allow greater access to lower levels of awareness in both "thin boundaries" and positive schizotypy. Evans (1997) directly addressed the relationship between schizotypy and subliminal processing. She employed a paradigm called *Semantic Activation Without Conscious Identification* and found a significant correlation between positive schizotypy and sensitivity to subliminal primes. Overall, it seems that there is an advantage for subliminal information among positive schizotypes, which may or may not also include psi. Levin, Gilmartin and Lamontanaro (1998–99) found that those with thinner boundaries, as identified by the BQ, had greater access to imagistic stimuli (in "image" or pictorial format) that were presented subliminally, than those with thicker boundaries. In the same study, boundary thinness was related to Rorschach boundary disruption, which indicates a greater openness to emotional stimuli (the Rorschach is employed to address the level of defensiveness to emotional stimuli).

Those with thinner boundaries were also more likely to recall their dreams,

---

*Later analysis has indicated an ESP effect where schizotypy is addressed in terms of clusters, such that those who score high on positive schizotypy and low on other forms of schizotypy demonstrated an attention-based psi effect (Holt and Simmonds-Moore, 2008).

which were considered to have greater subjective salience. Those who score high on positive aspects of schizotypy are also more likely to remember nightmares and enjoyable dreams (Claridge, Clark and Davis, 1997) and report hypnagogic imagery (Jakes and Hemsley, 1987). As such, thinner boundaried individuals seem to have more access to subliminal information of an emotional and image form than thicker boundaried individuals.

The hypothesis that there is increased psi amid usually subliminal information is supported by the similarity between subliminal perception and psi (Beloff, 1973; Carpenter, 2004, 2005; Roney-Dougal, 1986). Roney-Dougal suggests that both psi and subliminal percepts are weak inputs to the cognitive system and are good substrates for the study of how information moves from the subconscious to the conscious mind. Roney-Dougal's review of the literature demonstrates considerable overlaps between the correlates of subliminal perception and ESP. For example, they both influence conscious percepts and behavior, they are both associated with right hemisphere processes and occur more in altered states of consciousness. This is particularly the case with semantic and associational responses to stimuli. Finally, there is a similarity in physiological responses (e.g. by means of galvanic skin responses) to both psi and subliminally presented targets, particularly when these stimuli are emotional in nature. Direct experimental comparisons have revealed that the two forms of perception are actually related to one another in many contexts (see Roney-Dougal, 1986). Carpenter (e.g., 2004) has noted that ESP may work as an earlier stage in the perceptual processes, prior to subliminal perception. In this way, psi may work to *orient* the organism toward or away from a particular target or object. This would be seen in the laboratory as psi hitting or psi missing. He notes that many experiments exploring subliminal areas of mind may be applied to our understanding of ESP.

Increased awareness of subliminal information via decreased inhibition may otherwise be implicated in the mislabeling of mundane experiences as psychic. It may be that distracting information from lower levels of consciousness and unfiltered information from the external world may not be ignored by schizophrenics and schizotypes. As such, this may be involved in a "chain of semantic activation which may lead to intrusions of irrelevant information into consciousness" (Williams and Beech 1997, p. 77). In an experiment addressing the relationship between transliminality and performance at a subliminal card-guessing task, high transliminals outperformed low transliminals where they received subliminal primes as to the correct card choice (Crawley, French and Yesson, 2002). There was no difference where no primes were given, thus indicating that subliminal information is misattributed as psi among these individuals. Other work (Houran and Lange, 1998) has indicated a relationship between dream frequency and the reporting of precognition, which could indicate an increase in sense data which may be meaningfully related (coincidentally) to events in the real world.

ASSOCIATIONAL THINKING

A tendency toward making cognitive associations by having a "looser" cognitive style is also associated with a tendency toward new age beliefs and practices (which would include anomalous and paranormal experiences) (see Farias, Claridge, and Lalljee, 2005). Gianotti, Mohr, Pizzagalli, Lehmann, and Brugger (2001) have proposed that there is a continuum reflecting associative processing, and that this underlies the tendency to think creatively, experience paranormal cognition, and at higher levels have psychopathological delusions. Brugger (e.g., Brugger, 2001) has asserted that the tendency to make a type one error (or experience *apothenia;* seeing patterns where none are really there) explains the relationship between paranormal thinking and psychopathology. These researchers do not, however, entertain the possibility that paranormal ideation might also include genuine psi phenomena. Although they refer to the tendency as a continuum (with the tendency to make a type II error at the opposite end) they do not fully explore the notion that someone at the opposite end of the spectrum might be more prone to "miss" a genuinely psychic signal.

The associational tendency among those with "thinner boundaries" is illustrated by reference to Figure 2, which may simultaneously be considered cognitively *and* biologically in terms of perception and problem solving.

The "goal" is reached eventually by taking both pathways. In the thin-boundaried brain, processing is more associative, involving more connections, branches and ambiguity. In those who have thicker boundaries, processing is more linear and potentially faster, but the solution is less creative.

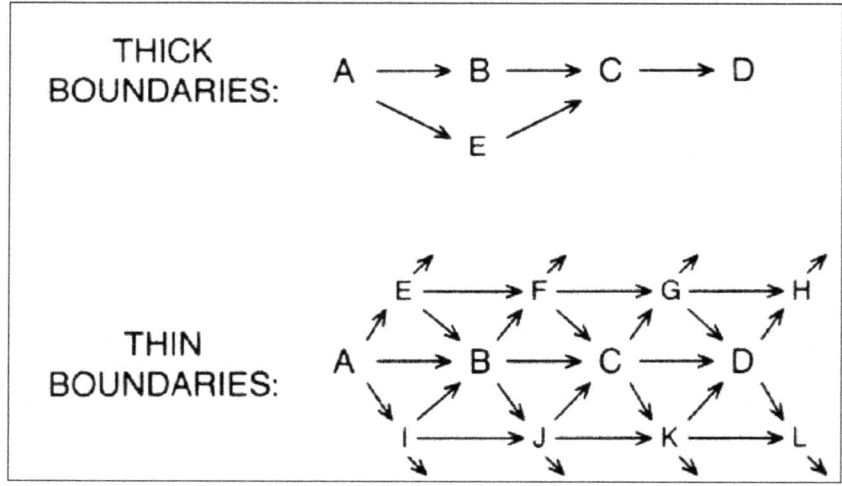

Figure 2: Boundary thinness (reproduced from Hartmann, 1991, p. 245).

Among those who score high on positive schizotypy, Evans (1997) found that there was an increase in the activity of automatic associational semantic networks lending empirical support to the idea that any stimulus might lead to more activations in memory in thinner boundaried individuals.

These tendencies may be underpinned by activity of structures within the limbic system. The hippocampus acts as the "key" to access the memory traces via its connections with the cortex. Brugger and Graves (1997) consider that a hyper-activation of the medial temporal lobes results in a disinhibition of associative processing among those who score high on positive schizotypy. Hypo-activation of the frontal association cortex in those who score low on positive schizotypy and high on negative schizotypy results in an inhibition of associative processing (or thicker boundaries). As noted previously, the amygdala has a role in attaching meaning to both external and internal experiences. An *over connection* between the limbic system and the cortex also causes extra meaning to be attached to sometimes mundane events (Skirda and Persinger, 1993). Brugger et al. (1999) have suggested that at the opposite end of the continuum individuals would be less likely to report seeing meaningfulness or perceiving a shape in randomness when one is actually there (the Type II error).

This has relevance for the psi and non-psi hypotheses. Roll (1966) and Irwin (1979) have both considered that the ESP response may be formed from the person's own memory traces. Greater connectivity would relate to access to more sense data and memories. Enhanced memory processes have been found to relate to psi (for example, Feather, 1967; Roll and Montagno, 1985) and another boundary related personality variable, temporal lobe lability (Persinger, 1996).

Positive schizotypy is also associated with making the type I error—perceiving something that is not present. For example, schizotypy has been associated with the likelihood of reporting hearing a song in white noise that was not actually played (Young, Bentall, Slade and Dewey, 1987); seeing a stimulus that was not present (Feelgood and Rantzen, 1994); reporting greater complexity of patterns observed in randomness (Jakes and Hemsley 1986); having greater confidence in the perceptual decision made regardless of accuracy (Nuchpongsai, Arakaki, Langman and Ogura, 1999); being more likely to see causality between two events (Jolley, Jones and Hemsley (1999) and being more likely to perceive meaningfulness (Brugger, et al.,1993). Little or no work explores the effects that disbelief or not having experienced any anomalies might have on the perception of a signal. The current author plans to explore this idea in future research.*

---

*This work is supported by the Bial Foundation, and will explore the perception of weak signals amid noise (visual and auditory contexts) for believers and disbelievers and those who score thin and thick in terms of boundaries. It will also include conditions where there is no signal and a condition where there is a psi signal for both contexts to explore apothenia, psi hitting and psi missing.

Synesthesia • Synesthesia has been suggested to be a building block of anomalous experiences (Irwin, 1999; Williams, 1997*).* Synesthesia is a blurring of sensory experiences where one modality is experienced when another modality is stimulated (Reber, 1985) and is considered by some authors (e.g. Marks, 2000) to be on a continuum in the general population. As such, a few individuals will be at an extreme and are classic "strong" synesthetes. Weaker forms of synesthesia, which are possibly those associated with thinner boundaries, are often associated with the experience of colored alphabets (where certain letters or words are experienced as particular colors) and musical experiences of colors (where certain notes are experienced as particular colors), which may be more of a cognitive form of boundary thinness. Different theories abound on the reasons for synesthesia, which include sequence learning, failure of neural pruning, sensory leakage of information in brain pathways, disinhibition of neural feedback, hybrid models and increased functioning of the limbic system (for reviews see Grossenbacher and Lovelace, 2001; Harrison, 2001; Marks, 2000).

In general, however, those prone to synesthesia, have less neural inhibitory processes than those who are not (Grossenbacher, 1997) and the majority of models would imply that synesthesia relates to a thinning of boundaries in the mind/brain. Indeed, synesthesia relates to psychometric measures of boundary thinness (Hartmann, 1991) to schizotypy (e.g., Williams and Beech, 1996) and to transliminality (Thalbourne, Houran, Alias and Brugger, 2001). It may well be that synesthesia can allow a person to see the world (or experience the world) in a different way, and as such have more access to psi phenomena, but this has yet to be explored directly in an empirical investigation.

INTERPERSONAL BOUNDARIES, SOCIETAL BOUNDARIES AND PSI

One of the original boundaries on Hartmann's original BQ (1991) was one relating to interpersonal boundaries, which indicated that an extremely thin boundaried person had a tendency to get "too close" to another individual. Previous work has indicated that close emotional and biological bonds may be associated with increased performance at a psi task. Dalton (1997), for example, has suggested that psi hitting is encouraged from emotionally close and biologically close pairs.

Sheldrake (2003) also found emotional closeness to be an important variable between individuals in his assessment of telephone telepathy. In a similar line of research, those who are biologically identical (monozygotic twins) were found to display EEG coherence, in other words they were acting as if there were no boundaries between them (Duane and Behrendt, 1965). More recently, the work of Grinberg-Zylberbaum, Delaflor, Attie and Goswami (1994) indicates that meditative "closeness" may also relate to paranormal communication. This work found that there was a physically observable evoked potential that was apparently *transferred* between the brains of pairs of participants who had got into a state of "deep communication" through shared meditation. This work has recently been replicated using EEG and fMRI (e.g., see Standish, Johnson, Kozak, and Richards, 2003).

At the level of society, one might expect that cultures based more on the idea of *community* and *connectivity* might experience more paranormal phenomena. This is reported anecdotally among Aboriginal societies. This is also supported by the proposal that meditation, as a means to experience subjective states of connection enables greater connectivity between people, society and the environment at a wider level. For example, it has been claimed that, according to the *Maharishi Effect*, if less than one percent of the world's population practiced Transcendental Meditation, then there would be increased peace in the world via increases in coherence in the collective unconscious (e.g., see Hamill, 2008). Recent work at the Monroe Institute (Radin and Atwater, 2006) found greater coherence of random number generators when a group of people were experiencing a similar meditative state induced by Hemi-Sync tapes, indicating an anomalous mind-matter interaction. Increased coherence may therefore potentially allow for more psi phenomena at a wider level.

Boundary Thinness as a State of Consciousness

As noted earlier, it seems that thin boundaries should be considered to be both state and trait. If there is a psi-conducive state in the brain/mind/body, this is accessible to everyone, but potentially more (in the waking state) among those who score psychometrically "thinner." Hartmann et al. (1998) have suggested that the thinking processes of those who are thicker boundaried may be akin to the waking state, while those who are thinner boundaried may exhibit thought processes more akin to thought processes nearer to sleep.

Specifically, Hartmann (1991) suggests that norepinephrine and serotonin are important neurotransmitters with regard to attention and boundaries. The effect of norepinephrine effectively serves to increase the signal to noise ratio, affecting inhibitory processes and sharpening and increasing focused attention. For example, increasing norepinephrine and serotonin in the cortex results in a thickening of boundaries while reducing norepinephrine and serotonin in the cortex results in a thinning of boundaries. Interestingly, these are the two main "chemicals of sleep" (Hobson, 1989) and are neuromodulators, which set the response mode of the brain. When we are wide awake, serotonin and norepinephrine are increased, while when we are asleep they are decreased, particularly in dreaming sleep (Hobson, 1989).

During the hypnagogic state, thoughts change from being realistic, coherent, undistorted verbal images to primary process thinking, including dissociation of thought and image and magical thinking (Vogel, Trosman and Foulkes, 1966). Vogel et al. (1966) suggest that the logic of hypnagogic thinking may be described as paralogical where everything may be related to everything else.

In a sense, thinner boundaried individuals should be considered to think *hypnagogically* during wakefulness. Hartmann (1991) suggests that those with thinner boundaries exhibit more halfway states of consciousness between waking and sleeping and exhibit brain activity normally localized only in REM sleep at other times. This is supported by the observation that positive schizotypes exhibit anomalies in their arousal systems which render them likely to experience changes in state at any time, even during daytime hours, which result in hypnagogic interruptions or "microsleeps" into waking awareness (McCreery, 1997). Positive schizotypy has been associated with hypnagogic experiences (e.g., Jakes and Hemsley, 1987; Pizzagali, et al., 2001), while negative schizotypy may reflect the opposite tendency, and is associated with a lack of lability in the nervous system. Zanes, Ross, Hatfield, Houtler and Whitman (1998) have also suggested that schizotypy may actually be better considered as a *state*.

When one is fatigued, it seems that one may experience an impairment of normal filtering processes associated with selective attention previously discussed as relating to anomalous and potentially psi experiences among schizotypes indicating a relationship between sleep-related and schizotypal thought.

As there is an association between hypnagogic thinking and ESP (e.g., Sherwood, 1998), it may be that those exhibiting positive schizotypy experience and perceive anomalous and paranormal experiences as if they are fully awake. Hypnagogic experiences do occur in wakefulness among all individuals (Foulkes and Fleisher, 1975), but may be more likely among those who have heightened positive schizotypy and temporal lobe lability.

The absorption variable (Tellegen and Atkinson, 1974) is associated with a proneness toward total attention that is directed to subjective reality; the internal world also seems important in the psi process as both a state and a trait (Irwin, 1985a). The idea of boundaries being considered as both state and trait has been proposed previously as being mediated by intense emotional states and driven by activation of the limbic system, which, via connectivity with the sensory cortex can produce anomalous phenomena (see Thalbourne, Crawley and Houran, 2003).

These ideas were explored empirically with regard to schizotypy and psi performance (Simmonds-Moore and Holt, 2007). Despite no significant psi effects overall, there was an inverse pattern for positive (and negative) schizotypes according to the state of consciousness the experiment was encouraging (a waking state ESP task and a ganzfeld ESP task).

MEDITATION AND THINNING BOUNDARIES?

Interestingly, meditation also thins boundaries between left and right hemispheres and between the cortex and subcortical structures. For example, hemispheric synchrony has been observed in transcendental meditation in terms of frontal coherence (a measure of functioning connectivity) and lateralized asymmetry (a measure of interhemispheric differences in power) (Travis and Arenander, 2006). In addition, the use of Hemi-Sync technology (to drive meditative states) has also been purported to increase synchronization between right and left hemispheres of the brain (e.g., see Atwater, 2004).

Atwater (2004) has also noted that the use of Hemi-Sync to drive meditative states also serves to vertically synchronize the activation of the brain, such that there is effectively more availability of limbic processes to the cortex. A similar observation may be made with regard to meditation, e.g., Yardi (2001) notes that there is less cortical control in meditative states, presumably allowing for more influence of subcortical processes.

Meditation, as a means to thinning boundaries may be associated with more efficient processing outside of the normal range of attention. Srinivasan and Baijal (2007), for example, found that meditation (both during and following the practice of Sudarsham Kriya yoga meditation) is associated with an increase in pre-attentive perceptual processes. As such, more of the subliminal components of the mind would hypothetically be available to conscious awareness.

It is of interest to note that in addition to being an aspect of personality, synesthesia can also be induced, and may be considered to be a state as well as a trait. For example, Simpson and McKellar (1955) describe how certain synesthesias are common in drug induced states, while, more recently, Walsh (2005) describes how synesthesia is possible in meditation. Work by Simmonds (2004) looking at a qualitative exploration of subjective paranormal experiences found that psychic experients often describe phenomena in a synesthetic manner.

Meditation and Hemi-Sync have both been related to anomalous experiences, including extrasensory perception (e.g., see Atwater, 2004, Palmer, Khamashta and Israelson, 1979; Rao and Rao, 1982). As noted earlier, it is yet to be seen whether synesthesia relates to veridical ESP.

CONSCIOUSNESS BINDING

Several authors have suggested that synchronization of 40 Hz (or gamma) activity in features of an object that are fused in the real world may be the necessary and sufficient condition for consciousness in the visual system and other areas of conscious awareness (e.g., Engel and Singer, 2001; see Hebert, Lehmann, Tan, Travis and Arenander, 2005 for a review). Recently, alpha has also been considered to be important in *binding* (see Hebert, et al., 2005). It is considered by this author that meditative and other states where boundaries are "thinned" (vertically and laterally) may allow for a *more efficient* unity of consciousness, which permit mystical, spiritual and possibly paranormal experiences. This is supported by recent empirical work by Hebert, et al. (2005) who found enhanced EEG alpha time-domain phase synchrony during transcendental meditation.

Work in parapsychology has also focused on the binding problem and the nature of preconscious paranormally derived information (e.g., Don, McDonough, and Warren, 1998). Event related potentials were recorded from participants performing a forced choice guessing task, in a study investigating gambling behavior. These authors compared ERP responses (at 40hz or the EEG gamma range) to targets and non targets and compared this to conscious guessing. Conscious target discrimination did not occur however there were different brain responses to targets and non-targets, which indicates that psi information was apparently detected at an unconscious level. The authors consider that psi information affected the neocortex but not to a large enough extent to be bound into consciousness. Don, et al.'s research has recently been replicated by Ogata, Smith and Zhang (2003).

Mental Health and the Manipulation of Boundary Thinness

If boundaries are considered as both a state and trait, it follows there may be neuro-behavioral influences on boundary thinness or thickness in addition to meditation. Hartmann (1991) has suggested that boundary thinness can be altered, but does not suggest how. Sleep variables were recently explored by Simmonds (2005) and there is some indication that sleep quality may statistically predict anomalies directly and indirectly via a relationship with boundary related personality types (see Figure 1). There was also a relationship between shorter sleep length and scoring on the schizotypy scale. Previous research has also addressed dissociation and reduced sleep quality and found that there was a strong relationship (Giesbrecht and Merckelbach, 2004). Due to the relationship between sleep quality and possibly sleep length and boundaries, it could be that sleep patterns could be manipulated in terms of thinning or thickening boundaries. If people can improve sleep quality, or sleep length experiences associated with reduced inhibition, effectively thinness of boundaries will be reduced during the daytime. This has implications for both mental health and anomalous phenomena.

Following a series of interviews with those who report subjective paranormal experiences, and those who practice as psychic healers, it seems that boundary thinness considered psychometrically are not sufficient to gain a complete understanding of anomalous experiences. Many individuals described how their boundaries had altered over time, starting off in a situation where they felt too open, but ending up being able to control their filter on the world. Individuals differed on when paranormal experiences started in their lives, some having experiences from childhood, while others began having experiences later on in life, around life changing moments. It looks as though very thin boundaries considered in themselves might be equivalent to an open unfiltered system. Information from a psi or non-psi source would enter the nervous system and reach conscious awareness. However, in the absence of effective inhibitory processes such as selective attention, there would be a reduced capacity to discern any signal from the noise at the conscious level (this would be the case in someone experiencing a schizophrenic breakdown). As a result, information would overload the system. A high scoring positive schizotype, can (often) cope with his or her experiences, which reflect an increased responsiveness to lower level processes, but not to the point where information is overwhelming.

To this author it seems that *some* boundaries would need to be thinned and some thickened in order for ESP or insights from subliminal areas of the mind to be integrated into the individual. As such, an ESP state may well be thin boundaried, but the outcome is balanced with some input from other modes of thinking (as described earlier with regard to intuitive and rational thinking styles). The mind of someone who is a balanced psychic experient, is potentially one who has developed both rational and intuitive thinking. This mind is thinner boundaried, but not an open flooded system.

Many participants talked about the manner by which they have developed boundaries, or selective boundaries over time, often overlapping with quests for spirituality. These often include meditation or meditative practices which seem to enable the individual to be both simultaneously thin and thick in mind; in other words to be able to dip into both modes of thinking. This has empirical support as observed in the previous section.

As such, boundaries may be manipulated by the processes of relaxation and meditation. This may thin boundaries in a way where one develops an ability to turn on the "state" when it is needed, via certain behavioral cues. Effectively, a state of consciousness becomes associated with certain metaphors, such as a ritual of "grounding" or setting up an imaginary filter.

It is of interest to note that a recent study demonstrated that spiritual transcendence was significantly higher among healers than non-healers (Palmer, Simmonds-Moore, and Baumann, 2006), and that spiritual transcendence has been related to several positive mental health measures. In order to be a healthy "psychic," and be able to use the information that may be perceived, it is necessary to keep boundaries open but not be flooded by information coming in (irrespective of whether this information is paranormal or normal in its origin).

It is also of interest to note that transliminality correlates with both panic attacks and kundalini experiences, which have been associated with awakening spirituality (Thalbourne and Fox, 1999). Kundalini awakening experiences have been described as emulating psychotic breakdown, and can be disturbing, but it is argued that spiritual transformation can occur by living through them (e.g., Clarke, 2000).

Hartmann (1991) suggests that the most healthy individuals exhibit both thick and thin boundaries, scoring somewhere in the middle of his scale. In terms of schizotypes, this might be equivalent to a person who is a happy schizotype (e.g., Goulding, 2004, 2005; Jackson, 1997) whereby boundary thinness is utilized in ways equivalent to the person being in control of their experiences, rather than experiences happening to them. Schizotypy is related to positive outcomes such as creativity (see Brod, 1997) and anomalous experiences that result from awareness of lower level mental processes (Bullen, Hemsley and Dixon, 1987). Anomalous experiences themselves are associated with subjective meaning in life (e.g., Kennedy, Kanthamani and Palmer, 1994).

Brod (1997) has suggested that coping strategies in high scoring schizotypes may be related to the level of intelligence in the high scoring schizotype. For example, "higher levels of intelligence supply a protective cloak for psychosis-prone individuals" (Brod, 1997, p. 282), this allows for more "flexible psychological resources" which would presumably permit more detachment from and integration of these anomalous experiences into the self.

It has often been suggested that Shamans of traditional societies are schizophrenic, however Noll (1983) and others have demonstrated that this is not the case as there is a control held over their experiences and these are employed for the benefit of the community in which they work. Shamans intentionally communicate with the non-physical world. There is a clear shared variance with creativity and psychopathology. This has been more recently argued to be due to schizotypy as the benign cognitive analogue of schizophrenia (Brod, 1997). Direct comparisons of mentally ill patients with highly creative normal controls demonstrate that both score identically on cognition indicative of boundary thinness (Nettle, 2006). However, creatives differ in that they do not exhibit negative schizotypal symptoms or "avolition." Others have speculated that differences in *inhibitory efficiency* may exist (Harnishfeger and Bjorklund, 1994). Highly creative normals may be able to ignore distracting information and focus their attention on some (relevant) information held in their conscious awareness. This may indicate that healthy experiences reflect those that are under the volitional control of the experiencer, the results of which are applied and used in the real world.

In summary, it may be that healthy paranormal experiences are indeed associated with thinner boundaries but more accurately, with an ability to dip into thin boundaried states of being whilst keeping the logical and rational aspects of the self available to awareness. What this implies is that thinner boundaries in themselves are not useful when there is not a simultaneous logical processing and integration of the information or perceived information. At the turn of the last century, Myers (1902/2002) described how a man of genius is able to consciously manipulate ideas that originated in his subliminal mind, which have projected into the conscious mind. He also suggests that genius lies in the increased control over subliminal mentation, whereby the person has attained a greater level of integration of his personality than the average person.

References

Alexander, C. H., and R. S. Broughton (1999). CL1-ganzfeld study: A look at brain hemisphere differences and scoring in the autoganzfeld. *Proceedings of Presented Papers from the 42nd Parapsychological Association Annual Convention*. 3–18.
Alvarado, C. (1998). ESP and altered states of consciousness: An overview of conceptual and research trends. *Journal of Parapsychology*, 62. 27–63.
Atwater, F. H. (2004). The Hemi-Sync process. http://www.monroeinstitute.com/PBWeditor/upload/File/the_hemisync_process_2004.pdf. Accessed on 29 February, 2008.
Beloff, J. (1973). The subliminal and the extrasensory. *Parapsychology Review*, 4. 23–27
Beloff, J. (1974). ESP: The search for a physiological index. *Journal of the Society for Psychical Research*, 47. 403–20.
Bergson, H. (1913). Presidential address. *Proceedings of the Society for Psychical Research*, 27. 157–175.
Braud, W. G. (1975). Psi-conducive states. *Journal of Communication*, 25 (1). 142–152.
Braud, W. G., D. Shafer and J. Mulgrew (1983). Psi functioning and assessed cognitive lability. *Journal of the American Society for Psychical Research*, 77 (3). 193–208.
Brod, J. H. (1997). Creativity and schizotypy. In G. Claridge (ed.), *Schizotypy: Implications for Illness and Health*. New York: Oxford University Press. 274–298.
Broughton, R. S. (1983). Brain Hemisphere specialization and ESP: What have we learned? *Proceedings of Presented Papers from the 26th Annual Parapsychological Association Convention*. 373–383.
Brugger, P. (2001). From haunted brain to haunted science: A cognitive neuroscience view of paranormal and pseudoscientific thought. In J. Houran and R. Lange (eds.), *Hauntings and Poltergeists: Multidisciplinary Perspectives*. Jefferson, NC: McFarland.
Brugger, P., A. Gamma, R. Muri, M. Schafer, and K. I. Taylor (1993). Functional hemispheric asymmetry and belief in ESP. *Perceptual and Motor Skills*, 77. 1299–1308.
Brugger, P., and R. E. Graves (1997). Testing vs. believing hypotheses: Magical ideation in the judgement of contingencies. *Cognitive Neuropsychiatry*, 2 (4). 251–272.
Brugger, P., M. Regard, T. Landis, N. Cook, D. Krebs and J. Niederberger (1993). "Meaningful" patterns in visual noise, effects of lateral stimulation and the observer's belief in ESP. *Psychopathology*, 26. 261–265.
Bullen, J. G., D. R. Hemsley and N. F. Dixon (1987). Inhibition, unusual perceptual experiences and psychoticism. *Personality and Individual Differences*, 8 (5). 687–691.
Carpenter, J. (2004). First sight: Part one, a model of psi and the mind. *Journal of Parapsychology*, 68. 217–254.
Claridge, G. (1967). *Personality and Arousal: A Psychophysiological Study of Psychiatric Disorder*. London: Pergamon Press.
Claridge, G. (1997). *Schizotypy: Implications for Illness and Health*. New York: Oxford University Press.

Claridge, G., K. Clark and C. Davis (1997). Nightmares, dreams and schizotypy. *British Journal of Clinical Psychology*, 36. 377–386.
Claridge, G., and T. Beech (1995). Fully and quasi-dimensional constructions of schizotypy. In A. Raine, T. Lencz, and S. A. Mednick (eds.), *Schizotypal Personality*. New York: Cambridge University Press. 192–216.
Clarke, I. (ed.) (2000). *Psychosis and Spirituality: Exploring the New Frontier*. London: Whurr.
Crawley, S. E., C.C. French and S. A. Yesson (2002). Evidence for transliminality from a subliminal card-guessing task. *Perception*, 31. 887–892.
Dalton, K. (1997). Exploring the links: Creativity and psi in the ganzfeld. *Proceedings of Presented Papers from the 40th Parapsychology Association Annual Conference*. 19–134.
Don, N. S., B. E. McDonough and C. A. Warren (1998). Event-related brain potential (ERP) indicators of unconscious psi: A replication using subjects unselected for psi. *Journal of Parapsychology*, 62 (2). 1270–145.
Duane, T. D., and T. Behrendt (1965). Extrasensory electroencephalographic induction between identical twins. *Science*, 150. 367.
Engel, A. K., and W. Singer (2001). *Trends in Cognitive Sciences*, 5 (1). 16–25.
Evans, J. L. (1997). Semantic activation and preconscious processing in schizophrenia and schizotypy. In G. Claridge (ed.), *Schizotypy: Implications for Illness and Health*. New York: Oxford University Press. 80–97.
Farias, M., G. Claridge and M. Lalljee (2005). Personality and cognitive predictors of New Age practices and beliefs. *Personality and Individual Differences*, 39. 979–989.
Feather, S. R. (1967). A quantitative comparison of memory and psi. *Journal of Parapsychology*, 31 (2). 93–98.
Feelgood, S. R., and A. J. Rantzen (1994). Auditory and visual hallucinations in university students. *Personality and Individual Differences*, 17 (2). 293–296.
Foulkes, D., and S. Fleisher (1975). Mental Activity in relaxed wakefulness. *Journal of Abnormal Psychology*, 4 (1). 66–75
Genovese, J. E. C. (2005). Paranormal beliefs, schizotypy, and thinking styles among teachers and future teachers. *Personality and Individual Differences*, 39. 93–102.
Gianotti, L., C. Mohr, D. Pizzagalli, D. Lehmann and P. Brugger (2001). Associative processing and paranormal belief. *Psychiatry and Cognitive Neurosciences*, 55. 595–603.
Giesbrecht, T., and H. Merckelbach (2004). Subjective sleep experiences are related to dissociation. *Personality and Individual Differences*, 37. 1341–1345.
Goulding, A. (2004). Schizotypy models in relation to subjective health and paranormal belief and experiences. *Personality and Individual Differences*, 37. 157–167.
Goulding, A. (2005). Healthy schizotypy in a population of paranormal believers and experients. *Personality and Individual Differences*, 38. 1069–1083.
Grinberg-Zylberbaum, J., M. Delaflor, L. Attie and A. Goswami (1994). The Einstein-Podolsky-Rosen paradox in the brain: the transferred potential. *Physics Essays*, 7. 422–427.
Grossenbacher, P. G. (1996). Perception and sensory information in synesthetic experience. In S. Baron-Cohen and J. Harrison (eds.), *Synaesthesia*. Oxford: Blackwell.
Grossenbacher, P. G., and C.T. Lovelace (2001). Mechanisms of synesthesia: Cognitive and physiological constraints. *Trends in Cognitive Science*, 5. 36–41.
Hamill, S. D. (2008). Sites for "Maharishi Effect" (Welcome to Parma) Spread Across U.S. http://www.nytimes.com/2008/02/22/us/22peace.html?_r=2&oref=slogin&oref=slogin. Accessed 18 June 2008.
Hansen, G. P. (2001). *The Trickster and the Paranormal*. Self-published: Xlibris.
Harnisherfeger, K., and D.F. Bjorklund (1994). A developmental perspective on individual differences in inhibition. *Learning and Individual Differences*, 6. 331–355.
Harrison, J. (2001). *Synaesthesia: The Strangest Thing*. Oxford: Oxford University Press.
Hartmann, E. (1991). *Boundaries in the Mind: A New Psychology of Personality*. New York: Basic Books.
Hartmann, E., R. Rosen and W. Rand (1998). Personality and dreaming: Boundary structure and dream content. *Dreaming*, 8 (1). 31–39.
Hebert, R., D. Lehmann, G. Tan, F. Travis and A. Arenander (2005). Enhanced EEG alpha time-domain phase synchrony during Transcendental meditation: Implications for cortical integration theory. *Signal Processing*, 85. 2213–2232.

Hobson, J. A. (1989). *Sleep*. New York: Scientific American Library.
Holt, N., and C. Simmonds-Moore (2008). *Creativity, Schizotypy, Paranormal Experiences and Mental Health: Developing a New Cognitive-Parapsychological Paradigm for the Assessment of Psi-Performance in the Laboratory.* Unpublished Final report of research findings for the Bial foundation.
Holt, N., C. Simmonds-Moore and S. Moore (2007). Psi and cognitive disinhibition: Exploring the filters of consciousness hypothesis. *Proceedings of Presented Papers of the 50th annual convention of the Parapsychological Association.* 192–194.
Holt, N., C. Simmonds-Moore and S. Moore (2008). Benign schizotypy: Investigating differences between clusters of schizotype on paranormal belief, creativity, intelligence and mental health. *Proceedings of Presented Papers of the 51st Annual Convention of the Parapsychological Association.*
Houran, J., and R. Lange (1998). Modeling precognitive dreams as meaningful coincidences. *Psychological Reports*, 83. 1411–4.
Irwin, H. J. (1979). *Psi and the Mind: An Information Processing Approach.* Metuchen, NJ: Scarecrow.
Irwin, H.J. (1985). Parapsychological phenomena and the absorption domain. *Journal of the American Society for Psychical Research*, 79 (1). 1–11.
Irwin H. J. (1999). *An Introduction to Parapsychology.* Third edition. Jefferson, NC: McFarland.
Irwin, H. J., and J. M. Young (2001). Intuitive versus reflective processes in the formation of paranormal beliefs. *European Journal of Parapsychology*, 17. 45–53.
Jackson, M. (1997). Benign schizotypy? The case of spiritual experience. In G. Claridge (ed.), *Schizotypy: Implications for Illness and Health.* New York: Oxford University Press. 227–250.
Jakes, S., and D. R. Hemsley (1987). Personality and reports of hallucination and imagery in a normal population. *Perceptual and Motor Skills*, 64. 765–766.
James, W. (2003). *The Varieties of Religious Experiences.* New York: Signet Classic.
Jolley, S., S. H. Jones and D. R. Hemsley (1999). Causal processing and schizotypy. *Personality and Individual Differences*, 27. 277–291.
Kennedy, J. E., H. Kanthamani and J. Palmer (1994). Psychic and spiritual experiences, health, well being and meaning in life. *Journal of Parapsychology*, 58 (4). 353–383.
Krippner, S., I. Wickramasekera and R. Tartz (2000). *Scoring Thick and Scoring Thin: The Boundaries of Psychic Claimants.* Unpublished manuscript.
Lange, R., J. Houran and L. Storm (2000). The revised Transliminality scale: Reliability and validity data from a Rasch top down purification procedure. *Consciousness and Cognition: An International Journal*, 9. 591–617.
Lawrence, T. R., and P. Woodley (1998). Schizotypy as a predictor of success in a free response ESP task. *Abstracts from the 22nd International Conference of the Society for Psychical Research.* 14.
Levin, R., L. Gilmartin and L. Lamontanaro (1998–1999). Cognitive style and perception: The relationship of boundary thinness to visual-spatial processing in dreaming and waking thought. *Imagination, Cognition and Personality*, 18 (1). 25–41.
Loughland, C. M., and L. M. Williams (1997). A cluster analytic study of schizotypal trait dimensions. *Personality and Individual Differences*, 23 (5). 877–883.
Marks, L. E. (2000). Synesthesia. In E. Cardena, S. J. Lynn, and S. Krippner (Eds.), *Varieties of Anomalous Experience: Examining the Scientific Evidence.* 121–149. Washington, D.C.: American Psychological Association.
Mason, O., G. Claridge and M. Jackson (1995). New scales for the assessment of schizotypy. *Personality and Individual Differences*, 18 (1). 7–13.
Mavromatis, A. (1987). *Hypnagogia: The Unique State of Consciousness Between Wakefulness and Sleep.* London: Routledge and Kegan Paul.
Merckelbach, H., E. Rassin and P. Muris (2000). Dissociation, schizotypy, and fantasy proneness in undergraduate students. *Journal of Nervous and Mental Disease*, 188. 428–31.
McCreery, C. (1997). Hallucinations and arousability: Pointers to a theory of psychosis. In G. Claridge (ed.), *Schizotypy: Implications for Illness and Health.* New York: Oxford University Press. 251–273.

McCreery, C., and G. Claridge (1996). A study of hallucinations in normal subjects—1. Self report data. *Personality and Individual Differences*, 21 (5). 739–747.
Myers, F. W. H. (1902/2002). *Human Personality and Its Survival of Bodily Death*. Charlottesville, VA: Hampton Roads.
Nettle, D. (2006). Schizotypy and mental health amongst poets, visual artists and mathematicians. *Journal of Research in Personality*, 40, 376–390.
Noll, R. (1983) Shamanism and schizophrenia: A state-specific approach to the schizophrenia metaphor. of shamanic states. *American Ethnologist*, 10. 443–59.
Nuchpongsai, P., H. Arakaki, P. Langman and C. Ogura (1999). N2 and P3b components of the event-related potential in students at risk for psychosis. *Psychiatry Research*, 88. 131–141.
Ogata S., M. M. Smith and H. Zhang (2003). An Experiment on unknown subconscious information transfer with auditory brain evoked potential. *Journal of International Society of Life Information Science (ISLIS)*. http://www.soc.nii.ac.jp/islis/sjis/journalJ/sampleJ0304.pdf. Accessed 19th June, 2008.
Palmer, J., K. Khamashta and K. Israelson (1979). An ESP ganzfeld experiment with transcendental meditators. *Journal of the American Society for Psychical Research*, 74. 333–348.
Palmer, J., C. Simmonds-Moore and S. Baumann (2006). Geomagnetic fields and the relationship between human intentionality and the hemolysis of red blood cells. *Journal of Parapsychology*, 70. 275–302.
Parker, A. (1999). Imaginal experiences and perceptual defence. *British Journal of Medical Psychology*, 72. 447–458.
Parker, A. (2000). A review of the ganzfeld work at Gothenburg University. *Journal of the Society for Psychical Research*, 64.1 (858). 1–15.
Parker, A., D. Grams and C. Pettersson (1998). Further variables relating to psi in the ganzfeld. *Journal of Parapsychology*, 62. 319–337.
Parker, A., and J. Westerlund (1998). Current research in giving the ganzfled an old and a new twist. *Proceedings of Presented Papers from the Parapsychological Association 41st Annual Conference*. 135–142.
Pekala, R. J., V. K. Kumar and G. Marcano (1995). Anomalous/paranormal experiences, hypnotic susceptibility, and dissociation. *Journal of the American Society for Psychical Research*, 89. 313–332.
Persinger, M. A. (1989). Psi phenomena and temporal lobe activity: The geomagnetic factor. In L. A. Henkel and R. E. Berger (eds.), *Research in Parapsychology 1988*. Metuchen, NJ: Scarecrow. 121–156.
Persinger, M. A. (1996). Hypnosis and the brain: The relationship between subclinical complex partial epileptic-like symptoms, imagination, suggestibility, and changes in self identity. In R. G. Kunzendorf, N. P. Spanos and B. Wallace (eds.), *Hypnosis and Imagination*. New York: Baywood. 283–305.
Persinger, M. A., and P. Richards (1991). Tobacyk's paranormal belief scale and temporal lobe signs: Sex differences in the experiences of ego-alien intrusions. Perceptual *and Motor Skills*, 73. 1151–1156.
Persinger, M. A., and K. Makarec (1987). Temporal lobe epileptic signs and correlative behaviours displayed by normal populations. *The Journal of General Psychology*, 114 (2). 179–195.
Persinger, M. A., and P. M. Valliant (1985). Temporal lobe signs and reports of subjective paranormal experiences in a normal population: A replication. *Perceptual and Motor Skills*, 60. 903–909.
Radin, D. I. (1997). Unconscious perception of future emotions: An experiment in presentiment. *Journal of Scientific Exploration*, 11 (2). 163–180.
Radin, D. I., and F. H. Atwater (2006). Entrained minds and the behaviour of random physical systems. *Proceedings of Presented Papers of the 49th Parapsychological Association Annual Conference*.
Rao, P. K., and K. R. Rao (1982). Two studies of ESP and subliminal perception. *Journal of Parapsychology*, 46. 185–207.
Rawlings, D., B. Williams, N. Haslam and G. Claridge (2008). Taxometric analysis supports a dimensional latent structure for schizotypy. *Personality and Individual Differences*, 44. 1640–1651.
Reber, A. (1985). *Dictionary of Psychology*. London: Penguin.

Rhine, L. E. (1953). Subjective forms of spontaneous psi experiences. *Journal of Parapsychology*, 17 (2). 77–114.
Richards, D. G. (1996). Boundaries in the mind and subjective interpersonal psi. *Journal of Parapsychology*, 60. 227–240.
Roll, W. G. (1966). ESP and memory. *International Journal of Neuropsychiatry*, (September–October). 505–521.
Roll, W. G., and E. Montagno (1985). System theory, neurophysiology and psi. *Journal of Indian Psychology*, 4 (2). 43–64.
Roney-Dougal, S. (1986). Subliminal and psi perception: A review of the literature. *Journal of the Society for Psychical Research*, 53 (804). 405–434.
Sanders, R., M. A. Thalbourne and P. S. Delin (2000). Transliminality and the telepathic transmission of emotional states: An exploratory study. *Journal of the American Society for Psychical Research*, 94. 1–24.
Schacter, D. L. (1976). The hypnagogic state, a critical review of the literature. *Psychological Bulletin*, 83 (3). 452–481.
Sheldrake, R. (2003). Experimental tests for telephone telepathy. *Journal of the Society for Psychical Research*, 67. 184–199.
Sherwood, S. J. (1998). Relationship between the hypnagogic/hypnopompic state and reports of anomalous experiences. *Proceedings of Presented Papers from the Parapsychological Association 41st Annual Conference*. 210–225.
Simpson, L., P. McKellar (1955). Types of Synaesthesia. *Journal of Mental Science 101*. 141–147.
Simmonds, C. A. (2003). *Investigating Schizotypy as an Anomaly-Prone Personality*. Unpublished Ph.D. thesis. University of Leicester/University College Northampton.
Simmonds, C. A. (2004). A qualitative investigation of source monitoring in the context of subjective paranormal experiences. Research Brief in *Proceedings of Presented Papers for the 47th Annual Convention of the Parapsychological Association*. 455–460.
Simmonds, C. A. (2005). Sleep patterns, personality and subjective paranormal experiences. *Proceedings of Presented Papers of the 48th Annual Convention of the Parapsychology Association*. 188–203
Simmonds-Moore, C., and N. Holt (2007). Trait, state and psi: An exploration of the interaction between individual differences, state preference and psi performance in the ganzfeld and a waking ESP control. *Journal of the Society for Psychical Research*, 71. 197–215.
Simmonds, C. A., and C. A. Roe (2000). Personality correlates of anomalous experiences, perceived ability and beliefs: Schizotypy, temporal lobe signs and gender. *Proceedings of Presented Papers from the Parapsychological Association 43rd Annual Conference*. 276–291.
Skirda, R. J., and M. A. Persinger (1993). Positive associations among dichotic listening errors, complex partial epileptic like signs, and paranormal beliefs. *Journal of Nervous and Mental Disease*, 181 (11). 663–667.
Srinivasan, N., and S. Baijal (2007). Concentrative meditation enhances pre-attentive processing: A MMN study. *Neuroreport*, 18. 1709–1712.
Standish, L., L. Johnson, L. Kozak and T. Richards (2003). Evidence of correlated functional magnetic resonance imaging signals between distant human brains. *Alternative Therapies*, 9. 121–125.
Stanford, R. G. (1974a). Unconscious psi-mediated instrumental response and its relation to conscious ESP performance. In W. G. Roll, R. L. Morris and J. D. Morris (eds.), *Research in Parapsychology, 1973: Abstracts and Papers from the 16th Annual Convention of the Parapsychological Association*. Metuchen NJ: Scarecrow. 99–103.
Stanford, R. G. (1974b). An experimentally testable model for spontaneous psi events: I. Extrasensory events. *Journal of the American Society for Psychical Research*, 68. 34–57.
Stanford, R. G. (1974c). An experimentally testable model for spontaneous psi events: II. Psychokinetic events. *Journal of the American Society for Psychical Research*, 68. 321–356.
Storm, L., and M. A. Thalbourne (2001). Studies of the I-Ching: II. Additional analyses. *Journal of Parapsychology*, 65. 291–309.
Tellegen, A., and G. Atkinson (1974). Openness to absorbing and self-altering experiences ("absorption"): A trait related to hypnotic susceptibility. *Journal of Abnormal Psychology*, 83 (3). 268–277.

Thalbourne, M. A. (1998). Transliminality: Further correlates and a short measure. *Journal of the American Society for Psychical Research*, 92 (4). 402–419.
Thalbourne, M. A. (1999). Transliminality: A review. Unpublished article submitted for publication to *International Journal of Parapsychology*.
Thalbourne, M. A. (2000). Transliminality and creativity. *Journal of Creative Behavior*, 34. 193–202.
Thalbourne, M.A., S. E. Crawley and J. Houran (2003).Temporal lobe lability in the highly transliminal mind. *Personality and Individual Differences*, 35. 1965–1974.
Thalbourne, M. A., and B. Fox (1999). Paranormal and mystical experience: The role of panic attacks and Kundalini. *Journal of the American Society for Psychical Research*, 93. 99–115.
Thalbourne, M. A., and J. Houran (2000). Transliminality, the mental experience inventory and tolerance of ambiguity. *Personality and Individual Differences*, 28. 853–863.
Thalbourne, M., J. Houran, A. G. Alias and P. Brugger (2001). Transliminality, brain function, and synesthesia. *Journal of Nervous and Mental Disease*, 189. 190–192.
Travis, F. T., and A. Arenander (2006). Cross-sectional and longitudinal study of effects of Transcendental Meditation practice on frontal power asymmetry and frontal coherence. *International Journal of Neuroscience*, 116. 1519–1538.
Vogel, G., H. Trosman and D. Foulkes (1966). Ego functions and dreaming during sleep onset. *Archives of General Psychiatry*, 14 (3). 238–248.
Walsh, R. (2005). Can synaesthesia be cultivated? Indications from surveys of meditators. *Journal of Consciousness Studies*, 12. 5–17.
Williams, C. (1997). *The Role of Imagination in the Construction of Anomalous Experience*. Unpublished Ph.D. Thesis. University of Edinburgh.
Williams, L., and A. Beech (1997). Investigations of cognitive inhibitory processes in schizotypy and schizophrenia. In G. Claridge (ed.), *Schizotypy: Implications for Illness and Health*. New York: Oxford University Press. 63–79.
Wolfradt, U., V. Oubaid, E. R. Straube, N. Bischoff and J. Mischo (1999). Thinking styles, schizotypal traits and anomalous experiences. *Personality and Individual Differences*, 27. 821–830.
Xiong, H. (2001). Is the activity of the cerebral cortex a "brake" on the functioning of the brainstem? Letter to the editor. *Journal of Scientific Exploration*, 14. 455.
Yardi, N. (2001). Yoga for control of epilepsy. *Seizure*, 10. 7–12.
Young, H. F., R. P. Bentall, P. D. Slade and M. E. Dewey (1987). The role of brief instructions and suggestibility in the elicitation of auditory and visual hallucinations in normal and psychiatric subjects. *Journal of Nervous and Mental Disease*, 175 (1). 41–48.
Zanes, J., S. Ross, R. Hatfield, B. Houtler and D. Whitman (1998). The relationship between creativity and psychosis-proneness. *Personality and Individual Differences*, 24 (6). 879–881.

About the Contributors

Daryl J. Bem, emeritus professor of psychology at Cornell University, has taught at Carnegie-Mellon, Stanford, Harvard, and Cornell, where he has been since 1978. He has published on several topics in psychology, including attitudes and public opinion, group decision making, self-perception, personality theory, sexual orientation and, most recently, psi (ESP). He is the coauthor of an introductory textbook in psychology and the author of *Beliefs, Attitudes, and Human Affairs* (1970). He is a fellow of the American Psychological Association and a charter fellow of the Association for Psychological Science.

Etzel Cardeña is the Thorsen Professor of Psychology at Lund University in Sweden. This professorship is the only one in the world dedicated to research in parapsychology and hypnosis. He is past president of the Society for Clinical and Experimental Hypnosis and Division 30 of the American Psychological Association, and was the senior editor of *Varieties of Anomalous Experience: Examining the Scientific Evidence* (2000). He is in 2009 president of the Parapsychological Association.

Jezz Fox currently works as a computer programmer and systems designer, having held lecturing posts at Liverpool Hope University and Liverpool John Moores University. He has also been an honorary research associate at the University of Manchester.

Rachel Fox worked as a research assistant at Goldsmiths College, University of London, and the University of East London for several years in both cognitive and health psychology. She now works in diabetes health care for the NHS diabetic retinopathy screening service.

Chris French is a professor of psychology and head of the Anomalistic Psychology Research Unit in the Psychology Department at Goldsmiths College, University of London. He is a chartered psychologist and a fellow of the British Psychological Society. He is also a fellow of the Royal Society for the Encouragement of Arts, Manufacturers & Commerce, and the Institute for Cultural Research, in addition to being a member of the Scientific Advisory Board of the British False Memory Society and the Advisory Board of the Center for Inquiry, London.

Victoria Hamilton was a research assistant at Goldsmiths College and Birkbeck College, University of London, for several years before returning to Australia to complete a Ph.D. in health psychology at Swinburne University of Technology in Melbourne.

Craig D. Murray is a senior lecturer in psychology in the School of Health and Medicine at Lancaster University. He has published widely on the topics of disability, health and illness, parapsychology, and technology. He is editor of the forthcoming book *Psychological Scientific Perspectives on Out-of-Body and Near-Death Experiences.*

Ciarán O'Keeffe is currently employed as a research associate at the University of Toulouse (Le Mirail) where he specializes in parapsychology and investigative psychology. His paranormal research has focused on testing mediums and psychics in the laboratory and also field work examining haunting experiences. He is the parapsychologist on the popular television show *Most Haunted* (Living TV).

Steve Parsons is a founding member of Para.Science, a group dedicated to the serious investigation of all types of ostensibly paranormal phenomena. He is currently researching the role that infrasound plays in haunting experiences.

Chris Roe is a senior lecturer in psychology at the University of Northampton and research leader for the psychology division. He is editor of the *Journal of the Society for Psychical Research* and is currently a board member of the Parapsychological Association, council member of the Society for Psychical Research, and international affiliate for England for the Parapsychology Foundation.

Julia Santomauro is a Ph.D. student in the department of psychology, Goldsmiths College, University of London. She is researching psychological aspects of sleep paralysis.

Simon J. Sherwood is a senior lecturer in psychology at the University of Northampton, where he specializes in teaching and supervising undergraduate and postgraduate research in parapsychology and the psychology of anomalous experiences. He has conducted research on sleep-related experiences, beliefs in anomalous phenomena, ESP in dreams, and allegedly haunted locations. He has collected reports of Black Dog apparitions from around the world via his website (www.blackshuck.info).

Christine Simmonds-Moore is a senior lecturer in psychology at Liverpool Hope University. Her research focuses on the relationships between personality and states of consciousness and how they relate to anomalous experiences.

Paul Stevens is a senior lecturer in psychology at Bournemouth University, leading a research program at the new Centre for Wellbeing and Quality of Life on the properties of certain environments that have restorative and therapeutic effects. He was a research fellow with the Koestler Parapsychology Unit at the University of Edinburgh for ten years, specializing in the study of people's physical interactions with their environment. He has been editor of the *European Journal of Parapsychology* since 2004.

Michael Thalbourne is a visiting research fellow at the University of Adelaide. He has a long-standing interest in the correlates of belief in the paranormal, and has developed several questionnaire measures of such belief which have been used widely in parapsychology and anomalistic psychology.

Caroline Watt is a senior lecturer in psychology at the University of Edinburgh and is a founding member of the university's Koestler Parapsychology Unit. She is a member of the Scientific Advisory Board for the Bial Foundation, and former president of the Parapsychological Association. She is the coauthor of *An Introduction to Parapsychology* (2007).

Richard Wiseman started his working life as a professional magician and currently holds Britain's only professorship in the "Public Understanding of Psychology" at the University of Hertfordshire. He is the author of several books, including *The Luck Factor* (2004) and *Quirkology* (2007).

Robin Wooffitt is a senior lecturer in the department of sociology at the University of York, where he is the director of the Anomalous Experiences Research Unit. He has a longstanding interest in the ways in which anomalous or exceptional experiences are mediated through language and social interaction, and he has studied how people describe anomalous experiences, and the interaction between psychic practitioners and their clients. He is currently examining the role of language in parapsychological experiments. His publications include *The Language of Mediums and Psychics: The Social Organisation of Everyday Miracles* (2006), *Conversation Analysis and Discourse Analysis: A Comparative and Critical Introduction* (2005), and *Telling Tales of the Unexpected: The Organisation of Factual Discourse* (1992).

INDEX

Aaronson, B.S. 95
absorption 42, 95, 137, 138, 143, 145, 146, 165, 166, 172, 182, 183, 196
AEI *see* Anomalous Experiences Inventory
Alarcón, A. 103
Alexander, C.H. 188
Ali, A.N. 39
Alias, A.G. 194
Alice in Wonderland (book) 10–11; *see also Through the Looking Glass*
alien contact experiences 3, 136–153
Allefeld, C. 42
Alpert, M. 146
altered states of consciousness 2, 25–49, 96, 102; definition 26
Alvarado, C.S. 27, 43, 44, 45, 77, 103, 110, 121, 161, 163, 165, 166, 168, 187
American Society for Psychical Research 27
Amsterdam 149
Andrews, S. 12
Angelini, R.F. 42
animal magnetism 93
anomalistic psychology 2
Anomalous Experiences Inventory 139, 143, 144, 145
anomaly-prone personality 183
anthropology 3
apothenia 192
apparitions 3, 27, 110, 115, 120–135
Appelle, S. 136
Arakaki, H. 193
Arenander, A. 197, 198
arousal 8, 59
Ås, A. 95
ASGS *see* Australian Sheep-Goat Scale
ASPR *see* American Society for Psychical Research
associational thinking 192
Atkinson, G. 137, 140, 196

Atkinson, J.M. 88
attention 14, 15, 17, 21, 22, 26, 27, 40, 41, 43, 44, 54, 66, 96, 98, 99, 100, 114, 125, 148, 160, 178, 180, 185, 187, 189–190, 195, 196, 197, 199, 200
Attie, L. 194
Atwater, F.H. 195, 197
Australian Sheep-Goat Scale 140, 144, 145

Back, K.W. 77
Baijal, S. 197
Bakan, P. 103
Baker, I. 14, 17, 20, 22, 108, 110, 115
Baker, R.A. 136
Bali 149
Ballard, J. 55
Bandy, D. 147
Banks, R. 167
Bányai, E.I. 96
Barabasz, A.F. 100
Barabasz, M. 100
Barber, T.X. 137, 146
Barnier, A. 95, 115
Barrett, T.R. 138, 140
Barry, J. 54
Bartholomew, R.E. 138
Bartlett, F.C. 26
Basterfield, K. 138
Baumann, S. 182, 187, 199
Baumeister, R.F. 136
Bayless, R. 121
Beech, A. 191, 194
Beech, T. 179, 180, 189
Behrendt, T. 194
Beloff, J. 26, 186, 191
Belvedere, E. 32
Bem, D.J. 1, 5, 36, 37, 38, 58, 68, 69
Bentall, R.P. 140, 146, 193
Bergson, H. 189
Bernstein, E.M. 140

Bertini, M. 33
Bessent, Malcolm 29
Besterman, T. 155
Bial Foundation 161, 193
Bierman, D.J. 6
Biles, C. 32
Binder, M. 13, 15
Bischoff, N. 180, 188
Bjorklund, D.F. 200
Black, D.L. 120
black dog apparitions 3, 120–135; Black Dog of Bungay 122, 129; explanations 126–132; Lancashire Skriker 125; Latin America 126, 132; Lincolnshire 125; as omen 125, 129
Blackmore, S.J. 141, 161, 162, 163, 164, 165, 166, 167, 168, 171
Blatterbauer, S. 137
body image 162, 165, 166, 167, 170, 171, 173, 174
Body Investment Scale 169
Bord, C. 122, 124, 125, 128, 129, 130, 131
Bord, J. 122, 124, 125, 128, 129, 130, 131
boundary thinness 178, 179, 181, 182, 183, 184, 192, 198, 199, 200
Bourque, L.B. 77
Bowers, J. 172
Boxer, A.M. 96
BQ *see* Hartmann's Boundary Questionnaire
Brady, C. 14, 15, 17, 20, 22
Braeunig, M. 40
Braffman, W. 100
Braithwaite, J. 76, 113, 114, 120, 128, 129, 130
Braud, L.W. 33, 44, 45
Braud, W.G. 12, 15, 17, 22, 32, 33, 44, 45, 53, 55, 186, 188
Braude, S.E. 121, 126, 130, 131, 132
Brenman, M. 95
Brier, R. 54
Broadbent, D. 189
Brod, J.H. 183, 200
Brodie, D. 167
Broughton, R.S. 37, 38, 188
Brown, D.P. 96
Brown, T. 121, 122, 123, 124, 125, 126, 132
Brugger, P. 116, 183, 188, 192, 193, 194
Büchi, S. 40
Buckner, R.L. 147
Bull, R. 149
Bullard, T.E. 138
Bullen, J.G. 190, 200
Burchell, S. 122, 124, 125, 126, 132
Bürkle, D. 15
Buss, A.H. 168

CA *see* Conversation Analysis
Cabeza, R. 147

Cabibbo, C. 13–14, 18, 85
Calverley, D.S. 146
Canter, D. 76
Cantrell, P. 169
Cappon, D. 167
Cardeña, E. 2, 41, 42, 44, 93, 95, 97, 101, 102, 103, 116
Carlson, E.B. 137
Carpenter, J.C. 191
Carroll, Lewis 5
CCTV 12
CES *see* Curious Experiences Survey
Chainey, S. 76
Chambers, R. 123
Chang, N. 140
Child, I.L. 31
Clancy, S.A. 136, 137, 138, 141, 142, 148, 149
Claridge, G. 179, 186, 189, 191, 192
Clark, K. 191
Clarke, D. 77
Clarke, I. 200
Clemmer, E.J. 32
coincidence 28
Collins, H.M. 73
Control of Imagery Questionnaire 163
Conversation Analysis 2, 78
Cook, A.M. 163
Cook, C.M. 76, 129
Coover, J.E. 12
Cornell, A.D. 109, 120, 121, 126
Cornell University 7
Costall, A. 149
Crawford, H.J. 97
Crawley, S.E. 183, 191, 196
creativity 183, 190, 192, 200
crisis telepathy 65
Crombag, H.F.M. 149
Crosby, Bing 146
Cross, P.A. 137
Curious Experiences Survey 140, 144
Curran, T. 146, 147, 148

Dale, A.M. 147
Dale, L.A. 27
Dale-Green, P. 125, 126, 132
Dalton, K. 32, 38, 77, 166, 194
D'Aquili, E.G. 102
da Silva, F.E. 39
Davey, S.J. 155
Davis, C. 191
Davis, O.C. 93
Daydreaming 39, 42
Deese, J. 136, 141
Deese/Roediger-McDermott (DRM) paradigm 136, 139, 141–142, 147, 148–149, 150
Delaflor, M. 194
Delanoy, D. 55, 73
Delin, P.S. 140, 182

Developing Perspectives on Anomalous Experience (conference) 1
developmental psychology 102
Dewey, M.E. 146, 167, 193
Diamond, M.J. 147
Diamond, S.G. 93
Dickson, K. 137
Didier, A. 94
Dijksterhuis, A. 7
Dill, C.A. 140
Dimensions of Attention Questionnaire 41
Dingwall, E. 94
direct mental interaction with living systems (DMILS) 12–13, 14, 53
discourse 77–86; monologic discourse 79–82
dissociation 3, 137, 146, 161, 166, 172, 183; *see also* dissociativity
Dissociative Experiences Scale 140
dissociativity 137, 138, 145; *see also* dissociation
Dixon, N.F. 190, 200
DMILS *see* direct mental interaction with living systems
Don, N.S. 186, 198
dreams 27, 30–33, 190–191, 195; dream ESP 30–33
DRM paradigm *see* Deese/Roediger-McDermott paradigm
Druffel, A. 138
Duane, T.D. 194
Dubreuil, S.C. 137
Duke University 72, 74, 87
Dukhan, H. 29, 30
Düzel, E. 148

EDA *see* electrodermal activity
Edge, H.L. 37, 85, 109
Edmonston, W. 102
EEG (electroencephalogram) 33, 40, 93, 97, 101, 187, 194, 195, 198
effect size 14, 22, 38, 39, 68, 69
Eisen, M.L. 137
electrodermal activity (EDA) 12, 55
electromagnetic fields (EMF) 111–113, 129, 130
Ellenberger, H.F. 95
Elliot, J. 140
Elliot-Carter, N.C. 95
EMF *see* electromagnetic fields
Engel, A.K. 198
Erickson, M.H. 96
ERP *see* event-related potentials
Ertel, S. 68
ESP *see* extrasensory perception
Evans, F.J. 43, 95
Evans, H. 138
Evans, J.L. 190, 193
event-related potentials (ERP) 148, 186, 198

experimenter effect 2, 12–24, 95
extrasensory perception (ESP) 1, 8, 13, 16, 25–49, 27, 52, 55–58, 61–70, 178, 179, 180, 186, 189, 190, 191, 193, 196, 197, 199; forced-choice ESP 57; free-response ESP 57
eyewitness testimony 110, 154–160

Faber, P. 93
Fabiani, M. 148
false memories 137, 138, 146–148, 149, 150
fantasy proneness 137–138, 145, 146, 147, 182
Farias, M. 192
Fassler, O. 43
Fayed, Dodi 149
Feather, S.R. 193
Feelgood, S.R. 193
Feldman, B.E. 97, 100
Fellows, B.J. 102
Fenigstein, A. 168
Ferrari, D.C. 52
Field, P.B. 95
Fielding, Y. 113
Finch, S.E. 147
Finkelman, D. 137
Fisk, G.W. 22
Fleisher, S. 196
Fleming, A. 122, 123
fMRI (functional magnetic resonance imaging) 147, 195
Fodor, N. 109, 113
folklore 76, 115, 121, 132
Fontana, D. 110
Foulkes, D. 32, 196
Fox, J. 2, 30, 39, 61, 65, 71, 136, 167, 169, 170, 171, 173, 180, 200
Fraser-Harris, D.F. 154
Freedman, D. 13
French, C.C. 3, 136, 137, 138, 141, 143, 146, 149, 150, 191
Freudian theory 162
Fromm, E. 96, 100

Gallagher, C. 139, 140
Gamma, A. 188
ganzfeld 33–39, 40, 41, 55, 58–59, 64, 65, 68, 72, 77–86, 180, 197; auto-ganzfeld 36, 38, 77; experimenter-participant interaction 83–86; meta-analyses 35–39, 68, 70; physiology 58–59; role of the sender 38, 65–66
Garoff-Eaton, R.J. 147
Garry, M. 149
Gauld, A. 94, 109, 120, 121, 126, 129, 130, 132
GDIS *see* Geodemographic Information Systems
Gearhart 129

Genovese 188
Geodemographic Information Systems (GDIS) 75, 76
Geographical Information Systems (GIS) 75, 76
geomagnetic fields (GMF) 111–112, 128, 129
Gervais, A. 164
ghosts 3, 108–119, 120, 121, 178
Gianotti, L. 192
Gibson, S. 172
Giesbrecht, T. 43, 198
Gifford-May, D. 102
Gill, M. 95
Gilmartin, L. 190
GIS *see* Geographical Information Systems
Gittelman, D.R. 148
Glicksohn, J. 138, 140, 166
Globus, G. 32
Glover, T.A. 137
GMF *see* geomagnetic fields
Goldberg, L.R. 140, 141
Goldsmiths College (University of London) 139
Gonsalves, B. 148
Goodpaster, J. 137
Gordon, M. 170
Gordon, R. 163
Goswami, A. 194
Gotlib, D. 138
Goulding, A. 39, 179, 200
Grams, D. 180
Granqvist, P. 115
Graves, R.E. 183, 193
Green, C.E. 120, 121, 125, 126, 131
Greening, E. 76, 110, 115, 120, 147, 157, 158
Greyson, B. 101
Grinberg-Zylberbaum, J. 194
Grossenbacher, P.G. 194
Gruber, E. 51, 52
Guerra, V. 15
Gurney, E. 27, 74, 120, 130

Haight, J.M. 51
hallucinations 146, 180
Hamill, S.D. 195
Hamilton, V. 136
Hampton Court Palace 129
Hansen, G.P. 178
Haraldsson, E. 120, 121
Hardy, C. 51
Harley, T.A. 41
Harnishfeger, K. 200
Harper, S. 33
Harribance, Lalsingh 29
Harris, K. 76
Harrison, J. 194
Hart, H. 120, 126, 130, 131, 167, 169, 170

Harte, J. 120, 122, 125, 126, 128, 129
Hartmann, E. 178, 179, 181, 183, 187, 194, 195, 196, 198, 200
Hartmann's Boundary Questionnaire 181, 182, 190, 194
Haslam, N. 180
Hatfield, R. 196
haunting experiences 3, 76, 108–119, 121, 129; definition 109–110; environmental factors 111–114; psychological factors 114–116; stone-tape theory 131
Hay, D. 77
Healey, F. 32, 76
Heaps, C. 137
Hearne, K. 28
Hebert, R. 198
Heinze, H.J. 148
Hemi-Sync 195, 197
Hemsley, D.R. 190, 191, 193, 196, 200
Heritage, J. 78, 79, 88
Hilgard, E.R. 96, 97, 101
Hilgard, J.R. 97
hippocampus 147, 193
Hiroka, R. 39
Hobson, J.A. 195
Hodgson, R. 155
Holden, K.J. 136, 138
Hollishead, M.T. 120
Holroyd, J. 102
Holt, N. 34, 39, 79, 85, 86, 179, 180, 189, 190, 196
homeostatic arousal 189
Honorton, C. 13–14, 18, 28, 29, 33, 35, 36, 37, 38, 39, 43, 44, 52, 58, 68, 69, 85, 94
Houdin, R. 94
Houran, J. 43, 108, 109, 110, 112, 114, 115, 116, 120, 121, 126, 128, 129, 179, 182, 183, 187, 191, 194, 196
Houtler, B. 196
Howard, G.S. 138
Howe, R.D. 93
Hufford, D.J. 127
Hunt, H.T. 102, 164
Hurst, C. 13
Hurt, S.W. 96
Hutchby, I. 78
Huxley, A. 96
Hyde, J.S. 169
Hyman, R. 32, 35, 36, 63
hyperaesthesia 182
hypnagogia 40, 41, 42, 127, 163, 173, 187–188, 191, 195, 196
hypnopompia 42, 127, 173
hypnosis 2, 42, 93–107, 149; and psi 94–95, 101; and transpersonal experiences 99
hypnotizability 42, 43, 95, 101
hypomania 183, 186

IAPS *see* International Affective Picture System
ICMIC *see* Inventory of Childhood Memories and Imaginings: Children's Form
imagination 28, 137, 146, 149
impulsive nonconformity 187
India 30
inference 62
inferior parietal cortex 148
infrasound 113–114, 128, 130
International Affective Picture System (IAPS) 8
intuitions 27
Inventory of Childhood Memories and Imaginings (ICMIC) 140, 143, 144, 145
Iobst, A.D. 137
Irwin, H.J. 42, 73, 74, 75, 77, 115, 120, 121, 125, 131, 163, 164, 165, 166, 167, 168, 170, 171, 173, 174, 188, 193, 194, 196
Israelson, K. 197

Jackson, M. 179, 200
Jakes, S. 191, 193, 196
James, W. 178
Jelicic, M. 43
Johnson, A. 120
Johnson, L. 195
Johnson, M.K. 138, 146, 148
Jolley, S. 193
Jones, L. 33
Jones, S. 131
Jones, S.H. 193
Jönsson, P. 93

Kanthamani, H. 181, 183, 200
Kelly, E.F. 25
Kemp, K. 75
Kennedy, J.E. 25, 181, 183, 200
Khamashta, K. 197
Kiemle, G. 167
Kirsch, I. 100
Knapp, P.H. 32
Knox, J. 43
Koestler Parapsychology Unit (University of Edinburgh) 73, 77
Koren, S.A. 76, 112, 113, 128, 129
Kot, T. 140
Kounios, J. 146
Koutstall, W. 147
Kozak, L. 195
Krippner, S. 30, 93, 95, 182
Kumar, V.K. 42, 95, 102, 115, 139, 140, 183
kundalini 200
Kurtz, P. 73

LaBerge, S. 13
Lacey, S.C. 137
Lalljee, M. 192
Lamont, P. 86, 160

Lamontanaro, L. 190
Lang, P.J. 8
Lange, R. 108, 109, 110, 112, 114, 115, 116, 120, 121, 126, 128, 129, 191
Langman, P. 193
Launay, G. 140
Launay-Slade Hallucination Scale (LSHS) 140, 144, 145, 146, 147
Laurence, J.R. 94
Lawrence, T.R. 38, 113, 114, 130, 180
Layton, B.D. 16
Leary, M.R. 167
Lehmann, D. 40, 93, 192, 198
Lenzenweger, M.F. 136
Leppink, J. 43
Levin, R. 190
Lewis, A.J. 154
Lewis, H.B. 33
Liverpool Hope University 1
Locke, R.G. 25
Lodge, O. 113
Loftus, E.F. 149
Loughland, C.M. 180
Lovelace, C.T. 194
LSHS *see* Launay-Slade Hallucination Scale
Ludwig, A.M. 39, 44, 96
Lynn, S.J. 43, 93, 95, 136

Mack, J. 138
MacKenzie, A. 121, 126
Maddern, C. 33
magical thinking 180, 182, 183, 196
magicians 157
Maharishi Effect 195
Maher, M.C. 14, 116, 120, 129
Maimonides Medical Center 30–33
Makarec, K. 179, 180, 181, 183
Mallot, J.M.
Mangun, G.R. 148
Manning, C.G. 149
Marcano, G. 42, 183
Marks, L.E. 102, 194
Marquis de Puységur 94
Martínez-Taboas, A. 42
Mason, O. 180
Mather, M. 146
Maurer, R. 95
Mavromatis, A. 127
May, E.C. 6
Mayer, A.R. 147
MBTI *see* Myers-Briggs Type Indicator
McClenon, J. 73, 77, 116, 127
McConkey, K.M. 95, 115
McCreery, C. 120, 121, 125, 126, 131, 189, 196
McCue, P. 120, 126, 130, 131
McDermott, K.B. 141, 147
McDonnell, R. 75
McDonough, B.E. 186, 198

McEwan, G.J. 124, 125, 132
McKellar, P. 197
McKenzie, E.A. 39
McKinley, N.M. 169
McNally, R.J. 136, 138
McNeill, K. 15
meditation 28–30, 36, 40, 101–102, 180, 195, 197, 199
mediums 63, 154
mediumship 178
Méheust, B. 94
memory 1, 5, 26, 55, 98, 137, 138, 142, 146–148, 149, 150, 162–163, 193
mental radio 55
mentation 31, 32, 33, 34, 35, 38, 41, 43, 52, 58 77–86, 138, 201
Merckelbach, H. 43, 146, 183, 198
Mesmer, F.A. 93, 94
mesmerism 93
Mesulam, M.-M. 148
meta-analysis 35–39, 52, 69–70, 94–95, 100, 101, 165
Miener, M. 40
Mikulincer, M. 169
Miles, C. 123, 124
Miller, K. 122, 124, 125, 126, 128, 131, 132
Milton, J. 25, 36, 37, 38, 68, 69
Mintz, S. 146
Mischo, J. 180, 188
Mitchell, D. 120
Mitra, S. 129
Mohr, C. 192
Moland, R.S. 76
Monroe Institute 195
Montagno, E. De A. 193
Moody, R.A. 111, 121
Moon, E. 95
Moore, S. 179, 189, 190
Moreau, C. 94
Morgan, A.H. 103
Morgan, R.F. 103
Morisy, A. 77
Morris, R.L. 15, 17, 22, 39, 73, 75, 109
Mulgrew, J. 186
Muri, R. 188
Muris, P. 183
Murphy, G. 27
Murray, C.D. 3, 161, 167, 169, 170, 171, 172, 173
Myers, F.W.H. 27, 65, 74, 120, 178, 185, 189, 201
Myers, S.A. 140
Myers-Briggs Type Indicator (MBTI) 33
mystical experience 76, 95, 101, 182

Nash, C.B. 54
Nash, M. 137
NDE *see* near-death experience
near-death experience (NDE) 101, 173, 174

NEC *see* Nocturnal Experiences Questionnaire
Necker Cube Fluctuation Test 163
negative expectancy 16
Neighbourhood Renewal Unit 76
Nelson, G.K. 77
Neppe, V.M. 128
Nettle, D. 200
Newberg, A.B. 102
Newman, L. 136
Newton, T. 167
Nickell, J. 110
nightmares 100, 191
Nijenhuis, E.R.S. 164, 170
Nocturnal Experiences Questionnaire (NEC) 141, 143
noise reduction model 43
Nolde, S.F. 146
Noll, R. 200
non-locality 53
non-verbal behavior 14
norepinephrine 195
Nuchpongsai, P. 193
Nyman, Andy 157

OBE *see* out-of-body-experiences
Oberlander, J.Z. 96
observational theories 51, 52, 53
O'Connor, R.P. 76
O'Donnell, E. 121
Ogata, S. 198
Ogura, C. 193
Okado, Y. 147
O'Keeffe, C. 3, 76, 108, 110, 113, 114, 115, 120
OLIFE (Oxford-Liverpool Inventory of Feelings and Experiences) 180
Orbach, I. 169
Orne, M.T. 95
Osis, K. 121, 132
Ost, J. 149
Ostvold, S. 95
Oubaid, V. 180, 188
out-of-body-experiences (OBE) 3, 161–176; Blackmore's Cognitive Theory 162; Irwin's Dissociational Theory 164–165; Palmer's Psychoanalytic Theory 162

Paller, K.A. 148
Palmer, J. 37, 38, 42, 109, 162, 164, 165, 166, 167, 168, 169, 173, 181, 182, 183, 187, 197, 199, 200
paranormal belief 138, 139–140, 145, 156, 157, 158, 159, 180, 181, 182, 188, 190
Parapsychological Association 51, 108
parapsychology 5, 12, 13, 16, 19, 22, 25, 26, 28, 50, 51, 52, 53, 55, 56, 57, 58, 59, 72, 73, 74, 75, 76, 77, 85, 86, 87, 108, 110, 121, 132, 198
parietal lobes 129

Paris 93, 149
Parker, A. 19, 22, 26, 33, 37, 38, 39, 40, 85, 180, 183
Parra, A. 39
Parrish, T.B. 148
Parsons, S. 3, 108, 114, 115
Patanjali 28
PCI *see* Phenomenology of Consciousness Inventory
Pekala, R.J. 41, 42, 95, 96, 98, 102, 115, 139, 140, 183
Peluso, J.P. 137
Perceptual Body Awareness Questionnaire 170
Perez-Aquino, K. 76
Perry, C. 94
Perry, P. 111, 121
Persinger, M.A. 76, 111, 112, 113, 120, 121, 128, 129, 179, 180, 181, 183, 193
Peterson, D.M. 12
Petterson, C. 180
Pettifer, S. 172
Pfeifer, G. 96
Phantasms of the Living (book) 27
Phenomenology of Consciousness Inventory 41, 98, 101, 102
philosophy 3
Physical Self-Efficacy Scale 170
physics 3, 50
Pilato, S. 39
pink noise 34
Pitman, R.K. 136
Pizzagalli, D. 192, 196
PK *see* psychokinesis
placebo 44, 115
Platt, R.D. 137
PMIR (psi-mediated instrumental response) 186
Podmore, F. 27, 74, 120
poltergeist 109, 113, 129, 131
Pomerantz, A. 80
Pope, K.S. 103
positive expectancy 16
Powers, S.M. 137
precognition 2, 5–11, 32, 52, 72, 191
precognitive aversion 8, 9–10
precognitive boredom 7, 8, 9–10
precognitive emotional arousal 5–11
precognitive habituation 7–8
presentiment 6, 10, 186
Price, D.D. 102
Price, H.H. 121, 130, 189
Princess Diana 149
PRL *see* Psychophysical Research Laboratories
probability 62–64, 68
psi 1, 8, 13–22, 25, 26, 28, 33, 35, 39, 40, 44, 50, 51–55, 57, 58, 59, 72, 73–78, 82, 86, 87, 93, 94, 95, 101, 129, 178, 180, 182, 185–196, 198, 199; psi-related experiences 42, 74–77, 95; and quantum theory 51; teleological model 51
psi-conducive experimenters 14
psi-inhibitory experimenters 14
psychic healing 199
psychokinesis (PK) 1, 53, 54, 72, 109, 130, 131, 178, 182, 186, 187
psychomanteum 111, 121
Psychophysical Research Laboratories (PRL) 35, 36
Puthoff, H. 51
Putnam, F.W. 140
Pütz, P. 40, 42

QiGong 187

Radin, D.I. 6, 22, 32, 51, 85, 111, 120, 121, 128, 186, 195
Rainville, P. 102
Rajaram, M. 129
Raju, T.R. 102
Ramakers, P. 15, 20
Ramsey, M., 13–14, 18, 85
Rand, W. 181
Randall, J.L. 110
Randles, J. 138
Rantzen, A.J. 193
Rao, K.R. 29, 30, 197
Rao, P.K. 197
Rao, S.M. 147
rapport 85
Rassin, E. 183
Ratcliffe, J. 76
Rawlings, D. 180
Raye, C. 138, 146
Reber, A. 194
Reber, P.J. 148
Rebman, J.M. 111
recurrent spontaneous psychokinesis (RSPK) 109
Reeve, C. 122, 123, 125, 129
Reiman, E. 147
reincarnation 178
Rejeski, W.J. 167
religious studies 3
REM (rapid eye movement) sleep 31, 32, 33, 196
remote helping 12–24
remote staring 12, 13
remote viewing 51, 52
replicability 1, 13, 36
Rhine, J.B. 72, 94
Rhine, L.E. 27, 28, 65, 72, 74, 87, 178
Rice, T.W. 77
Richards, D.G. 166, 182
Richards, P.M. 112, 181
Richards, T. 195
Richardson, J. 102
Richet, C. 63, 65
Robbins, M.A. 169

Robinson, K.B. 141, 142
Rodeghier, M. 137
Roe, C.A. 2, 25, 32, 33, 34, 38, 39, 85, 180
Roediger, H.L. 141, 142, 147
Rogez, R. 94
Rogo, D.S. 138
Roll, W.G. 112, 116, 120, 129, 193
Roney-Dougal, S.M. 30, 189, 191
Rorschach 190
Rosch, E. 101
Rose, N.J. 141
Rosen, B.R. 147
Rosen, R. 181
Rosenthal, R. 100
Ross, S. 196
RSPK *see* recurrent spontaneous psychokinesis
Rubin, D.B. 100
Ruch, J.C. 103
Rudkin, E.H. 125, 126, 129
Rush, J.H. 26, 27, 53, 109
Ryckman, R.M. 169, 170

Sacerdote, P. 95
Sacks, H. 78, 80, 82
sacred sites 76
Sah, S. 55
Saltmarsh, H.F. 74
Sanders, R. 182
Sannwald, G. 27, 74
Santomauro, J. 136, 138
Sargent, C.L. 41
Schacter, D.L. 136, 146, 147, 148
Schafer, M. 188
Schechter, E.I. 94
Schegloff, E. 78, 80
Scheier, M.F. 168
schizophrenia 179, 191, 200
schizotypal personality 183
schizotypy 179–180, 183, 184, 185, 188, 190, 191, 193, 194, 196, 198, 200; cognitive disorganisation 180; impulsive nonconformity 180; introvertive anhedonia 180; negative schizotypy 180, 193, 196–197; positive schizotypy 179–180, 183, 188, 189, 190, 193, 196–197, 199, 200
Schlitz, M.J. 13, 15, 22, 42, 51, 52, 74, 85, 95
Schmeidler, G.R. 14, 29, 37, 39, 44, 85, 120
Schmidt, H. 51, 55, 58
Schmidt, S. 12, 55
Schmitz-Gropengiesser, F. 40
Schneider, R. 12, 13–14, 15, 55
Schouten, S.A. 27, 74, 75
Schwarz, B.E. 138
séance 3, 154, 155
Self-Consciousness Scale 168, 169
self-hypnosis 96, 100, 101
sensory isolation 33
serotonin 195

Serper, M. 140
Shafer, D. 12, 15, 186
shamans 200
Shearing-Johns, S. 164
Sheldrake, R. 194
Sherman, S.E. 97
Sherman, S.J. 149
Sherwood, S.J. 32, 33, 34, 39, 41, 44, 85, 108, 115, 120, 122, 123, 126, 127, 196
siddhis 29
Sidgwick, E.M. 27, 120
Sidgwick, H. 120, 121
Siegel, R.K. 102
Simmonds, C. 32, 39, 179, 180, 183, 188, 189, 197, 198; *see also* Simmonds-Moore, C.
Simmonds-Moore, C. 3, 177, 179, 180, 182, 187, 189, 190, 196, 199; *see also* Simmonds, C.
Simpson, L. 197
Singer, J.L. 102
Singer, W. 198
Skinner, J.C. 32
Skirda, R.J. 193
Slade, P.D. 140, 146, 167, 193
sleep paralysis 138, 139, 141, 143, 145, 149
Slotnick, S.D. 147
Smeets, T. 43
Smith, M.D. 13, 14, 115, 155, 157, 158
Smith, M.M. 198
Smith, P.K. 7
Social Physique Anxiety Scale 169, 170
Society for Psychical Research (SPR) 27
sociology 2, 72–91
Solfvin, J. 30
somatoform dissociation 164, 166; *see also* Somatoform Dissociation Questionnaire
Somatoform Dissociation Questionnaire 164, 168, 170, 172; *see also* somatoform dissociation
Spanos, N.P. 136, 137
spatial parapsychology 74–77
Spencer, J. 138
Spiegel, D. 95, 116
Spinhoven, P. 164
Spinks, R. 148
spirit 123, 126, 131–132, 154, 160, 178
spiritual experiences 99, 198
spiritualism 110
spirituality 199, 200
Spottiswoode, S.J.P. 6
SPR *see* Society for Psychical Research
Srinivasan, N. 197
Stadler, M.A. 148
Standish, L. 195
Stanford, R.G. 13, 40, 41, 42, 44, 94, 186
Stark, C. 147
statistical significance 8, 9, 63, 68
Stein, A.G. 95
Steinkamp, F. 32

Stern, D.N. 102
Stevens, P. 2, 50, 58, 76, 110, 115, 120
Stevenson, I. 132
Storm, L. 42, 68, 182
Straube, E.R. 180, 188
Strauch, I. 40
subliminal processing 7, 9, 177, 185, 190, 191, 197, 199
suggestibility 95
suggestion 157, 158
Summers, J. 39
synesthesia 96, 164, 165, 194, 197

Taddonio, J.L. 16
Taft, R. 147
Tan, G. 198
Tandy, V. 113, 114, 120, 129, 130
Targ, E. 42, 74
Targ, R. 51
Tart, C.T. 25, 45, 96, 97, 101, 102, 103
Tartz, R. 182
TAS *see* Tellegen's Absorption Scale
Taylor, K.I. 188
tectonic stress 76, 111, 129
telepathy 50, 53, 55–56, 57, 62, 64, 65, 67, 72, 130–131, 178, 194
Tellegen, A. 137, 140, 196
Tellegen's Absorption Scale (TAS) 140, 144, 145
temporal lobe 76, 128, 129, 147, 179, 180, 181, 183, 184, 186, 193, 196
Tennessee Self-concept Scale 169
Terhune, D. 93, 108, 115, 116
Thalbourne, M.A. 42, 43, 110, 136, 138, 140, 179, 182, 183, 187, 194, 196, 200
Thayer, R.E. 53
theology 3
Thompson, N.L. 102
Thornton, B. 169
Through the Looking Glass (book) 5; *see also Alice in Wonderland*
Titchener, E.B. 12
tonic arousal 189
Townsend, M. 76, 113, 114, 129, 130
Transcendental Meditation 195, 197, 198
transliminality 42, 43, 179, 182, 183, 184, 187, 188, 190, 191, 194, 200
Travis, F. 164, 197, 198
Trosman, H. 196
Trubshaw, B. 122, 126
Tulving, E. 148
Turnbull, B. 16
Turner, K.H. 111
twins 194
type I error 192, 193
type II error 192, 193
Tyrrell, G.N.M. 110, 120, 121, 126, 130, 131

UFO 139, 149
Ullman, M. 30

University of Edinburgh 77
Upchurch, I. 38
Utts, J. 12, 55, 57, 68, 70

Vaitl, D. 39, 44
Vallee, J. 138
Van de Castle, R. 27, 28, 31, 32, 33, 94
van der Hart, O. 164
Vanderlinden, J. 164
van de Ven, V. 146
van Dyke, R. 164
van Koppen, P.J. 149
Venkatesh, S. 102
Villanueva, J. 39
virtual reality 170, 171, 172
visual perception 54
Vogel, G. 196
Vrij, A. 149

Wackermann, J. 39, 40, 42, 44
Wagenaar, W.A. 149
Wagner, A.D. 147
Walach, H., 12, 13, 15, 55
Walker, E.H. 51
Walsh, R. 197
Warren, C.A. 186, 198
Wasserman, T. 13
Watson, D. 42
Watt, C. 2, 12, 16, 17, 20, 22, 73, 75, 76, 85, 110, 115, 120
Weitzenhoffer, A.M. 95
Wessels, P.M. 148
West, A. 172
West, D.J. 22, 154
Westerlund, J. 39, 180
Westwood, J. 125
White, R.A. 27, 28, 73
white noise 34, 44, 58, 81, 147, 193
Whitman, D. 196
Wickramasekera, I. 182
Wilde, D. 169
Wilkinson, H.P. 129
Williams, B. 180
Williams, B.J. 121, 128, 129
Williams, C. 38, 183, 194
Williams, L.M. 191, 194
Willin, M.J. 37
Wilson, K. 137, 149, 150
Wilson, S. 34
Wilson, S.C. 137
Wilson-Barber Inventory of Childhood Memories and Imaginings: Children's Form (ICMIC) 140
Winkelman, M. 102, 103
Winograd, E. 137
Winsper, A. 114
Wiseman, J. 155
Wiseman, R. 3, 13, 22, 36, 37, 38, 68, 70, 76, 85, 110, 115, 120, 129, 154, 155, 157, 158, 160

Witkin, H.A. 33
Wolfradt, U. 180, 188
Wood, R. 33, 45
Woodley, P. 180
Wooffitt, R. 2, 72, 78, 79, 84
Wright, T. 39
Wulff, D.M. 101, 102

Yardi, N. 197
Yesson, S.A. 191
Yim, S. 39

yoga 28–29, 30, 197
Yonelinas, A.P. 148
Young, C.A. 76
Young, H.F. 146, 193
Young, J.M. 188
Yun, L.S. 147

Zajonc, R.B. 6
Zanes, J. 196
Zhang, H. 198
Zingrone, N.L. 77, 110, 121, 163, 165, 166

www.ingramcontent.com/pod-product-compliance
Ingram Content Group UK Ltd.
Pitfield, Milton Keynes, MK11 3LW, UK
UKHW041952140426
5217IPUK00015B/768